A Brief Guide to AutoCAD® 2000

A Brief Guide to AutoCAD® 2000

Scott E. Davis
Montana State University

Prentice Hall

Upper Saddle River, New Jersey
Columbus, Ohio

Library of Congress Cataloging-in-Publication Data
Davis, Scott E.
A brief guide to AutoCAD 2000 / Scott E. Davis.
p. cm.
ISBN 0-13-088985-7
1. Computer graphics. 2. AutoCAD. I. Title.

T385.D397 2001
620′.0042′02855369--dc21 00-032668

Vice President and Publisher: Dave Garza
Editor in Chief: Stephen Helba
Acquisitions Editor: Debbie Yarnell
Associate Editor: Michelle Churma
Production Editor: Louise N. Sette
Production Supervision: Lisa Garboski, bookworks
Design Coordinator: Robin G. Chukes
Cover Designer: Thomas Borah
Text Designer: STELLARViSIONs
Production Manager: Brian Fox
Marketing Manager: Chris Bracken

This book was set in Palatino by STELLARViSIONs. It was printed and bound by Courier Kendallville, Inc. The cover was printed by Phoenix Color Corp.

All screen captures for the text were made using SuperClip™ screen capture software by AndroSoft™.

Prentice Hall

10 9 8 7 6 5 4 3 2 1
ISBN 0-13-088985-7

Preface

A Brief Guide to AutoCAD® 2000 is a beginner's guide to AutoCAD® 2000 software to create 2D computer-aided drawings. This text provides a method that enables the reader to learn to use the software in the easiest possible manner. The information is based on a generic systems approach. Moreover, the approach taken in writing the text was to define and explain the terms most commonly used in creating, editing, displaying, plotting, and printing drawings. Thus, readers can understand the basics for using the software and then apply these to their own areas of expertise.

This text should appeal to students and teachers at the secondary and collegiate level, including those who are involved in Technology Education and Industrial Technology programs. *A Brief Guide to AutoCAD® 2000* is not meant to be all-inclusive. CAD users will need to consult more detailed manuals to address specific questions and to learn to produce advanced drawings.

The following features in the text make it unique as a learning and teaching tool:

Key Concepts listed at the start of each chapter specify commands and new content reviewed in the chapter.

Margin definitions provide explanations of new terms introduced in the chapter and reinforce Key Concepts. Because some of the terminology may be new to the reader, margin definitions help the reader understand and review new terms when they are used in context.

"Try This" activities woven throughout every chapter are abbreviated lessons and drawing activities that give the reader a chance to practice a command or concept immediately after it has been introduced.

Drawing Activities located at the chapter end provide a more in-depth use of the commands and concepts covered in the chapter. Drawing activities cover creating both mechanical parts and architectural drawings.

In addition to these features, *A Brief Guide to AutoCAD® 2000* provides chapter content that is sequenced logically and arranged so that the content learned in one chapter is applied in later chapters. Chapters 1 through 5 focus on creating objects using AutoCAD® 2000 layout techniques and drawing tools. Readers will learn commands to:

- create a drawing sheet template;
- place geometric figures on the drawing sheet;
- use drawing aids that help improve the layout of a drawing;
- change how objects are displayed on the computer screen; and
- use object snaps, drawing tools that help in drawing more precisely.

As users draw, it is inevitable that they will make mistakes. AutoCAD® 2000 editing commands make correcting these mistakes easy and also help the user locate dimensions correctly. In addition, some common mistakes can be avoided with the use of template files that have predefined characteristics consistent from drawing to drawing. Chapters 6 through 8 cover commands that help the reader to:

- correct drawing errors;
- properly locate and use dimension variables; and
- use template files.

Once the drawing and editing stages have been completed, the next step is to plot and print the file. Chapters 9 and 10 provide a brief discussion of how to:

- plot and print drawings and
- set dimension variables so that they appear correctly on mechanical and architectural drawings.

Finally, because drawings can be complex in nature, users often find it necessary to identify object properties, such as layer, length, and distance. AutoCAD® 2000 has built-in commands that help the user determine object properties. Other commands help the user create objects that can be used from one drawing to the next. Chapter 11 discusses:

- commands for determining object properties and
- block commands for inserting objects into drawings.

Readers will find this text easy to use. The numerous illustrations throughout the text assist the reader in grasping the concepts discussed. In addition, the level and scope of the technical content covered in the text enable the reader to create drawings almost immediately—giving the reader that early sense of accomplishment so important to beginning users.

Contents

A Brief Guide to AutoCAD® 2000

CHAPTER

1

Introduction to AutoCAD 2000

AFTER READING THIS CHAPTER, YOU WILL BE ABLE TO:

- Open the AutoCAD 2000 software in a Windows environment.
- Identify drawing editor components.
- Recognize drawing editor menus.

KEY CONCEPTS:

- Command prompt
- Drawing editor
- Icon
- Layout
- Model space
- Paper space
- Pull-down menu
- Screen menu
- Startup dialog box
- Toolbar
- User coordinate system (UCS)

The information presented in this chapter provides a general overview of how AutoCAD 2000 operates. Understanding how the software enables you to create drawings is an important first step in being able to use AutoCAD 2000 correctly.

WINDOWS OPERATING PLATFORM

AutoCAD 2000 software functions in a variety of operating systems; however, for the purposes of this book, AutoCAD 2000 operation is reviewed only in the Windows 95/98 and Windows NT systems. Software application is discussed as it relates to desktop PCs commonly used either at home or in an office setting.

Icon—a graphical symbol representative of a command.

The Windows desktop can take on a variety of appearances. Typically, a number of programs have been loaded on the PC (see Figure 1–1). In order to open AutoCAD 2000, double click on the shortcut AutoCAD 2000 icon. If the icon is not on the desktop, then click on the Start icon located in the lower left corner of the screen. Locate the Program button near the top of the column and click on it. A listing of programs is displayed. Locate the AutoCAD 2000 button and click on it. A listing of AutoCAD 2000 options is displayed in the dialog box. If you have any problems opening the software, check your installation manual for troubleshooting help, or call your software dealer.

STARTUP SCREEN MENU OPTIONS

The startup screen menu (Figure 1–2) provides several options for starting the software. The series of button icons located along the top left of the dia-

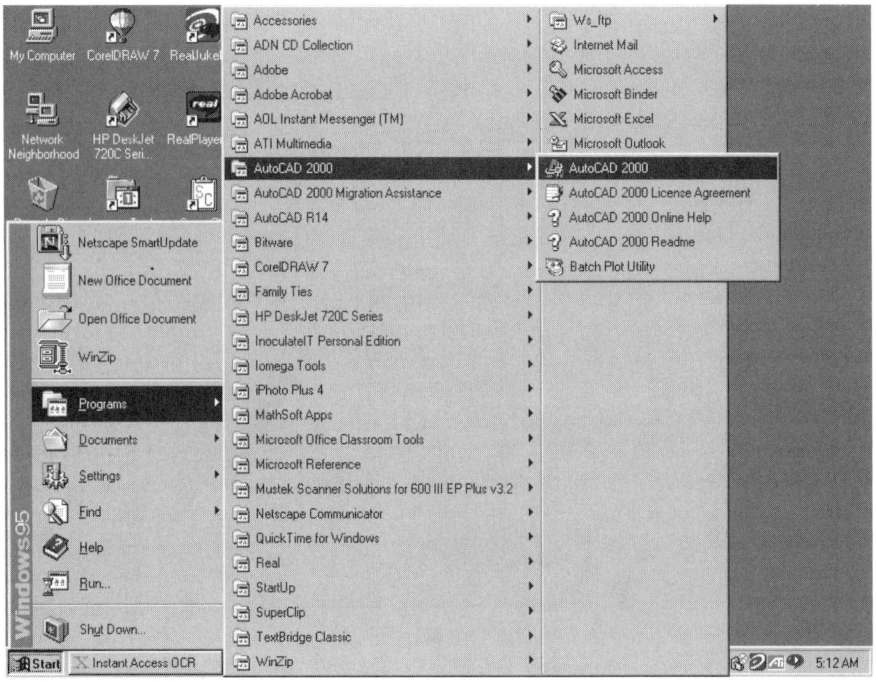

Figure 1–1
Program files.

Figure 1–2
Wizard dialog box.

log box include options for entering the drawing editor. The Open File icon allows you to open an existing file. The second button icon from the left is the Start from Scratch button. If it is selected, there are only two options available: use either English or Metric units. The third button icon in Figure 1–2 allows you to select a template file for starting AutoCAD 2000. Use a Wizard is the fourth button icon from the left, and the options associated with Use a Wizard are displayed.

Use a Wizard

There are two options, Advanced Setup or Quick Setup, if the Use a Wizard option is selected. Both options allow you to set various drawing parameters before entering the drawing editor. Drawing parameters that can be set in the Advanced Setup dialog box (Figure 1–3) include Units, Angle, Angle Measure, Angle Direction, and Area. The Units variable option can be set to Decimal, Engineering, Architectural, Fractional, or Scientific. Once you have set the variables for these options, you are defaulted into the drawing editor. The Quick Setup in the Use a Wizard option allows for the setting of two variables, Units and Area.

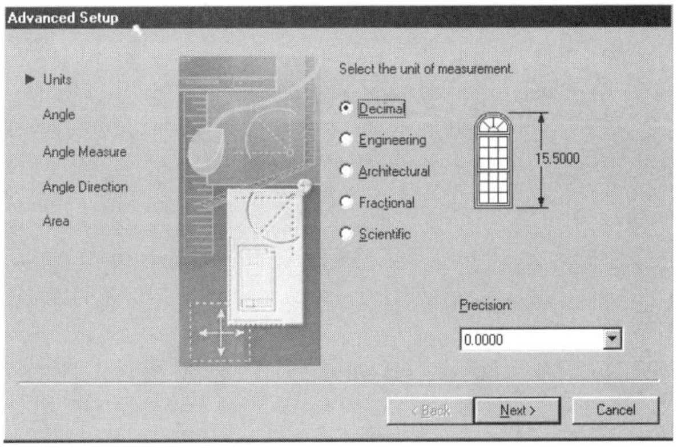

Figure 1–3
The Advanced Setup screen.

TRY THIS

Open AutoCAD 2000 and use the Advanced Startup option to set up the following drawing parameters. In the Units option select **Decimal** and set the Precision to two decimal places. In the Angle option select **Decimal Degrees,** and set the **Precision** to two decimal places. Set both the Angle Measure option and the Angle Direction to **East**. In the Area option set the **Width** to **10** and the Length to **8**.

Use a Template

A template drawing file has predefined parameters that are set by the software. These template files correspond to the different sizes of paper used to create printed/plotted drawings. Different border styles are used based on the particular application (e.g., architectural, engineering, English, or German). The Use a Template dialog box is displayed in Figure 1–4. Borders and title blocks are placed in paper space, whereas the actual drawing of the object occurs in model space. Any drawing file can serve as a template if it is saved with a .dwt file extension.

TRY THIS

Open AutoCAD 2000 and select the **Use a Template** option. Load the template **ANSI A named plot styles. dwt**. Repeat the process and load the following templates:

Architectural, english units, named plot styles.dwt
Metric layout templates.dwt

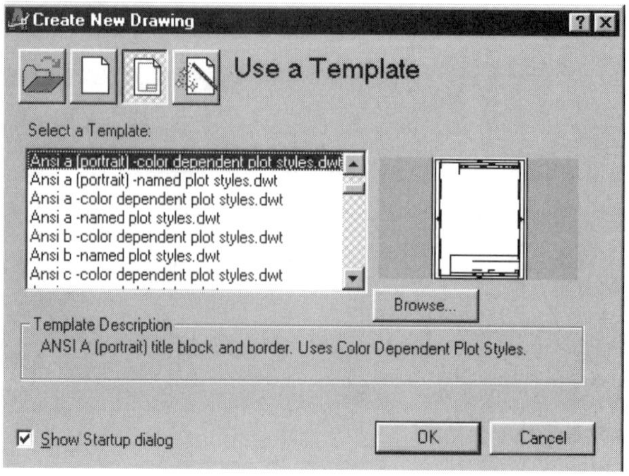

Figure 1–4
The Use a Template dialog box.

Figure 1–5
Start from Scratch dialog box.

Start from Scratch

If you are beginning a new drawing and do not want the wizard to set any parameters or use a template, click on the Start from Scratch icon and you will automatically default into the drawing editor. The Start from Scratch icon is the second from the left in the Create New Drawing dialog box (see Figure 1–5). The only parameter you can choose in the Start from Scratch option is whether the drawing will be in feet and inches or metric.

Open a Drawing

Another of the options in the Startup dialog box is Open a Drawing. If you want to edit an existing drawing, use this method for opening it. You must know the directory path (for example, A:\ or c:\temp) to the drawing file in order to open it in the drawing editor. In Figure 1–6 two previously created drawing files are listed for selection. This option is available only when you first start AutoCAD. In order to edit an existing drawing once you have already opened AutoCAD, you must use the Open command in the File pull-down menu, or type open at the command prompt.

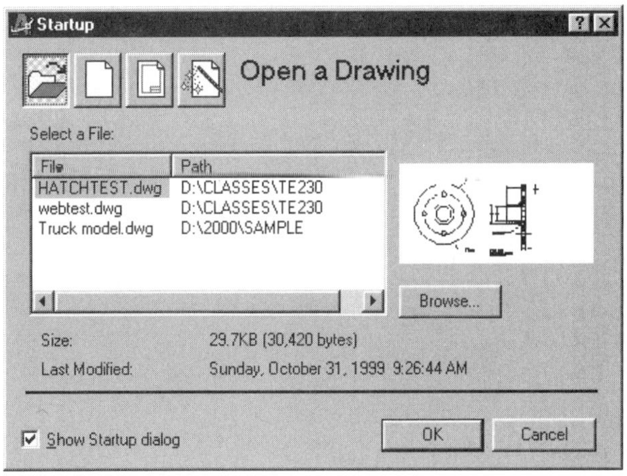

Figure 1–6
Open a Drawing dialog box.

THE DRAWING EDITOR

No matter which option you choose (Start from Scratch, Use a Wizard, etc.) to enter the drawing editor, those elements that make up the drawing editor exist in all options. The drawing editor (Figure 1–7) is that part of the software program that enables you to create entities. These entities are created by entering commands.

The **pull-down menu bar** includes the following options: File, Edit, View, Insert, Format, Tools, Draw, Dimension, Modify, Express, Window, and Help.

Commands in the drawing editor are initiated in a variety of ways, including using the pull-down menu bar, the screen menu, toolbars, or typing the command at the command prompt. Across the top of the drawing editor is the **pull-down menu bar** containing the options File, Edit, View, Insert, Format, Tools, Draw, Dimension, Modify, Express, Window and Help (Figure 1–8). Beneath each of these terms are submenus that make up the numerous commands that AutoCAD 2000 uses to perform its operations.

Toolbars contain tools, represented by icons, that start commands.

Below the pull-down menu items in Figure 1–7 are three rows of horizontal toolbars. There are also two columns of toolbars along the left side of the drawing editor. Toolbars are composed of **icons** that represent individual commands or functions used in AutoCAD. There are multiple toolbars with icons that allow point-and-click operations. Toolbars can be activated or turned off through the Toolbars dialog box. To display the Toolbars dialog box, click on the View pull-down menu option and select Toolbars (Figure 1–9). In Figure 1–10 the Dimension, Draw, and Modify toolbars were selected for display.

Screen menu—command list typically located on the right side of the drawing editor screen.

The **screen menu** is the column of commands found on the right side of Figure 1–7. Submenus are linked to each term, that when selected allow access to more commands. The default setting for the screen menu is typically off, so it will not always be displayed when you enter the drawing editor. If you are comfortable using the pull-down menu, selecting an icon, or

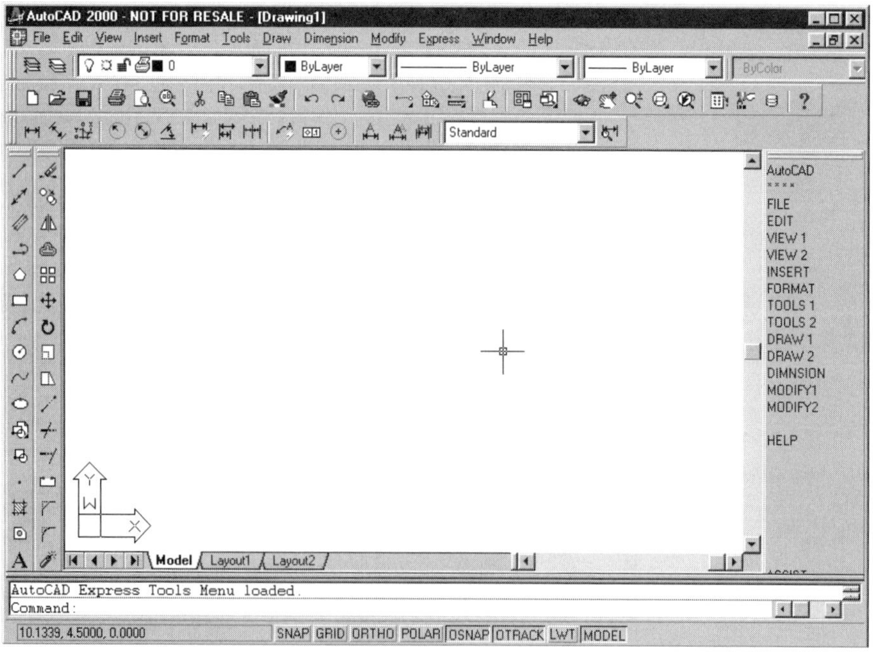

Figure 1–7
AutoCAD 2000 drawing editor.

Figure 1–8
Pull-down menu options.

Figure 1–9
Displaying toolbars.

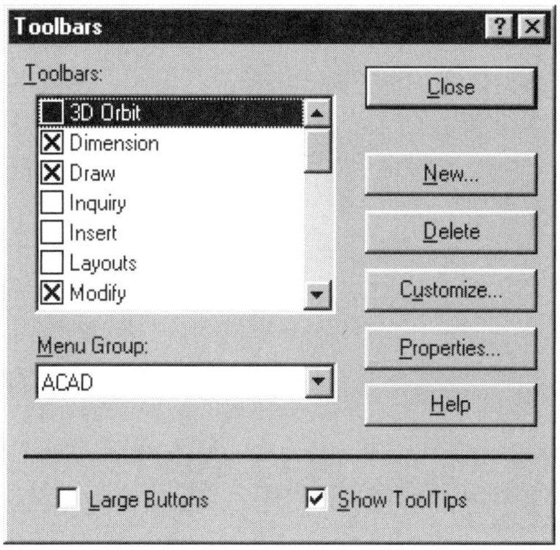

Figure 1–10
Toolbars dialog box.

entering commands at the command prompt, it is not necessary to have the screen menu on. In order to display the screen menu, go to the Tools pull-down menu and select Options. The Options dialog box (see Figure 1–11) will appear with several tabs along the top. Select the Display tab. To display the screen menu, select the Display screen menu option. To turn the display menu off, simply deselect the box.

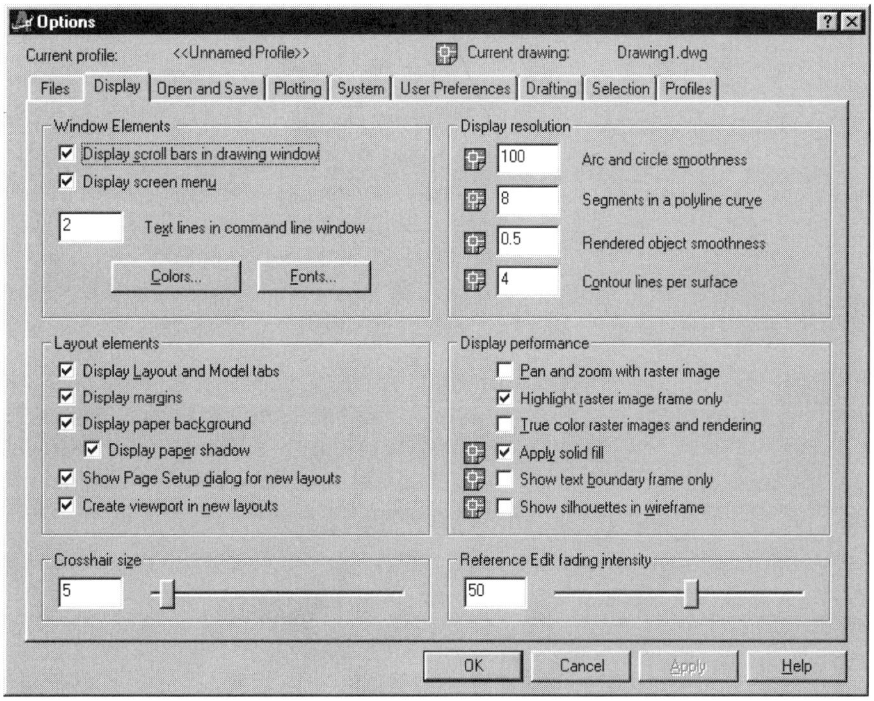

Figure 1–11
Options dialog box.

Figure 1–12
Button icons.

Figure 1–13
Coordinate display.

Model space Paper space

Figure 1–14
UCS icon in model space and paper space.

Paper space—an area that is used for creating a finished layout for printing or plotting, as opposed to doing drawing.

Model space—that viewport where most or all of the drawing is created

The **UCS icon** (Figure 1–14) represents the orientation of the X, Y, and Z axes and the position of the current UCS origin.

Along the bottom of the drawing editor screen is a row of **button** icons (see Figure 1–12). These buttons control the **snap** setting distance; the **grid** spacing and display; the **ortho** mode; the **polar** tracking mode, which when on displays the distance and angle of direction; the **osnap** mode, the **otrack** mode (object snap tracking displayed); the lineweight mode **(LWT)**, and whether you are in **model** space or **paper** space. Clicking on a button can either activate or deactivate the command or function associated with it.

To the left of the button icons located near the bottom of the drawing editor is the coordinate display (see Figure 1–13). The numerical readout typically displays the position of the cursor on the X and Y axes.

In the lower left-hand corner of the drawing editor is the user coordinate system (UCS) icon as seen in model space (see Figure 1–14). It represents the orientation of the X, Y, and Z axes. The icon will change when you go into layout or paper space.

Model and Layout

Objects are typically drawn in what is known as **model space**. Near the lower left corner of the drawing editor are tabs labeled Model, Layout1, and Layout2. Model refers to model space. When the Model tab is selected, you can create two-dimensional or three-dimensional drawings in model space. The drawing shown in Figure 1–15 was created in model space.

The Layout tabs allow you to set up the paper size on which you are going to plot/print and also to design or lay out your model drawing for plotting. A layout typically consists of a title block, one or more viewports, and any annotations. The dashed lines that appear on a layout sheet represent the printable area based on the printer/plotter that is selected. Figure 1–16 depicts the same drawing as seen in Figure 1–15 except that it is shown in layout format.

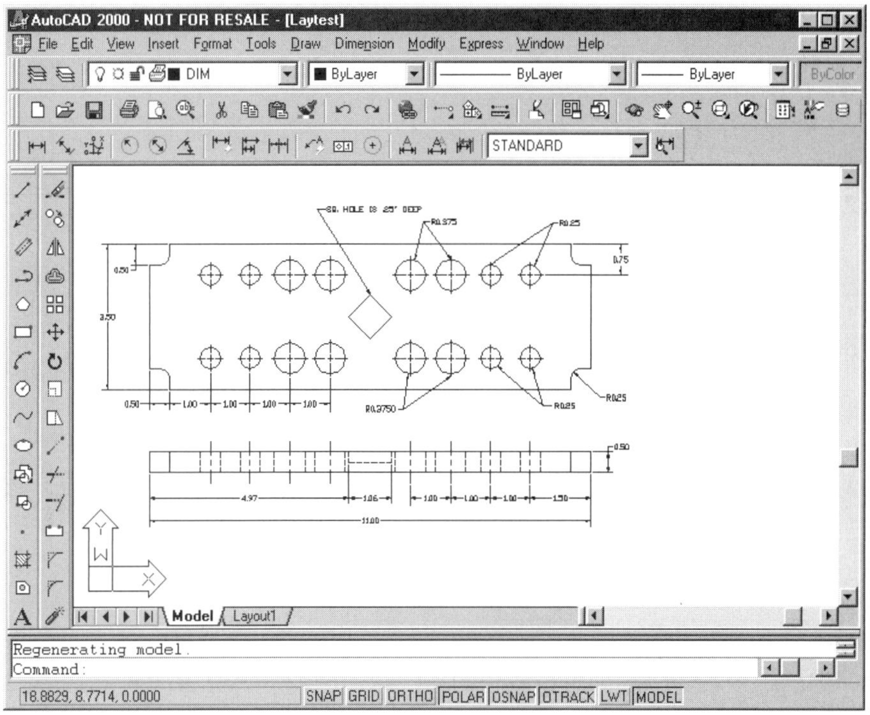

Figure 1–15
Drawing in model space.

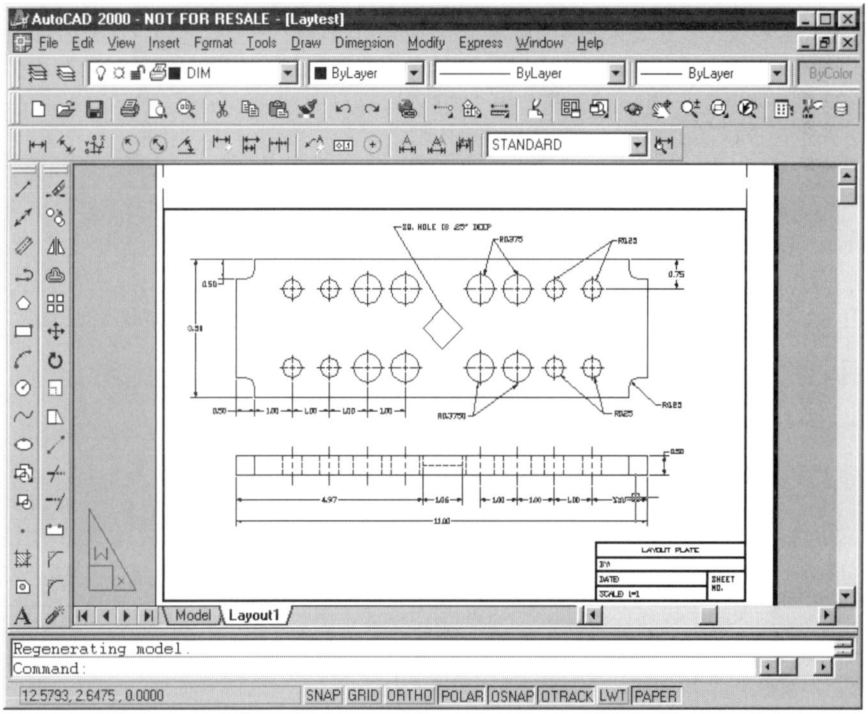

Figure 1–16
Layout.

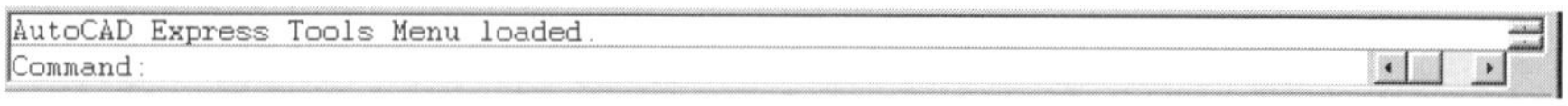

Figure 1–17
Command prompt areas.

Command Prompt

Command prompt—that area in the drawing editor where text can be entered to start commands.

Located between the coordinate display readout and the Model and Layout tabs is the command prompt area. In Figure 1–17 two command prompt areas can be seen. The top command prompt area (AutoCAD Express Tools Menu loaded.) has scroll bars located at the right end of the box. This command prompt area allows you to scroll through and review all the commands that you have executed since entering the drawing editor. The bottom command prompt area (Command:) is where you can type in English word commands.

SETTING DRAWING PARAMETERS

In order to create a drawing that correctly represents the image you want to relate to the viewer, you must set certain parameters. Most of these parameters are located in the Format pull-down menu. Parameters that need to be set include color, limits, layers, linetypes, and units (see Figure 1–18).

Each option listed in the pull-down menu is a submenu. Some of the parameters are also located in the screen menu, and the English word equivalent can be typed at the command prompt.

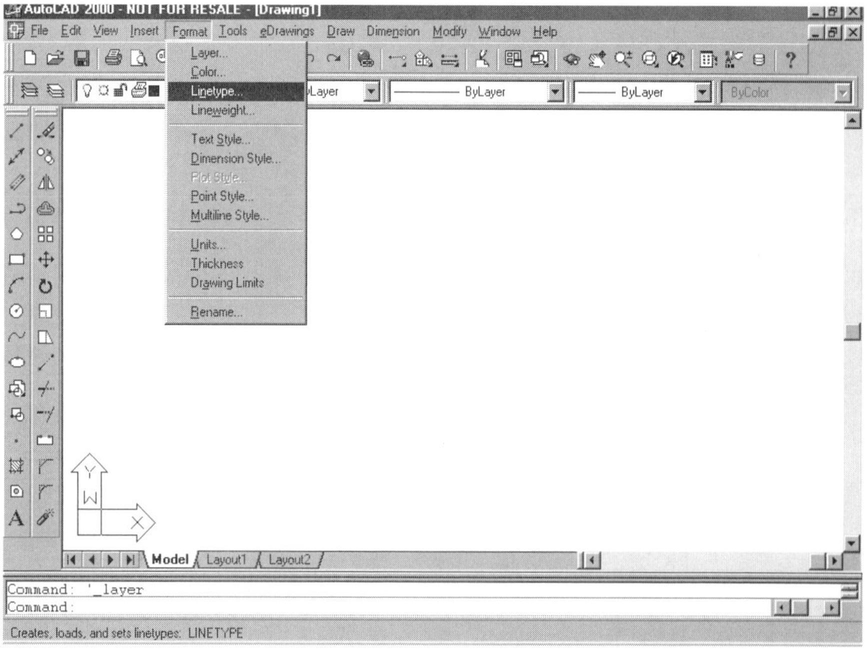

Figure 1–18
Drawing format options.

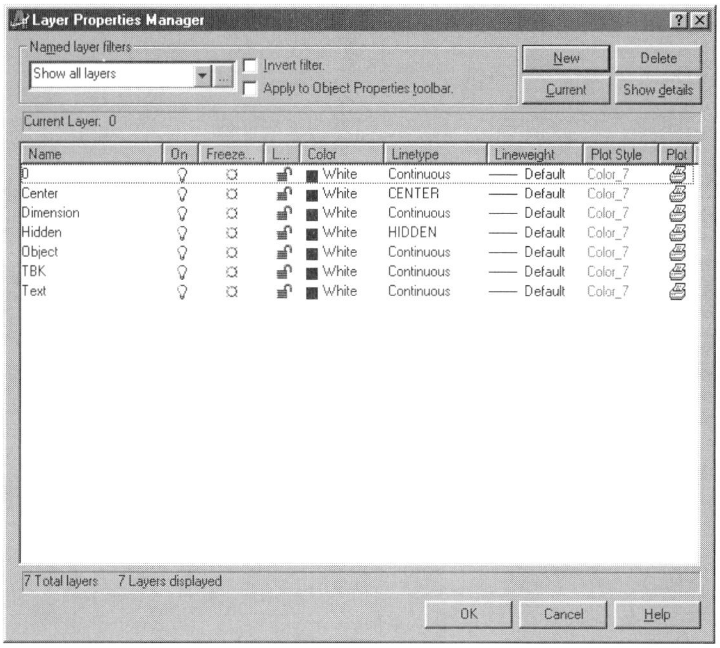

Figure 1–19
Layer Properties Manager dialog box.

Color, Layers, and Linetypes

Layers are similar to multiple sheets of paper on which certain characteristics of a drawing are assigned. Entities are drawn on certain layers. Each layer is assigned a name and has specific attributes such as color and linetype assigned to it. Clicking on Layer in the Format pull-down menu opens the Layer dialog box. Figure 1–19 depicts the Layer Properties Manager dialog box.

In order to create a new layer in the dialog box, click on the New button. The new layer name should appear in the layer window. Specific naming conventions are used for naming layers. Layers can be turned off, which means the entities on that layer do not show on the drawing screen. Layers can also be frozen. No editing can take place on a frozen layer.

Now let's see how to save a drawing once you have made one.

SAVING DRAWING FILES

This section provides information on those options associated with creating an archival drawing file. There are three commands that are associated with creating an archival drawing file: **quit, save,** and **saveas.** Archival files will have a file extension of .dwg.

Two of the options, Save and Save As, are found in the File pull-down menu or by clicking the save icon. The screen that appears at the saveas

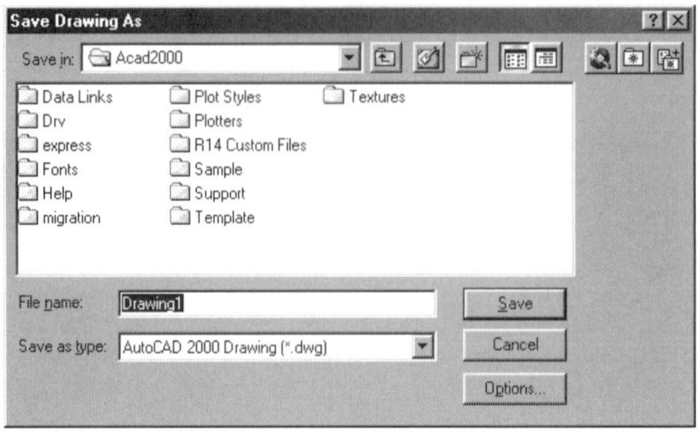

Figure 1–20
Save Drawing As dialog box.

command is displayed in Figure 1–20. When Save As is selected, the format and name of the drawing file can be selected.

The save command can also be typed at the command prompt.

At the command prompt, type save

If the drawing is named, AutoCAD displays the Save Drawing As dialog box.

If a different file name is entered, AutoCAD saves a copy of the drawing under the specified name.

If the drawing is unnamed, AutoCAD displays the Save Drawing dialog box.

If the current drawing has not been named, AutoCAD displays a dialog box in which you name the drawing before exiting.

The quit command exits AutoCAD if there have been no changes since the drawing was last saved. If the drawing has been modified, AutoCAD displays the Save Drawing As dialog box to prompt you to save or discard the changes before quitting.

If a template drawing is used, and you choose to save the drawing, the Save Drawing As dialog box will appear when the Save command is selected.

Chapter 1 ■ Activities

Activity 1–1

Use the AutoCAD Learning Assistance Tutorials to Become More Familiar with Using AutoCAD in the Windows Environment

ACTIVITY STEPS:

1. From the AutoCAD Help menu select Learning Assistance.
2. Select Tutorials.
3. In the right-hand window there should be several underlined bulleted items in blue text. These bulleted items represent a list of tutorials in which you can either watch multimedia presentations and/or try sample activities.
4. Select Introduction to AutoCAD in the Windows Environment.
5. Select the Executing Commands text.
6. Near the top of the right-hand column should be a Play Video icon. Select the Play Video icon. A multimedia presentation should then start playing.
7. After watching the multimedia presentation select the Try it! Option, and follow the instructions to complete the activity.

Activity 1–2

Use the AutoCAD Learning Assistance Tutorials to Become More Familiar with Organizing Your Project

ACTIVITY STEPS:

1. From the AutoCAD Help menu select Learning Assistance.
2. Select Tutorials.
3. In the right-hand window there should be several underlined bulleted items in blue text. These bulleted items represent a list of tutorials in which you can either watch multimedia presentations and/or try sample activities.
4. Select the Organizing Your Project text.

5. Select the Wizards text.
6. Near the top of the right-hand column should be a Play Video icon. Select the Play Video icon. A multimedia presentation should then start playing.
7. After watching the multimedia presentation select the Try It! option, and follow the instructions to complete the activity.

ACTIVITY 1–3

Identify Drawing Editor Components

In the Create New Drawing dialog box, select the Start from Scratch option. After you enter the drawing editor, go to the View pull-down menu and select Toolbars. The Toolbars dialog box should appear. Make sure the following toolbar options have been selected to show in the drawing the editor: Dimension, Draw, Modify, Object Properties, and Standard toolbar. If you move the cursor over a toolbar icon and let it briefly rest on an icon, a window will appear that indicates the command the icon represents. Move the cursor over the button icons and familiarize yourself with the commands the icon represents.

ACTIVITY 1–4

Layout Development

ACTIVITY STEPS:

1. From the AutoCAD 2000 help pull-down menu select Learning Assistance.
2. Select Concepts from the window on the right.
3. The Contents tab should appear in the left window. A listing of options should appear.
4. Select Concepts: Layout.
5. A right-hand and a left-hand window should now appear. Read through the information in the right-hand window. At the top of the right-hand window a Play Video option should be showing. Select the Play Video option and watch the multimedia presentation.
6. After watching the multimedia presentation, select the underlined blue Layouts term in the first sentence in the right-hand column. New information about layouts should now be shown.
7. Select the Play Video option and watch the multimedia presentation.
8. After watching the video, complete the Try It! activity.
9. After completing the Try It! activity, exit the Learning Assistance Program

CHAPTER

2

2D Object Creation

AFTER READING THIS CHAPTER, YOU WILL BE ABLE TO:

- Use a limited number of commands for object creation.
- Use the absolute, polar, and relative coordinate systems to enter object starting and ending points.

KEY CONCEPTS:

Arc (a)
Circle (c)
Donut
Ellipse (el)
Hatch
Line (l)
Mline (ml)
Polar coordinates
Polygon
Polyline (pl)
Rectangle
Relative coordinates
Solid
Text

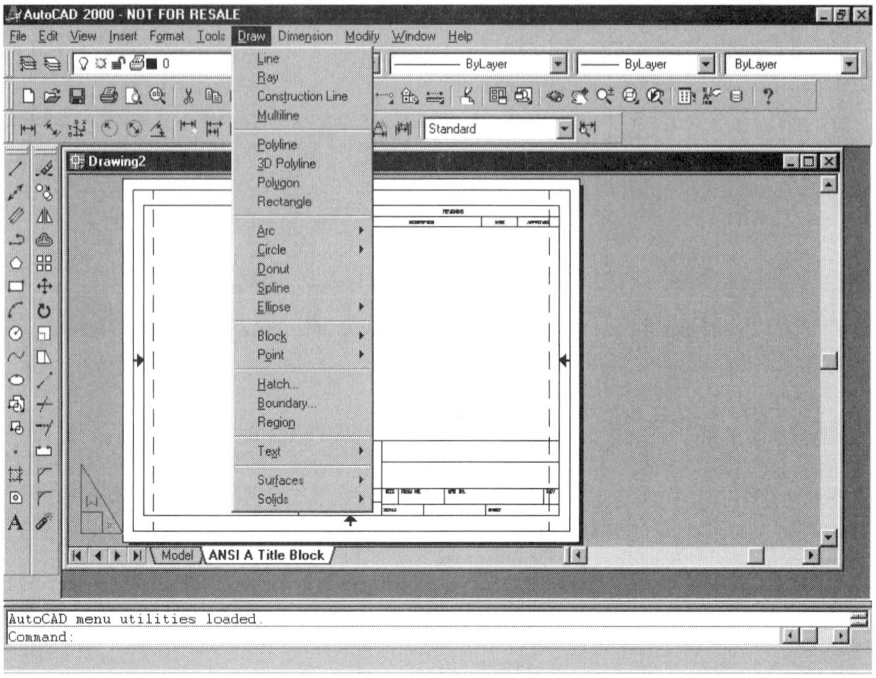

Figure 2–1
Draw pull-down menu.

Objects are created in numerous ways. Common commands for creating objects are either selected from pull-down menus or screen menus, or the English word equivalent is typed at the command prompt.

The pull-down menu in Figure 2–1 was activated by clicking once on Draw in the menu bar. Figure 2–1 displays the Draw menu commands available for creating objects. The more common commands used to create objects include **arc (a), mline** (ml), **line** (l), **construction line, ellipse** (**el**), **circle** (c), **donut, hatch, polyline** (pl), **polygon, rectangle, solid,** and **text**. Some commands have what are known as **hot keys**. Hot keys are single or multiple letters that represent the command associated with it. For example, typing l at the command prompt would activate the line command. Typing c at the command prompt would activate the circle command.

The method for selecting commands for creating objects again will vary depending on the system the user implements; however, the side bar menu has two draw menus. Commands can be selected from either the DRAW 1 or the DRAW 2 menu.

Text for general notes as well as for title blocks is created with the text command. Text is also used in creating dimensions. Dimensions (DIM) commands for describing objects and displaying the size of objects are also located in the Dimension pull-down menu file structure. There are several variables that affect the dimensions that are used in a drawing.

COORDINATE TYPES

All drawings are superimposed on an invisible grid, or coordinate system, with a horizontal X axis and a vertical Y axis (Autodesk, Inc., 1997, p. 46). The Z axis is perpendicular to the X and Y axes. As you are looking at the initial drawing editor when you open AutoCAD, think of the Z axis as com-

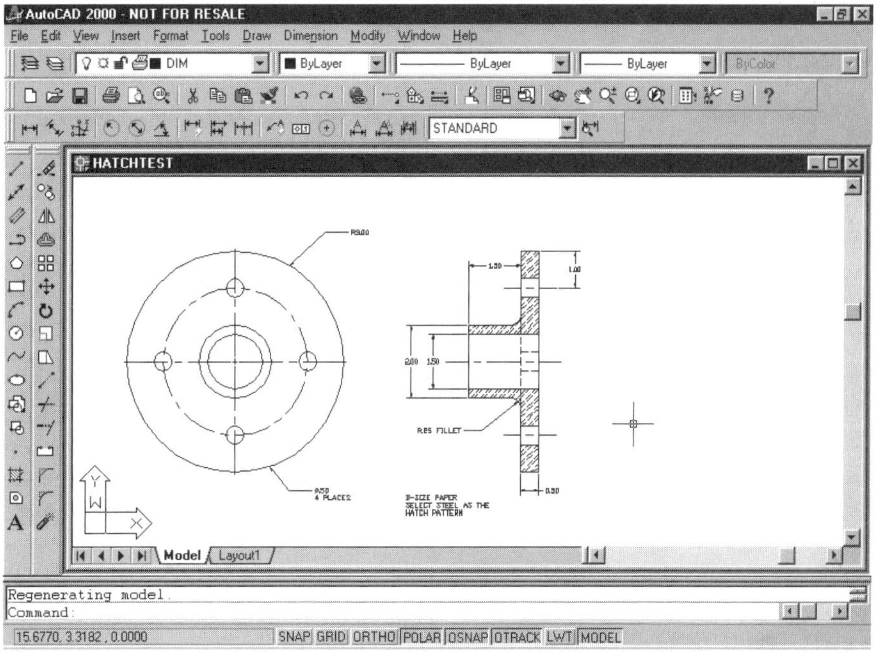

Figure 2–2
UCS icon depicting X, Y, and Z axes.

ing out of the computer screen. In Figure 2–2, the UCS icon in the lower left corner of the drawing editor depicts the position of the X, Y, and Z axes.

As you draw, you can enter coordinate values to locate a point. There are three common coordinate systems that can be used to enter points. The **absolute coordinate** system uses values based on the origin point of 0,0. The **relative coordinate** system uses values based on the last point entered. The **polar coordinate** system uses a distance and angle.

Entering Absolute Coordinates

To draw a line a from a beginning point that has an X value of 1.5 and a Y value of 2, and an ending point that has an X value of 5 and a Y value of 5, make the following entries on the command prompt line.

Try This

Open the AutoCAD system program and start a drawing from scratch.

1. At the Command prompt, type **l** and press **<Enter>**, or press the right mouse key. (This is the same as pressing the <Enter> key.)
2. At From Point: type **1.5,2** and press **<Enter>**.
3. At To Point: type **5,5** and press **<Enter>**.
4. At To Point: press **<Enter>** to exit the command.

A diagonal line should appear on the drawing screen that starts at 1.5,2 and goes to 5,5.

Entering Relative Coordinates

Relative coordinate points are used when you know the position of a point in relation to a previous point. To locate a point relative to 1.5,2 type the @ symbol before entering the next coordinate.

TRY THIS

Open the AutoCAD software program and start a drawing from scratch.

1. At the Command prompt, type **l** and press **<Enter>** or press the right mouse key. (This is the same as pressing the <Enter> key.)
2. At From Point: type **1.5,2** and press **<Enter>**.
3. At To Point: type **@3.5,3** and press **<Enter>.**
4. At To Point: press **<Enter>** to exit the command.

A diagonal line should appear on the drawing screen that starts at 1.5,2 and goes to 5,5.

This sequence should draw the same line that appeared in the previous example.

Entering Polar Coordinates

Polar coordinates are entered as a distance and angle. The values are separated with the angle bracket (<) symbol. To draw a line with a starting point of 1.5,2 and 3″ in length at a 45° angle enter the following commands. If the polar button icon is selected to be on, polar tracking will automatically be displayed. Polar tracking shows the distance and angle of an entity from a starting point. In Figure 2–3, the distance and angle of the proposed endpoint of the line are displayed.

TRY THIS

Open the AutoCAD software program and start a drawing from scratch.

1. At the Command prompt, type **l** and press **<Enter>** or press the right mouse key. (This is the same as pressing the <Enter> key.)
2. At From Point: type **1.5,2** and press **<Enter>**.
3. At To Point: type **@3<45** and press **<Enter>**.
4. At To Point: press **<Enter>** to exit the command.

A diagonal line should appear on the drawing screen that starts at 1.5,2 and goes to 5,5.

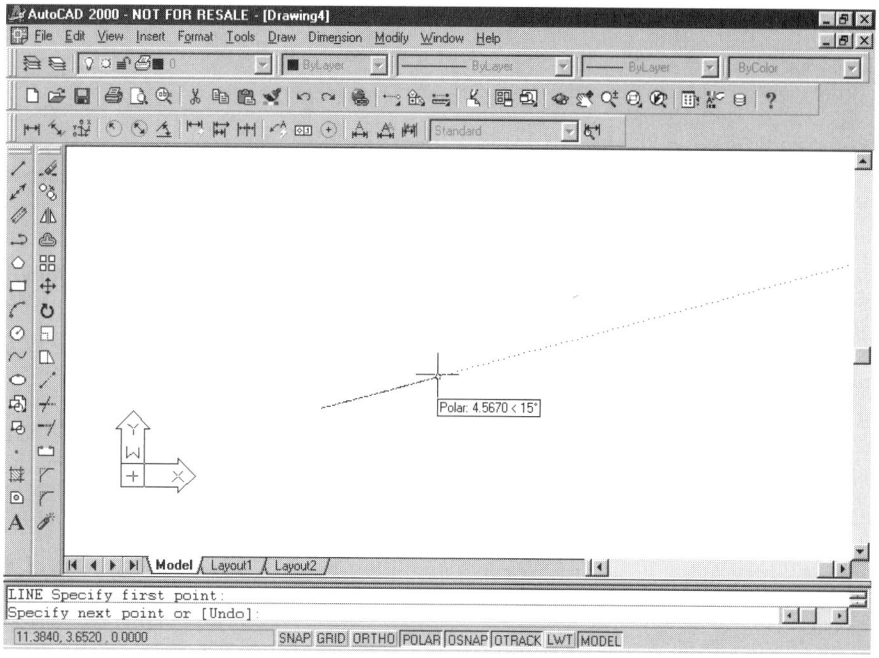

Figure 2–3
Polar tracking.

CREATING OBJECTS

Lines and Polylines

Common commands used to create lines include **line (l)** and **polyline (pl)**. A **line** is one segment or a series of connected segments; however, each segment is an individual object. A **polyline** is a connected sequence of line or arc segments and is treated as a single object (Autodesk, Inc., 1997). When you create a line, AutoCAD requests the starting point and the ending point. Starting and ending points can be determined in a variety of ways.

To draw a line:

1. From the Draw pull-down menu, select Line.
2. Specify the starting point.
3. Specify the endpoint.
4. Specify the endpoints of any other line segments.
5. Press <Enter> to complete the line.

TRY THIS

Draw a box by typing in or selecting the following coordinates:

1. From the Draw pull-down menu or the toolbar menu, select the **Line** command.
2. For the starting point, enter or select the coordinates 2,2.

3. Next point: 4,2.
4. Next point: 4,4.
5. Next point: 2,4.
6. Next point: 2,2.
7. Press <Enter> to exit the line command.

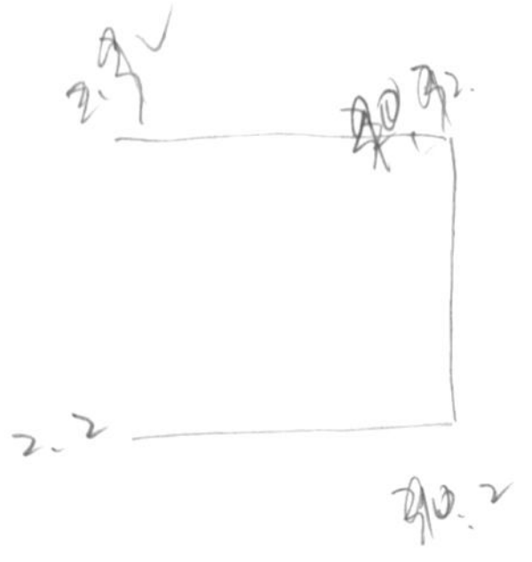

A rectangular box should now be showing on the screen.

Note: Repeat the preceding example but instead of entering the last point (2,2), type c (for close).

Lines can also be created by typing in the relative or polar coordinates. For example (Figure 2–4), to draw a 6″ long horizontal line from the point 1,1 (absolute coordinates), the command would be @6<0 (polar coordinates). Recall that the @ symbol indicates a distance relative to the initial point. The result would be a horizontal line 6″ long that has a starting point at 1,1. The @ symbol indicates a position relative to the initial point.

TRY THIS

Enter the following distances and angles to draw a rectangle that measures 3″ × 2″.

1. From the Draw pull-down menu, select **Line**.
2. Type **1,1** as the starting point.

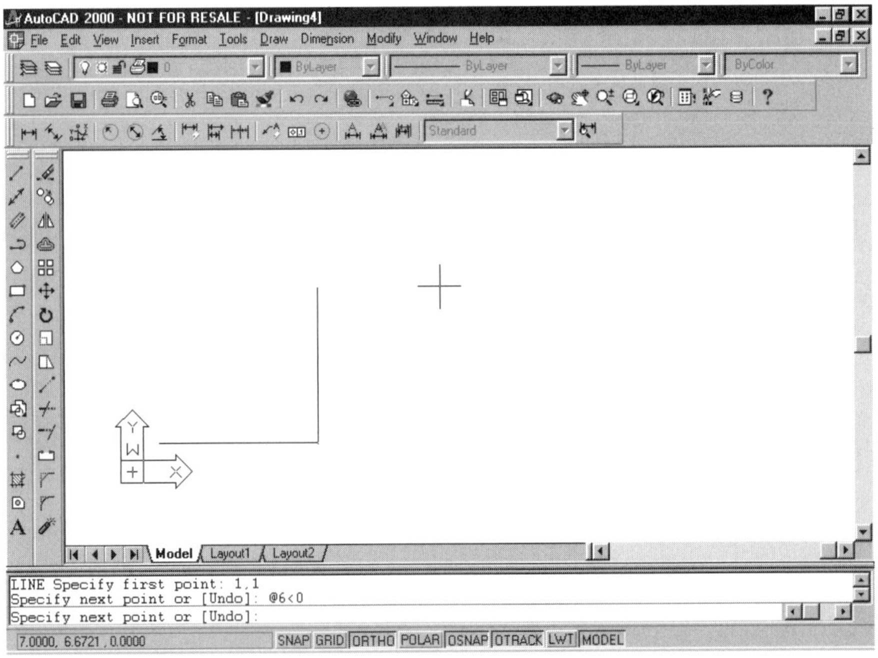

Figure 2–4
Using the polar coordinate system for entering data.

3. Type @3<0 and press <Enter>. (A horizontal line 3 units long should appear.)
4. Type @2<90 and press <Enter>. (A vertical line 2 units long should be drawn from the endpoint of the previous line.)
5. Type @3<180 and press <Enter>. (A horizontal line 3 units long should be drawn from the endpoint of the previous line.)
6. Type c (close) to draw a line from the endpoint of the previous line to the original starting point.
7. Press <Enter>.

Lines may also be drawn by manually selecting two points using the mouse and selecting points. It is recommended that if you use this method, you turn the grid on and set the snap distance to the smallest increment. A **grid** is a visual representation of the drawing area. Grid points can be set to different values. A **snap** setting restricts the movement of the crosshairs by a distance you define. The relationship between the grid and snap is determined by the spacing of the visual reference points of the grid and the smallest increment the crosshairs move as determined by the snap setting (see Chapter 3).

Polyline–a connected sequence of line or arc segments created as a single object

Pline is an acronym for polyline. The pline (pl) command allows for the creation of multisegmented lines that are connected at the endpoints of each segment. Even though there may be many different segments, a polyline is treated as a single object. Plines are also different from lines in that plines can be assigned width. The pline in Figure 2–5 has a width of .03″. Plines are edited through the **pedit** command.

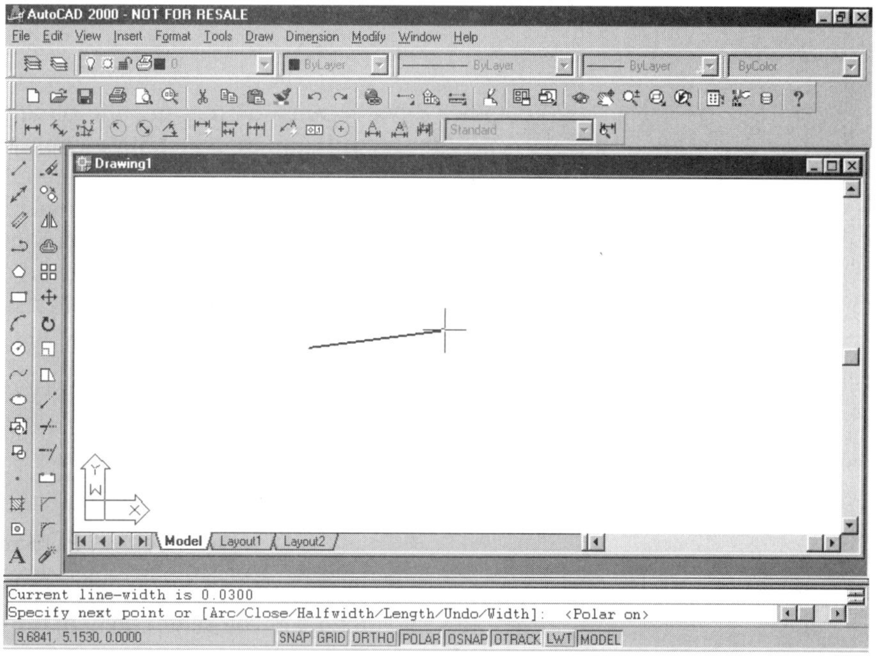

Figure 2–5
Creating a polyline.

Try This

Create a horizontal pline that is 4 units long and .03″ wide. The starting point of the pline is at .5,.5.

1. From the Draw pull-down menu, select **Polyline**.
2. Starting point is **.5,.5**.
3. Next type **W** for entering the width of the line. Type **.03**″ for width value, both starting and ending.
4. Enter the polar coordinate **@4<0** for the next point.
5. Select **<Enter>** to exit the polyline command.

The pline command is also used to create arcs that have pline characteristics.

Try This

1. From the Draw menu, select **Polyline**.
2. Specify a starting point: **1,1**.
3. Specify an endpoint: **1,2**.
4. Enter **a** to switch to Arc mode.
5. Specify the endpoint of the arc (select a point).
6. Enter **l** to return to the line mode.
7. Press **<Enter>** to end the command, or type in the endpoint coordinates. The drawing should look similar to that in Figure 2–6.

Other draw commands that use the pline characteristic for creating objects include the **polygon** and **rectangle** commands. A polygon is a multisided object that has between 3 and 1024 equal-length sides. A polygon is drawn by inscribing it in, or circumscribing it about, an imaginary circle. Polygons can also be drawn by specifying the endpoints of one of the edges of the polygon.

Inscribed polygons are used when you want to specify the distance between the center of the polygon and each vertex (Autodesk, Inc., 1997).

Try This

Draw an inscribed square.

1. From the Draw menu, select **Polygon**.
2. Enter **4** to specify the number of sides for the polygon.
3. Enter **4,4** as the center point of the polygon.

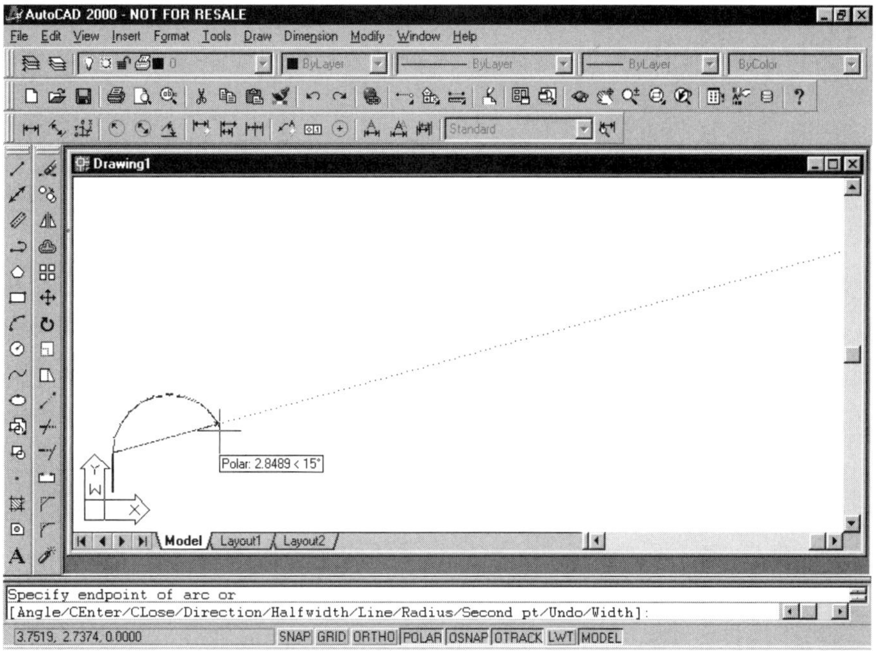

Figure 2–6
Pline and arc commands.

4. Enter **I** (inscribed in circle).
5. Specify the radius as 3.

Circumscribed polygons are used when you want to specify the distance between the center of the polygon and midpoint of each side.

TRY THIS

Draw a circumscribed octagon.

1. From the Draw menu, select **Polygon**.
2. Enter **8** to specify the number of sides for the polygon.
3. Enter **3,4** to specify the center of the polygon.
4. Enter **c** (circumscribed about a circle).
5. Specify the radius length as **2**.

Figure 2–7 depicts a five-sided polygon that was inscribed.

The term *construction line* usually refers to xlines. Construction lines are used as references for creating other objects. Construction lines extend to infinity but have no effect on the extents of the drawing. Construction lines are typically created on a separate layer that can be turned off so that they will not plot.

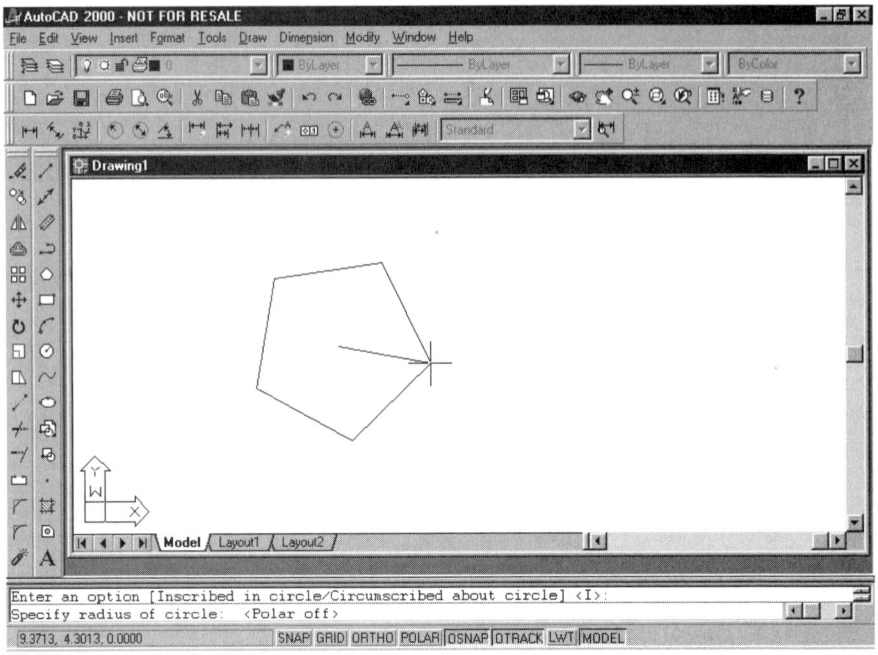

Figure 2–7
Five-sided polygon.

Multilines (ml) consist of between 1 and 16 parallel lines. The lines, called *elements,* are positioned by specifying the desired offset of each element from the origin of the multiline. You can create and save multiline styles. From the Format pull-down menu, select Multiline Style. A dialog box will appear (see Figure 2–8) where style options, Element properties, and Multiline properties can be set. The color and linetype of each element can be set and saved as a particular style.

TRY THIS

Create a series of lines using the Multiline command.

1. From the Draw menu, select **Multiline**.
2. At the command prompt, type **st** to select a style.
3. To list the available styles, type the style name or enter **?**.
4. To justify the multiline, enter **j** and select from top, zero, or bottom.
5. To change the scale of the multiline, enter **s** and enter a new scale. The scale affects the distance between the lines. A scale of 0 would create a single line, since the distance between the lines would be 0.
6. Draw the multiline.
7. Specify a starting point.
8. Specify a second point.
9. Specify a third point.
10. Specify a fourth point, or enter **c** to close the multiline, or press **<Enter>**.

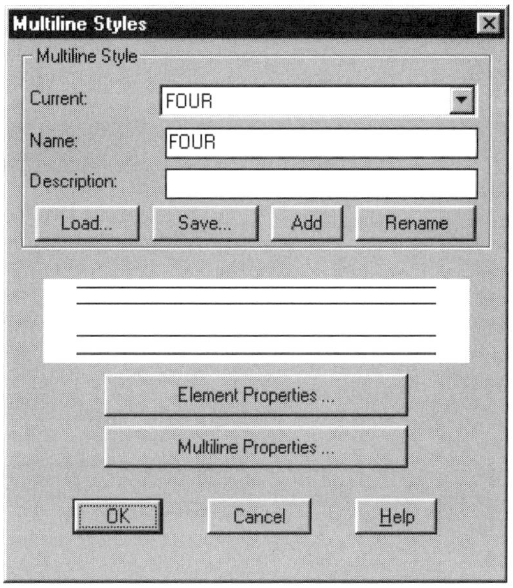

Figure 2–8
Multiline dialog box.

Arc

The Arc command is used to create a curved edge. There are several submenus for creating arcs (see Figure 2–9). The submenu options are represented by various letters such as (S) start, (C) center, (D) distance, (E) end, or (R) radius. These options are used in a variety of combinations to create an arc. For instance, the SER prompt would enable you to create an arc through the following process:

1. Select a start point (S).
2. Select an endpoint (E).
3. Determine the radius (R) of the arc by either typing in a value or moving the crosshairs to the selected point.

TRY THIS

Create an arc.

1. From the Draw menu, select **Arc**.
2. Select the **SER** option for creating this arc.
3. Pick a start point.
4. Pick an endpoint.
5. Enter a radius value for the arc.

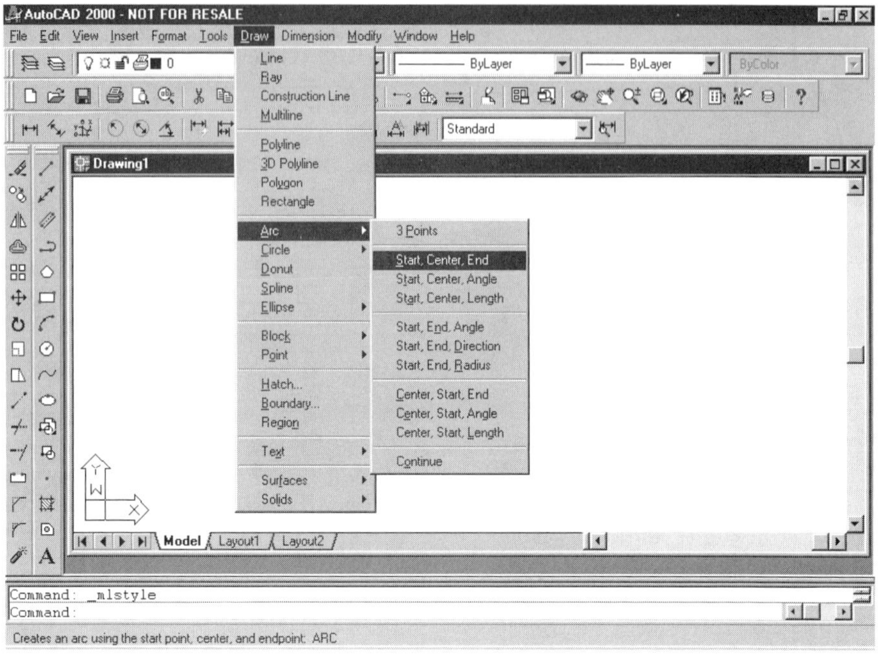

Figure 2–9
Arc command options.

Circle

Circles are created by picking a center point and then inputting a radius or diameter value. The center point of a circle can be selected by moving the cursor crosshair to a point for the circle center or by typing in the coordinates of the circle's center. The second prompt of the circle command determines the circle size based on the radius or diameter. Press <Enter> after typing in the diameter value. In Figure 2–10 the circle command was selected from the pull-down menu.

TRY THIS

Draw a circle by specifying the center point and radius.

1. From the Draw pull-down menu, select **Circle**.
2. Select **Center, Radius**.
3. Specify the center point at **3,3**; press **<Enter>**.
4. Specify a radius of **2**; press **<Enter>**.

Ellipse

There are two methods for creating an ellipse. The first method involves selection of the center of the ellipse. After selecting the center of the ellipse you can either click the mouse to pick axis endpoints or type in values at

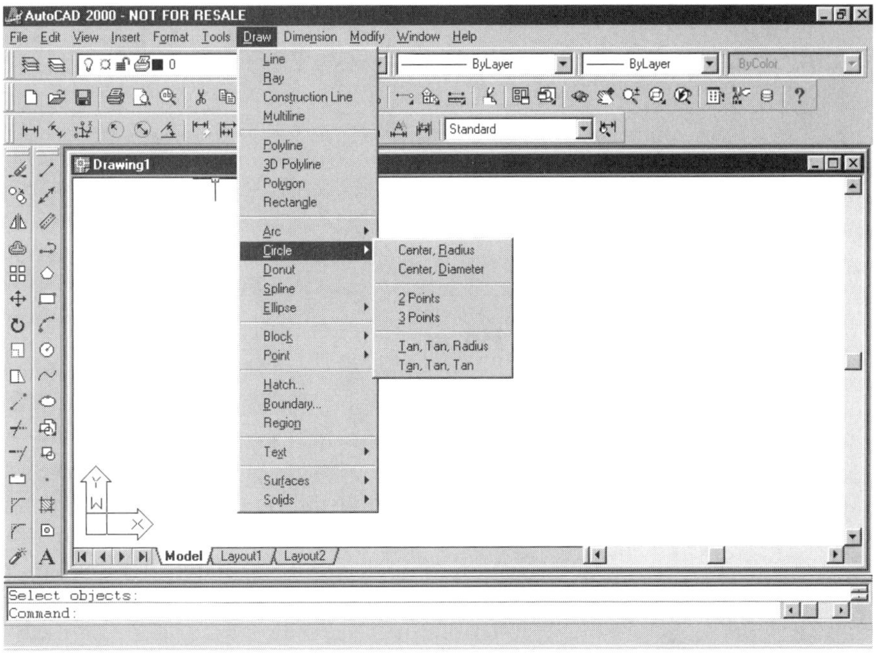

Figure 2–10
Using the pull-down menu to create a circle.

the command prompt (see Figure 2–11). The second method for creating an ellipse is to define the size of the major and minor axes.

TRY THIS

Draw an ellipse using endpoints and a distance.

1. From the Draw pull-down menu, select **Ellipse**.
2. Select option **<Axis Endpoint 1>**.

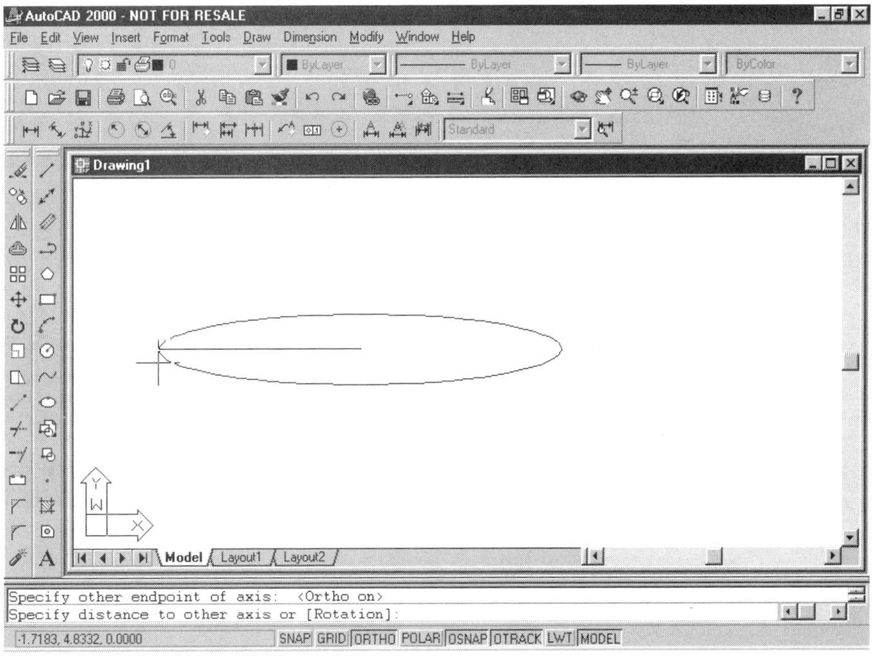

Figure 2–11
Creating an ellipse.

3. Specify the first endpoint of the first axis.
4. Specify the second endpoint of the first axis.
5. Move the pointing device from the midpoint of the first axis and click to specify a distance.

Hatch

Hatch fills an area with a pattern. AutoCAD has numerous predefined hatch patterns in the program. A hatch is applied by picking a point within an enclosed area or by picking an object that has closed endpoints. Hatch patterns are visual representations of materials. When the Hatch command is chosen from the Draw pull-down menu, a series of dialog boxes with options that pertain to hatch parameters appears (see Figure 2–12). Hatch properties include the pattern, scale, and angle. After selecting the pattern and setting the scale and angle, the next step would be to select either a point inside a closed boundary or the boundary itself.

If you choose the Pick Points option, a dialog box appears that asks you to select an internal point. This prompt appears at the command prompt. After an internal point has been selected, the screen will display the original hatch dialog box.

The advanced options of the hatch command allow you to define the objects that determine the boundary. The boundary style of the hatch can also be set in the Advanced tab of the Boundary Creation dialog box (see Figure 2–13). This determines the hatch style for the selection of objects. This command can be executed by selecting Boundary from the Draw pull-down menu.

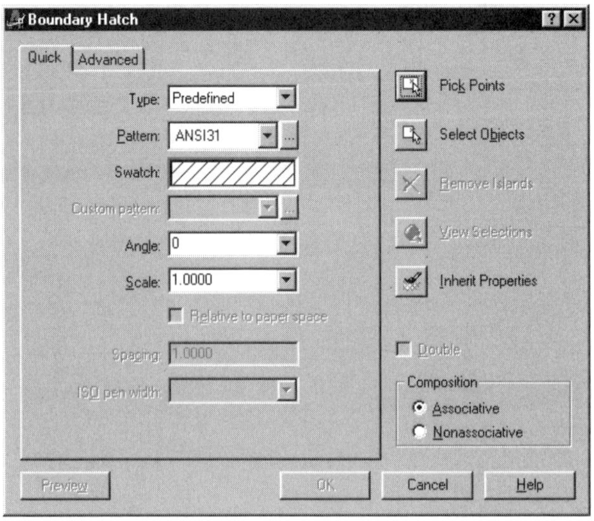

Figure 2–12
Hatch pattern dialog box.

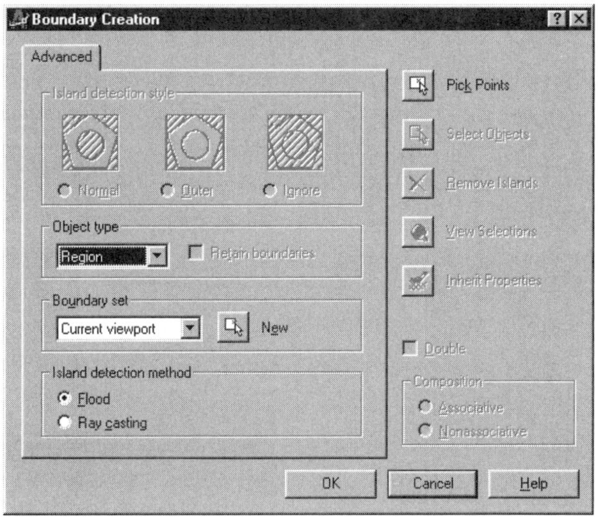

Figure 2–13
Advanced hatch options dialog box.

TRY THIS

Hatch a circle using the Bhatch command.

1. Create a circle with a center point of 3,3 and a radius of 2.
2. At the command prompt, type **Bhatch** (boundary hatch).
3. Change the hatch pattern to **ANSI33**.
4. Pick **Select Objects**.
5. Pick the edge of the circle and right click on the mouse, or press **<Enter>**.
6. Preview hatch to check the angle and scale of the pattern.
7. Apply Hatch.

Hatch patterns are defined as graphic objects, so the more hatches a drawing has, the larger the file size and the longer it takes to regenerate a drawing.

Text

There are three commands that can be used to enter text. These include typing Text at the command prompt, or selecting Text from the Draw pull-down menu, or selecting mtext (multiline text) or dtext from the screen menu. One of the first questions you will be asked when using the text command is to locate the starting point of the text on the drawing. You must also determine the justification style that you will use. There are a variety of text justification methods that can be used. Selecting text from the Draw pull-down menu is shown in Figure 2–14. Text justification options include the following:

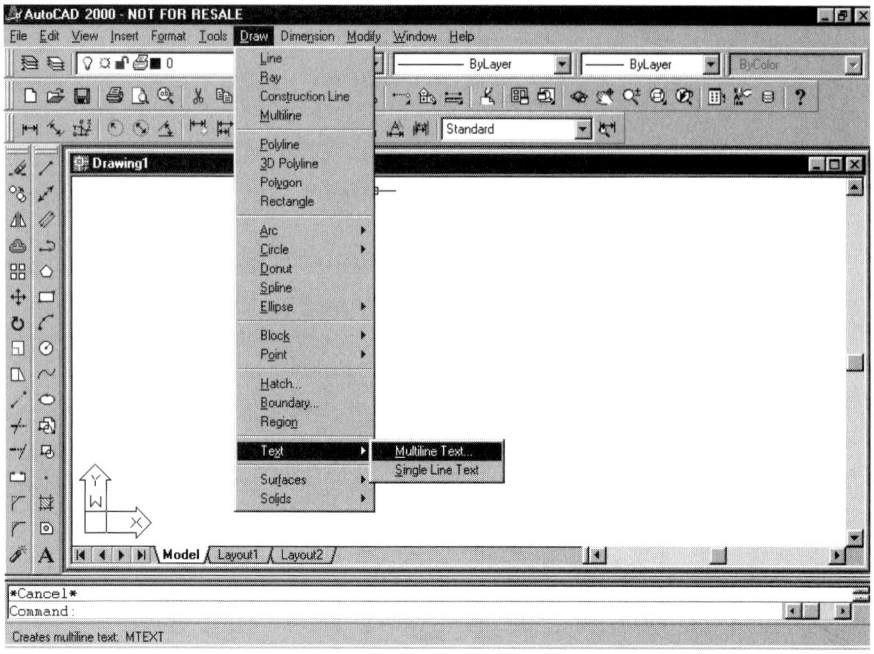

Figure 2–14
Text justification options.

Align	Provides the option of aligning the text to an object.
Fit	The text is fit between two points.
Center	Center of the text is based on a selected point.
Middle	Text is centered around a selected point.
Right	Text justifies to the left of a picked point.
TL	Top Left
TC	Top Center
TR	Top Right
ML	Middle Left
MC	Middle Center
MR	Middle Right
BL	Bottom Left
BC	Bottom Center
BR	Bottom Right

Text size also must be entered after the justification option has been selected. The rotation of the text can also be changed if the text is to be rotated. The default value for text rotation is (0) based on the X axis.

Another option is to set the text style. Figure 2–15 is one dialog box that contains a variety of text styles. From the Format pull-down menu, select Text Style in order to view this dialog box.

TRY THIS

Create a line of text.

1. From the Draw pull-down menu, select **Text**.
2. Select the **Single Line Text** option.

MTEXT
SCALETEXT

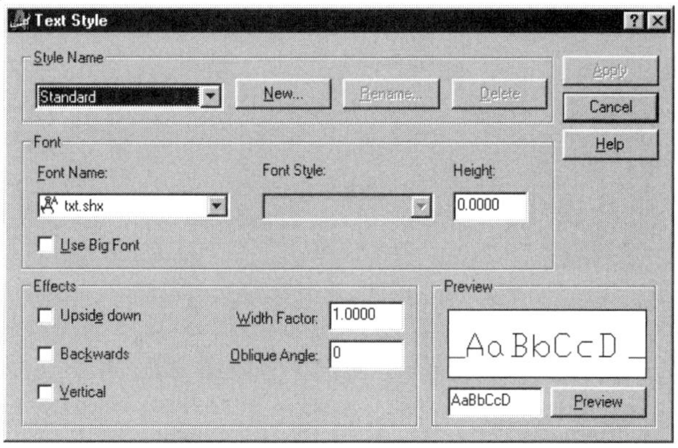

Figure 2–15
Text style dialog box.

3. Click on the starting point for the first character. If you press the **<Enter>** key, the text entry point will default to the last text you entered.
4. Specify the text height.
5. Specify the text rotation. (Accept the default.)
6. Enter the text. (Type any line of text.)
7. When you select **<Enter>** on a blank line, you exit the text command.

The **Dtext** command stands for dynamic text. If you use this command, your characters appear on the screen as you type them. If you use the Text command, the characters will not appear until you are finished typing and exit the command.

If you need to create or import text in paragraph form, use the Multiline (Mtext) text command. When using this command, you will have to define the space in which you want to place the text. You do this by selecting opposite corners of a text box. The command sequence is:

Command: Mtext
Specify first corner:
Specify opposite corner or Height/Justify/Rotation/Style/Width:

After you have selected the opposite corner, a dialog box appears in which you can type your text or import your text from a word processor file. If you use a word processing program to create a file, you should save the text in ASCII text format.

An advantage of using Mtext is that individual words or characters can be formatted. Also, Multiline text has more editing options than either Dtext or Text.

TRY THIS

Create multiline text.

1. From the Draw pull-down menu, select **Text**, and then at the next menu select **Multiline Text**.

2. Specify the first corner of the rectangle in which you want to place the text.
3. Specify the width of the text boundary by moving the pointing device to the left or right of the insertion point and clicking.
4. Specify the text flow by dragging the pointing device either up or down. Click when you have determined the approximate height.
5. In the Multiline Text Editor, enter the text, allowing it to wrap naturally to the next line.

Rectangle

A rectangle is a four-sided object that is constructed out of a polyline. The lines that make up a rectangle are joined at the endpoints. You cannot edit one line without affecting the other lines. Since the lines of a rectangle are polylines, they can have width assigned to them. When selecting the **Rectangle** command for use, you must pick opposite corners in order to create the image (see Figure 2–16). If you know the coordinates of two diagonal corners, you can type them in at the command prompt in order to create the rectangle. Rectangle options include Chamfer, Elevation, Fillet, Thickness, and Width. If Chamfer is selected, the size of the chamfer must be specified. The Elevation option allows for changing the elevation from its current setting to a new setting. The Fillet option allows you to determine corner radii of the four corners.

TRY THIS

Create a rectangle that is 5 × 3 units in size.

1. From the Draw pull-down menu, select **Rectangle.**

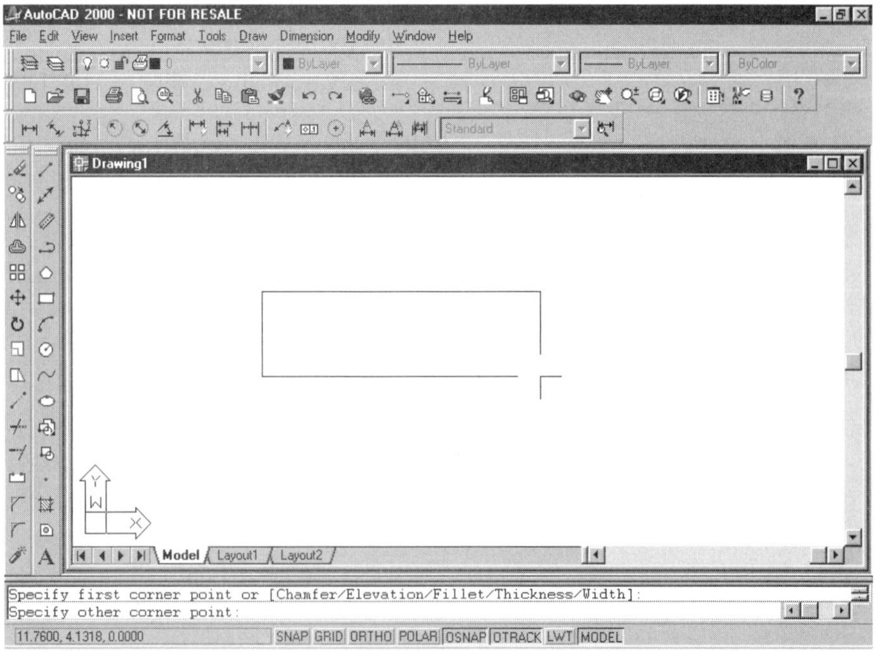

Figure 2–16
Rectangle command.

2. Type **F** for fillet, and enter a radius of **.25**.
3. Type **W** for width, and enter a value of **.03**.
4. Enter a starting point of **2,2**.
5. Enter an ending point of **7,5**.

Donut

The **donut** command allows you to create a solid filled circle that has a hole in the center. In order to create a donut you must know the outside and inside diameter of the object. For instance, Figure 2–17 depicts a donut that has an outside diameter of 1″ and an inside diameter of .5″.

TRY THIS

Create several donuts of varying sizes.

1. From the Draw pull-down menu, select **Donut**.
2. Set the inside diameter to **.75**.
3. Set the outside diameter to **1.25**.
4. Select a point to place the donut in the drawing.
5. Press **<Enter>** twice to cancel and restart the command.
6. Change the diameters to different values, and place these new donuts on the drawing.

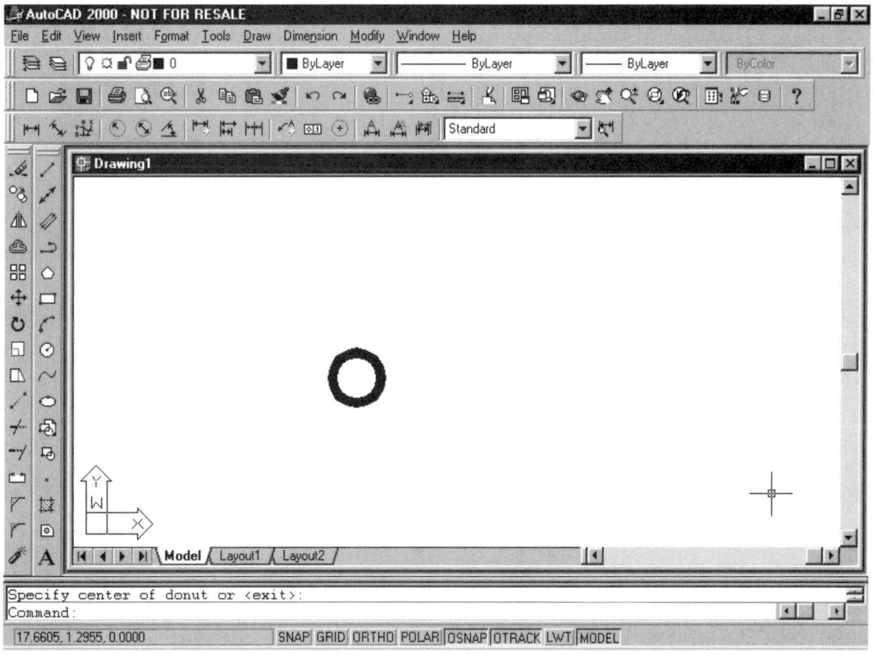

Figure 2–17
Donut command.

Solid

The **solid** command is used to fill a closed object, either triangular or quadrilateral in shape. The solid area will show only if the Fillmode command is on. In order to start the solid command, type or enter solid at the command prompt, or select Surfaces from the Draw pull-down menu, then 2D Solid.

After selecting the Solids command, you must answer a series of prompts in order to successfully create the solid. You must select points on the object to create a solid surface.

Command:	Solids
First Point:	(must select a point on the object)
Second Point:	(must select a point on the object)
Third Point:	(must select a point on the object)
Fourth Point:	(must select a point on the object)

Press <Enter> to exit the command.

Figure 2–18 shows three examples for creating a 2D solid. The numbers on each object represent the sequence of picked points.

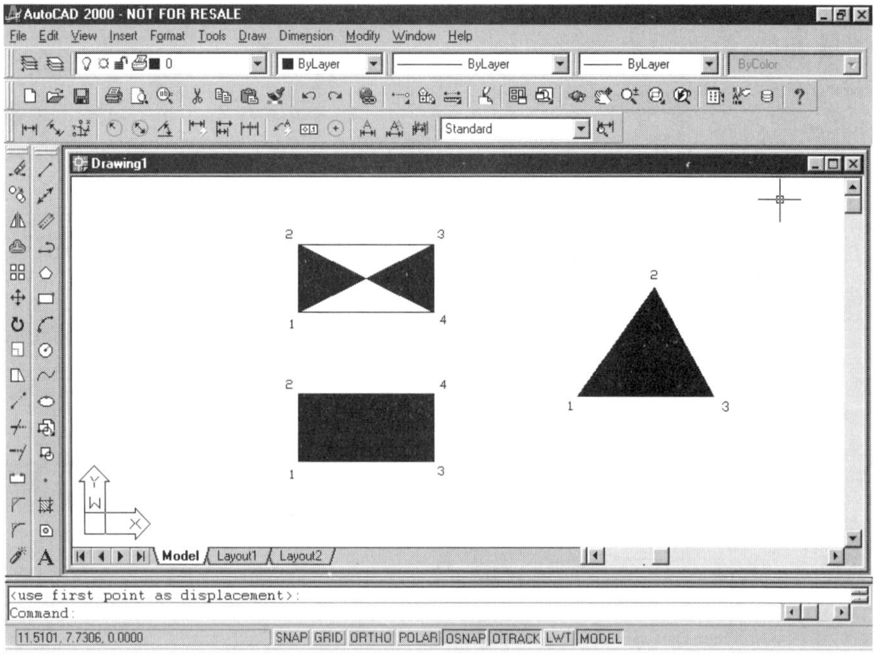

Figure 2–18
2D solid examples.

Chapter 2 ■ Activities

There are four drawing activities associated with this chapter. The first two activities involve the creation of two border template files, one for A-size paper and one for B-size paper. Activities 3 and 4 deal with object creation.

Activity 2–1

Create an A-Size Border Template

The purpose of this activity is for you to create a title block and border for A-size paper (see page 38). The English drawing sheet size for A-size paper is 11″ × 8.5″. When you take into consideration the mechanical limits of most plotters/printers, you cannot use the full sheet of paper. In this particular activity, you will create an A-size border and title block that measures 10″ × 7.7″.

ACTIVITY STEPS:

1. Open the AutoCAD software program and select Start from Scratch.
2. From the Tools pull-down menu select Wizards, then Create Layout.
3. A dialog box should appear that lists several options that allow you to set up a custom layout.
4. The first option is to rename the layout; call it Bordera.
5. The second option is to select the output device (printer/plotter in most instances) that you will use for outputting the drawing.
6. Option 3 allows you to select the paper size you are using for output.
7. Option 4 allows you to pick the orientation of the paper, either portrait or landscape. Select the option based on your printer.
8. Option 5 allows you to select one of the predefined title blocks or none at all. Since you are creating your own title block, select None.
9. The Define Viewport is the next option. Select Single, and in the Viewport scale option, select 1:1.
10. The next option is the Pick Location option that lets you determine where the viewport is displayed as well as the size of the viewport. Click on the Select Location option. Specify the first corner at 0,0 and the second corner at 10, 7.7.
11. Select Finish. A viewport window that is designated by a solid rectangle should now appear.

12. From the File pull-down menu select Page Setup. Reset the X and Y plot offset origins so that the viewport window appears inside the dashed lines.
13. Type z <Enter> then a (all) and press <Enter> to zoom to full screen.
14. At the command prompt, type layer. A dialog box should appear that lists all the current layers and their properties. Click on the New button, create a new layer called border, and make it current.
15. From the Draw pull-down menu select Polyline to start the pline command.
16. At the From point: prompt enter 0,0.
17. At the Endpoint of line: prompt, enter w (width) and then <Enter>.
18. At the Starting width: prompt, type .03 <Enter>.
19. Accept the default ending width by pressing <Enter>. It should read .03.
20. At the prompt Endpoint of line: type 10,0 <Enter>.
21. At the prompt Endpoint of line: type 10,7.7 <Enter>.
22. At the prompt Endpoint of line: type 0,7.7 <Enter>.
23. At the prompt Endpoint of line: type c (close). An outside borderline should be visible.
24. Press <Enter> to restart the pline command.
25. At the prompt From point: type 6,0 <Enter>.
26. At the prompt Endpoint of line: type @1.5<90 <Enter>.
27. At the prompt Endpoint of line: type @4<0 <Enter>.
28. The command prompt line should be blank, and there should be a rectangular box in the lower right corner of the drawing screen.
29. Press <Enter> to restart the pline command.
30. At the From point: command, type 6, .375 <Enter>.
31. At the Endpoint of line: command, type 9, .375 <Enter>.
32. Press <Enter> twice, once to exit the command and once to restart the command.
33. At the From point: command, type 6, .75 <Enter>.
34. At the Endpoint of line: command, type 10, .375 <Enter>.
35. Press <Enter> twice, once to exit the command and once to restart the command.
36. At the From point: command, type 6, 1.125 <Enter>.
37. At the Endpoint of line: command, type 10, 1.125 <Enter>.
38. Press <Enter> twice, once to exit the command and once to restart the command.
39. At the From point: command, type 9, 0 <Enter>.
40. At the Endpoint of line: command, type 9, .75 <Enter>.
41. Press <Enter> to exit the pline command.
42. From the File pull-down menu select Save.
43. Name the drawing Borda and change the File type to .dwt.

The title block and borderlines for an A-size sheet of paper should be completed. The second part of this activity will be to add text to the title block.

1. At the command prompt, type z (zoom). Use the cursor crosshairs to create a window around the title block in the right corner of the drawing.
2. From the Tools pull-down menu, select Drafting Settings. Change the Snap setting for X and Y to .0625″. Be sure to check the ON box for the snap. The cursor will move at .0625″ intervals.
3. Change the Grid setting for X and Y to .25″. Be sure to check the ON box for the snap. The grid points should be displayed at .25″ intervals.
4. From the Format pull-down menu, select Layer. The Layer dialog box should now appear.
5. In the Layer dialog box, select New. Type Text as the new layer. In this same dialog box and in the same row as the Text layer, select the black square next to the word Continuous. This square represents the color assigned to this layer. After you have selected the square, a Color dialog box should appear. At the top of the dialog box is a row of the Standard Colors. Click on the color blue. Press <OK> to exit the Color dialog box. The square next to the word Continuous should now appear blue.
6. If the layer Text is not highlighted, click on the word Text. Near the center and top of the dialog box there is a button that makes the layer you have highlighted current. Click on it to make Text the current layer. The current layer name should appear to the right of the word Current.
7. Click <OK> to exit the Layer dialog box.
8. At the command prompt, type Text. At the Starting point prompt, pick a point in the lower right section of the title block. With the snap on, you should be able to move the cursor crosshairs to a point that is two snap points above the bottom line and two snap points from the left vertical line. Press <Enter>.
9. At the Text height: prompt, type .125 <Enter>.
10. Leave the Rotation angle at 0. Press <Enter>.
11. At the Text: prompt, type Scale: <Enter>. Repeat the Text command and place text similar to that in the example (Figure 2–19).
12. Save the drawing before exiting.

ACTIVITY 2–2

Create a B-Size Border Template

The purpose of this activity is for you to create a title block and border for B-size paper (see page 41). The English drawing sheet size for B-size paper is 17″ × 11″. When you take into consideration the mechanical limits of most plotters/printers, you cannot use the full sheet of paper. In this particular activity, you will create a B-size border and title block that have a measurement 15.5″ × 10″.

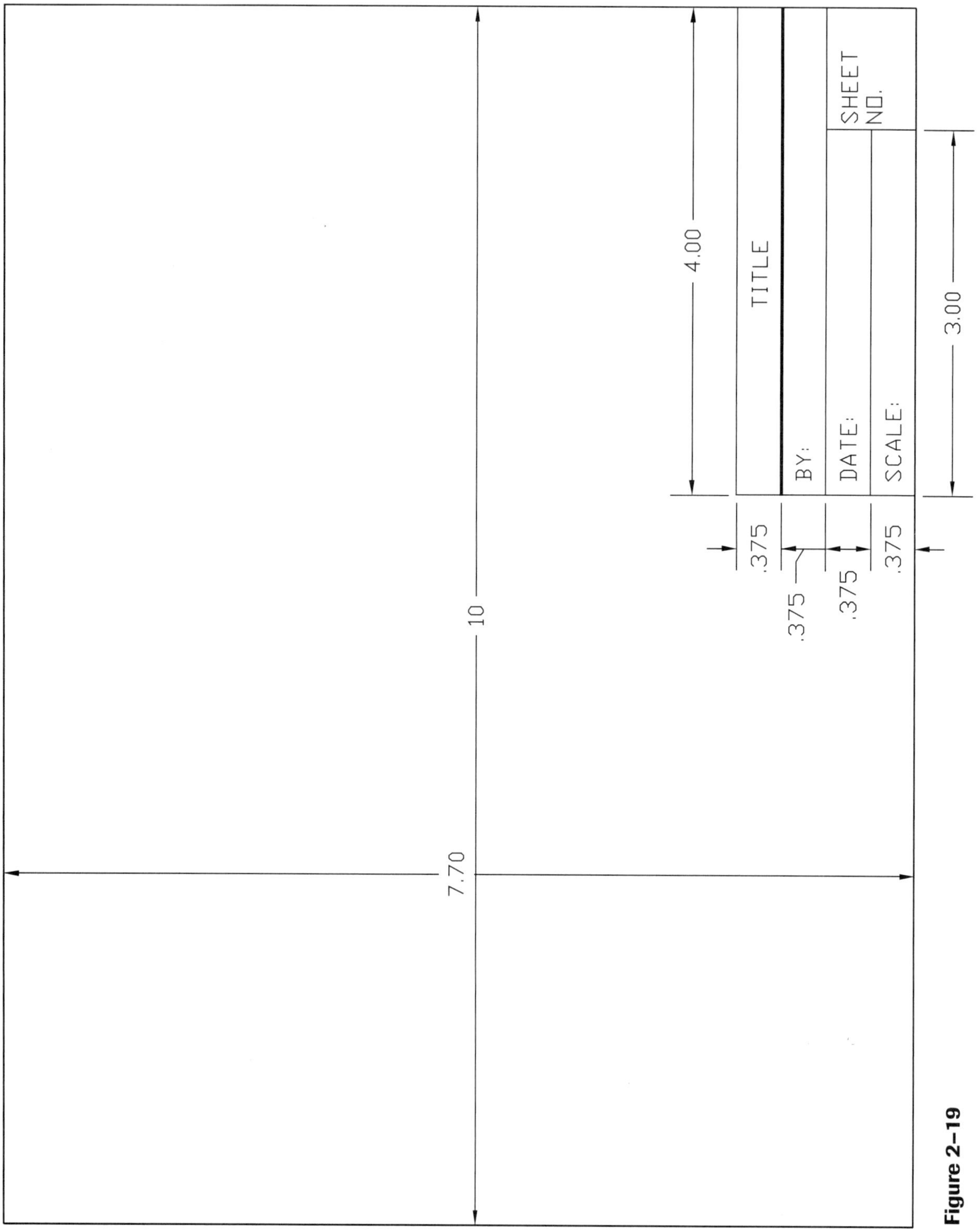

Figure 2–19

ACTIVITY STEPS:

1. Open the AutoCAD software and select Start from Scratch.
2. From the Format pull-down menu, select Drawing Limits.
3. Accept the default (press <Enter>) of 0,0 for the lower left corner.
4. Type 15.5,10 <Enter> at the command prompt to change the settings for the upper right-hand corner.
5. Type z <Enter> then a (all) <Enter> to zoom to full screen.
6. Double click on the MODEL (model space) button at the bottom of the screen to switch to paper space (ps).
7. Type mview (mv) then 0,0 and <Enter> at the (First point) prompt.
8. At the Other corner prompt, type 15.5,10 <Enter>. A rectangular box should be showing on the screen. This is a viewport box.
9. Type z (zoom) <Enter> then a (all) <Enter> to zoom full screen in paper space.
10. From the Format pull-down menu, select Drawing Limits. The limits must be reset in paper space. Set the limits to 0,0 and 15.5,10.
11. Type z (zoom) <Enter> then a (all) <Enter> to zoom full screen.
12. From the Draw pull-down menu, select pline to start the pline command.
13. At the From point: prompt, enter 0,0.
14. At the Endpoint of line: prompt, enter w (width) and then <Enter>.
15. At the Starting width: prompt, type .03 <Enter>.
16. Accent the default ending width by pressing <Enter>. It should read .03.
17. At the prompt, Endpoint of line:, type 15.5,0 <Enter>.
18. At the prompt, Endpoint of line:, type 15.5,10 <Enter>.
19. At the prompt Endpoint of line:, type 0,10 <Enter>.
20. At the prompt Endpoint of line:, type c (close). An outside borderline should be visible.
21. Press <Enter> to restart the pline command.
22. At the prompt From point:, type 11.5,0 <Enter>.
23. At the prompt Endpoint of line:, type @1.5<90 <Enter>.
24. At the prompt Endpoint of line:, type @4<0 <Enter>.
25. The command prompt line should be blank. There should be a rectangular box in the lower right corner of the drawing screen.
26. Press <Enter> to restart the pline command.
27. At the From point: command, type 11.5, .375 <Enter>.
28. At the Endpoint of line: command, type 14.5, .375 <Enter>.
29. Press <Enter> twice, once to exit the command and once to restart the command.
30. At the From point: command, type 11.5, .75 <Enter>.
31. At the Endpoint of line: command, type 15.5, .75 <Enter>.
32. Press <Enter> twice, once to exit the command and once to restart the command.
33. At the From point: command, enter 11.5, 1.125 <Enter>.

34. At the Endpoint of line: command, type 15.5, 1.125 <Enter>.
35. Press <Enter> twice, once to exit the command and once to restart the command.
36. At the From point: command, type 14.5,0 <Enter>.
37. At the Endpoint of line: command, type 14.5, .75 <Enter>.
38. Press <Enter> to exit the pline command.
39. From the File pull-down menu, select Save.
40. Name the drawing Bordb and change the File type to .dwt.

    The title block and borderlines for a B-size sheet of paper should be complete.

The second part of this activity will be to add text to the title block.

1. At the Command: prompt, type z (zoom). Use the cursor crosshairs to create a window around the title block in the right corner of the drawing.
2. From the Tools pull-down menu, select Drawing Aids. Change the Snap setting for X and Y to .0625″. Be sure to check the ON box for the snap. The cursor will move at .0625″ intervals.
3. Change the Grid setting for X and Y to .25″. Be sure to check the ON box for the snap. The grid points should be displayed at .25″ intervals.
4. From the Format pull-down menu, select Layer. The Layers dialog box should now appear.
5. In the Layer dialog box, select New. Type Text as the new layer. In this same dialog box and in the same row as the Text layer, select the black square next to the word Continuous. This square represents the color assigned to this layer. After you have selected the square, a Color dialog box should appear. At the top of the dialog box is a row of the Standard Colors. Click on the color blue. Press <OK> to exit the Color dialog box. The square next to the word Continuous should now appear blue.
6. If the layer Text is not highlighted, click on the word Text. Near the center and top of the dialog box there is a button that makes the layer you have highlighted current. Click on it to make Text the current layer. The current layer name should appear to the right of the word Current.
7. Click <OK> to exit the Layer dialog box.
8. At the command prompt, type Text. For a Starting point pick a point in the lower right section of the title block. With the snap on, you should be able to move the cursor crosshairs to a point that is two snap points above the bottom line and two snap points from the left vertical line. Press <Enter>.
9. At the Text height prompt, type .125 <Enter>.
10. Leave the Rotation angle at 0. Press <Enter>.
11. At the Text prompt, type Scale: <Enter>. Repeat the Text command and place text similar to that in the example (Figure 2–20).
12. Save the drawing before exiting.

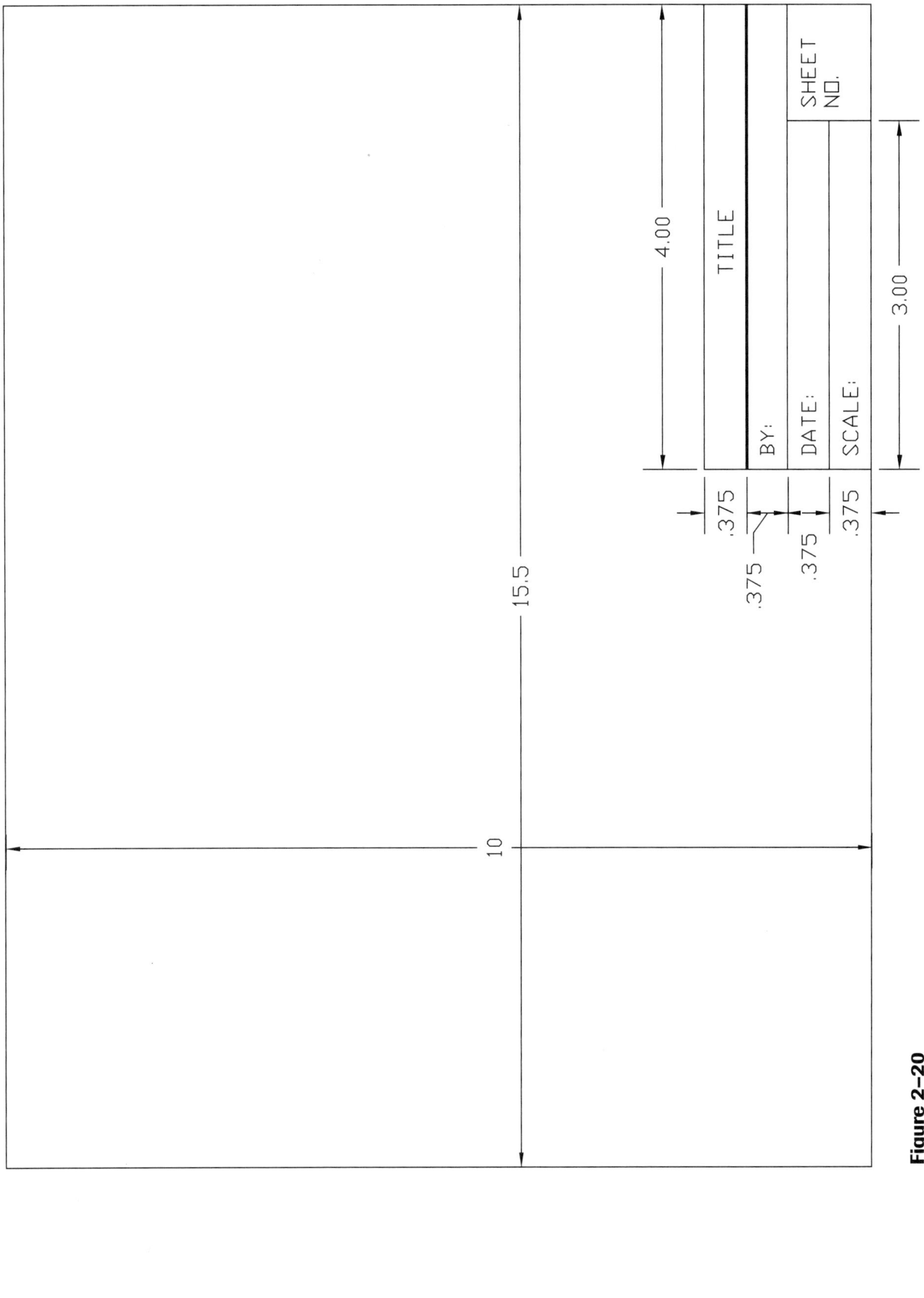

Figure 2–20

ACTIVITY 2–3

Drawing Assignment #1: Entities

Plotter paper size: A

Suggested settings:	Grid	.25″
	Snap	.125″
	Layers (3)	**0** (default border)
		Object, Linetype continuous, Color: black
		Text, Linetype continuous, Color: blue
	Units	Decimal

Hints:

1. At the Startup dialog box, select Use a Template. Load the template file Bordera.
2. Switch to Model space before changing any of the listed settings. Make the suggested settings, and be sure to create the layers listed. All text height is .125″.
3. Review Figure 2–21, following this page. Use the pull-down menu, the floating toolbar, and the screen menu, or type in the command to create the objects. Make sure to create the drawing objects with the accompanying text in Model space. Both the Pline and the Rectangle have line widths of .03″. The Donut has an inside diameter of .5″ and an outside diameter of 1. The only objects that should exist in Paper space are the borderlines and the border text.
4. Switch to Paper space to update the text in the Title block with the appropriate information. You have to be in Paper space in order to edit the objects that were created in Paper space. The name of the drawing is ENTITIES.
5. Once you have completed the drawing, there are two different ways to exit the drawing editor. Before exiting, always save the drawing. From the File pull-down menu select Exit. At the command prompt type quit. If you have made any changes, you will be asked if you want to save those changes.
6. To save your drawing without leaving the drawing editor, type save and press <Enter>. At this point you must give your file a name. Be sure to include the drive designation.

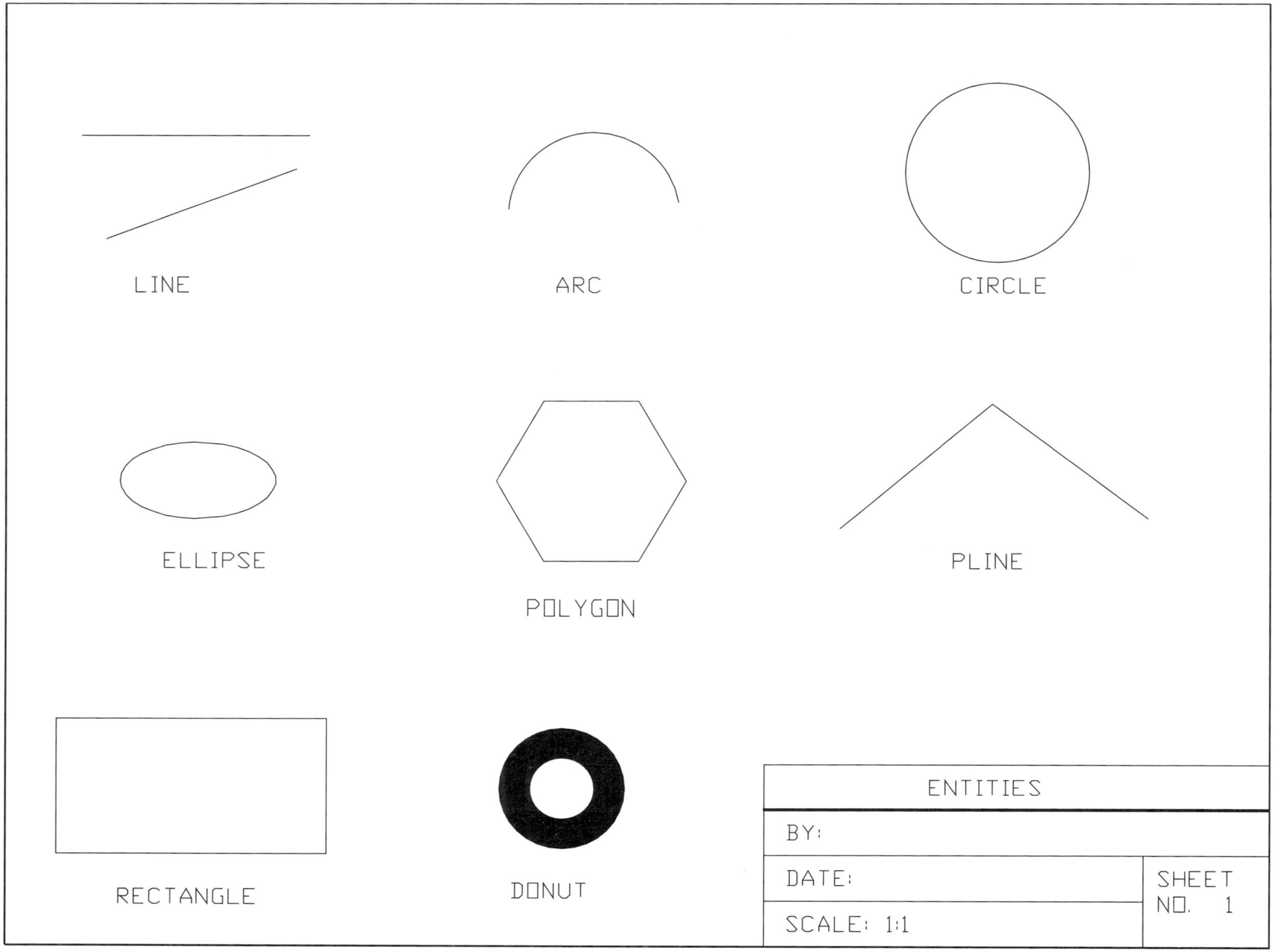
LINE
ARC
CIRCLE
ELLIPSE
POLYGON
PLINE
RECTANGLE
DONUT
ENTITIES
BY:
DATE:
SCALE: 1:1
SHEET NO. 1

Figure 2–21

ACTIVITY 2–4

Drawing Assignment #2: Shim

Plotter paper size: A		
Suggested settings:	Grid	.25″
	Snap	.125″
	Layers (3)	**0** (default border)
		Object, Linetype continuous, Color: black
		Text, Linetype continuous, Color: blue
	Units	Decimal

Hints:

1. At the Startup dialog box, select Use a Template. Load the template file Bordera.
2. Switch to Model space before changing any of the listed settings. Make the suggested settings, and be sure to create the layers listed.
3. Review Figure 2–22, following this page. Use the pull-down menu, the floating toolbar, and the screen menu, or type in the command to create the objects. Make sure to create the drawing objects with the accompanying text in Model space. **Note:** The spacing between the objects is 1.5″. **Do not** include dimensions on the drawing.
4. Switch to Paper space to update the text in the Title block with the appropriate information. You have to be in Paper space in order to edit the objects that were created in Paper space. The name of the drawing is SHIM. Name the file you save SHIM also.
5. Once you have completed the drawing, there are two different ways to exit the drawing editor. Before exiting, always save the drawing. From the File pull-down menu select Exit. At the command prompt type quit. If you have made any changes, you will be asked if you want to save those changes.

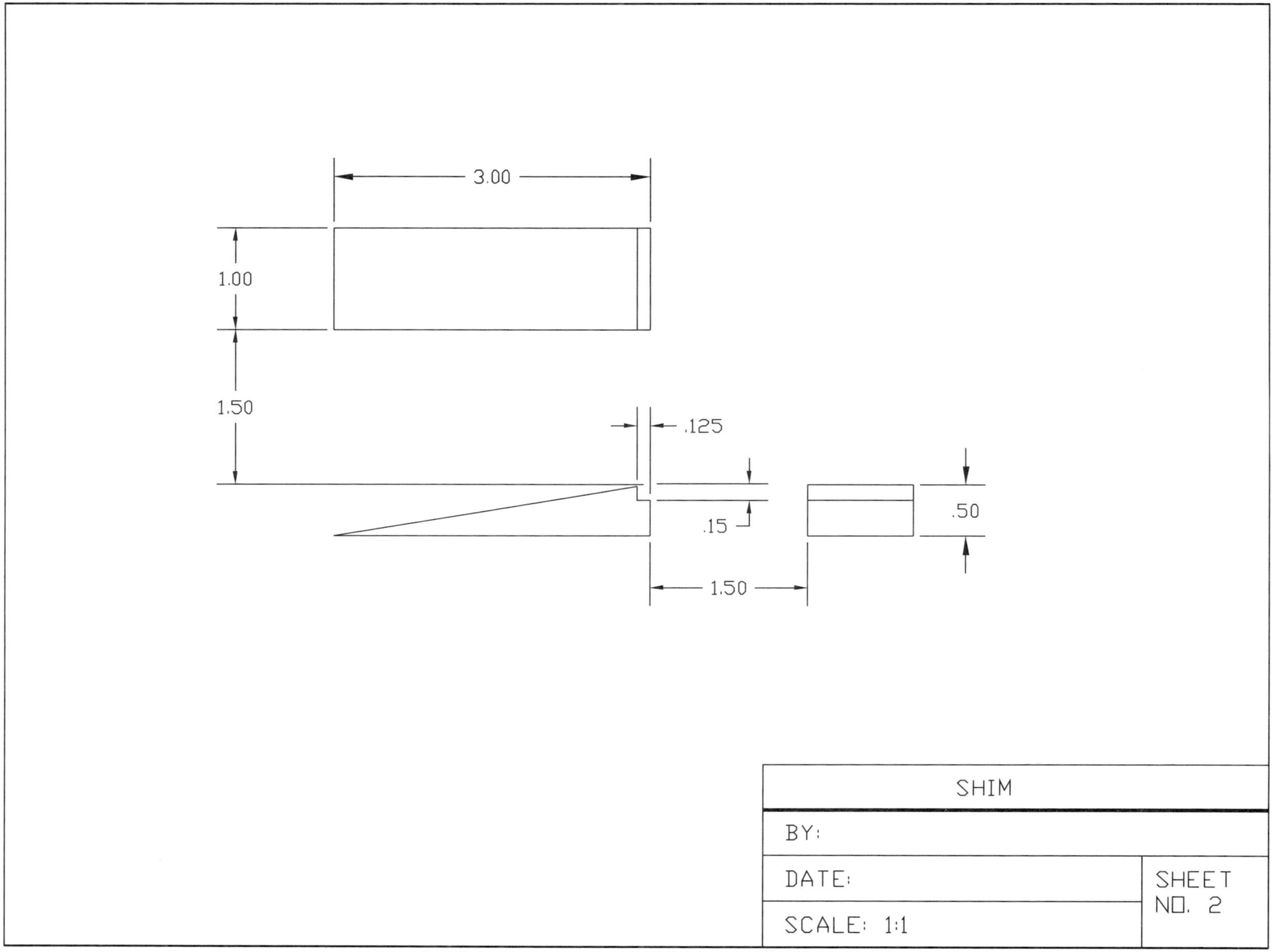

Figure 2–22

CHAPTER

3

Drawing Aids

AFTER READING THIS CHAPTER, YOU WILL BE ABLE TO:

- Use AutoCAD 2000 commands that aid in setting up a drawing sheet.

KEY CONCEPTS:

- Grid
- Limits
- Polar Tracking
- Snap
- Units

When working in the drawing editor and doing drawing layout, it is beneficial to set certain parameters to aid in producing a drawing. This chapter reviews some of the more common drawing aids that can be used to correctly set up a drawing.

LIMITS

The **Limits** command is linked to the size of the drawing. *Drawing limits* refer to the electronic drawing screen that determines the actual size of the drawing area on which an object is created. Two different limits must be set: those in model space and those in paper space. Images are drawn full size, so the limits in model space are set to allow for creating images full size. For example, if you were drawing a house that measured 40′ × 30′, you might set the limits at 60′ × 40′.

Paper space limits are typically the same size as the sheet of paper on which the output is going to occur, and in AutoCAD 2000 they are automatically set when creating a layout. Paper space limits are determined by the output device used to create a plot/print of the drawing. When you are working in a paper space layout, the scale factor represents a ratio between the actual size of the model displayed in the viewports and the size of the layout (Autodesk, Inc., 1999). When the limits in model space are different from the limits of paper space, a zoom ×P factor has to be entered in model space so that the drawing will be plotted at the correct size and scale.

Drawing limits can be set from the Format pull-down menu (see Figure 3–1) or through the Use a Wizard options of Quick Setup or Advanced Setup.

The word limits can also be typed at the command prompt in order to set drawing size. When the command is typed, two relative coordinate points must also be set. Typically the lower left corner is left at 0,0 and the upper right point is set to an (X,Y) point that allows a drawing to be drawn at full size, or the (X,Y) point relates to the size of the sheet of paper on

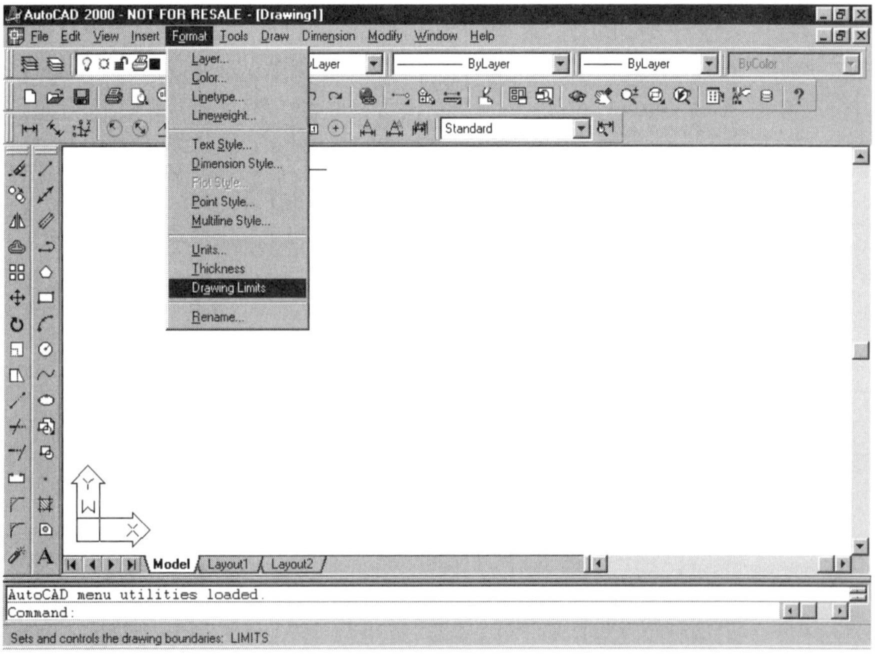

Figure 3–1
Drawing Limits command.

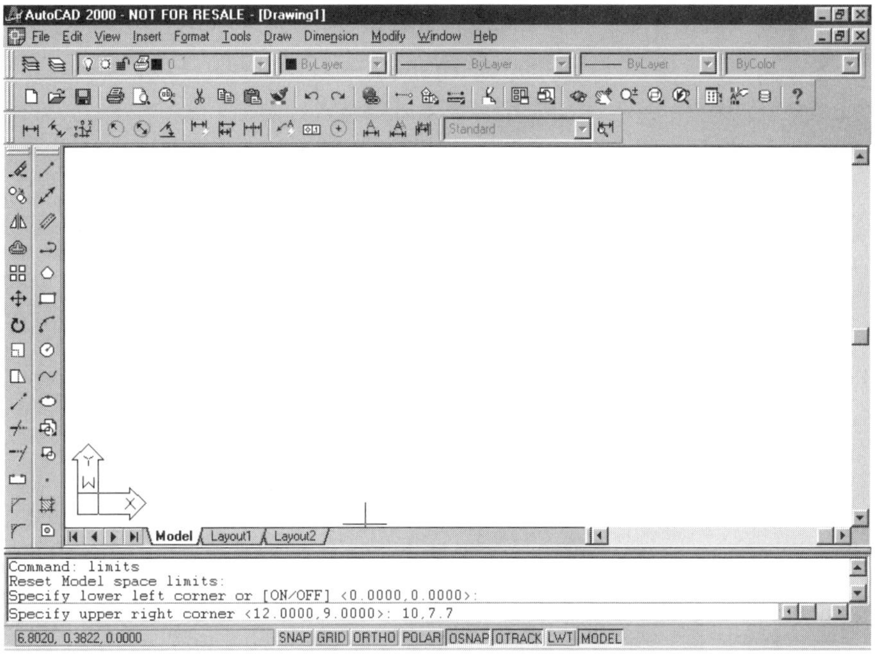

Figure 3-2
Entering limits at the command prompt.

which the drawing will be printed (see Figure 3–2). Limits can be set or changed any time during the drawing process.

TRY THIS

Practice setting the limits in both model space and paper space.

1. Open the AutoCAD software program.
2. In the Startup dialog box, select **Start from Scratch**.
3. From the Format pull-down menu select **Drawing Limits**.
4. At the command prompt change the limits to **0,0** for the lower left corner and **10,7.7** for the upper right corner.
5. At the Command prompt type **z** (for zoom) and then **a** (for all).
6. Repeat the **Limits** command and set the limits to **0,0** for the lower left corner and **15.5,10** for the upper right corner.

UNITS

The **Units** command determines the format of the presentation of the information. There are five different unit types in which the information can be expressed, namely, Scientific, Decimal, Engineering, Architectural, and Fractional.

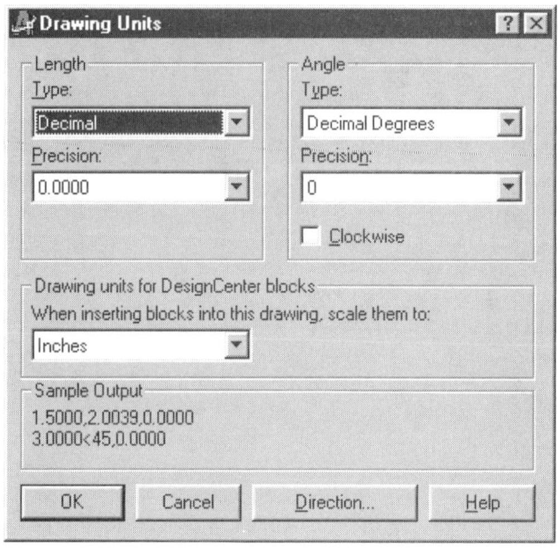

Figure 3–3
Drawing Units dialog box.

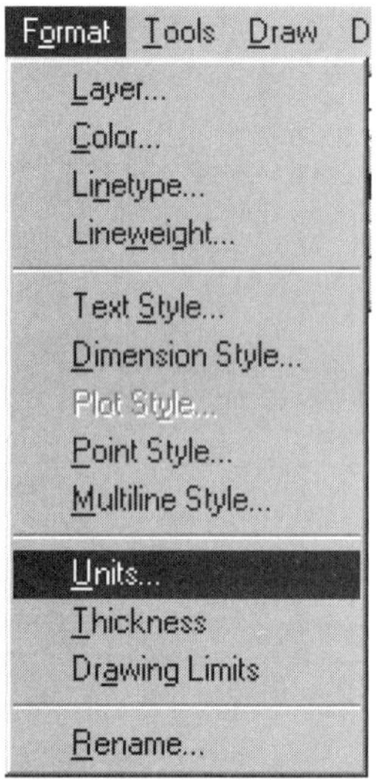

Figure 3–4
Units selected from the Format pull-down menu.

Units are set through the Use a Wizard options of Quick Setup or Advanced Setup. When units is entered at the command prompt, a dialog box appears and displays the following prompts (see Figure 3–3).

The options in the Length portion of the dialog box let you pick the type and the precision level (number of decimal places). Options in the Angle portion of the dialog box allow you to determine how the angle will be measured and the angle measurement precision. You can also indicate whether you want the angle measured clockwise instead of the standard clockwise measurement.

The last variable that can be set in the Drawing Units dialog box determines the format in which blocks will be inserted into the drawing.

You also can select Units from the Format pull-down menu (see Figure 3–4).

TRY THIS

Practice setting up drawings with different units.

1. Open the AutoCAD software program.
2. In the Startup dialog box, select **Start from Scratch**.
3. From the Format pull-down menu select **Units**.
4. In the Drawing Units dialog box select **Architectural** and set the **Precision** to **1/8"**.
5. Select **OK** to exit the Units dialog box.
6. Check the coordinate readout display along the bottom of the screen. It should read in feet and inches.

Repeat the preceding steps and try changing the units to Engineering, Scientific, and Fractional. When you exit the drawing editor, answer **NO** when asked whether to save changes.

GRID

A **blip mark** is a temporary mark in the shape of a plus sign (+) that appears where you specify a point.

The **grid** is used for visual reference. The distance between grid points is based on the size of the electronic drawing sheet. Grid points are not plotted and are not part of the drawing or any drawing object. The shortcut key for toggling the grid on/off is F7. When the grid is turned either on or off, an automatic redraw occurs, and any **blip marks** that are on the screen are removed. The grid can also be turned on/off by double clicking on the GRID button located at the bottom of the drawing editor screen.

In order to access the grid through the pull-down menu, select Tools and then Drafting Settings. The dialog box should appear as shown in Figure 3–5. By clicking in the appropriate boxes, you can enter numerical values for both grid spacing and snap spacing. You can also set grid options by typing grid at the command prompt.

Separate grids exist for model space and paper space, and the grid spacing can be set separately for each.

TRY THIS

Practice setting the grid to different values.

1. Open the AutoCAD software program.
2. In the Startup dialog box, select **Start from Scratch**.
3. Make sure you are in **Model space**.
4. From the Tools pull-down menu, select **Drafting Settings**.
5. Select the Grid On box to turn the grid on.
6. For the Grid X spacing enter .5.
7. For the Grid Y spacing enter .5.
8. Select **OK** to exit the dialog box.

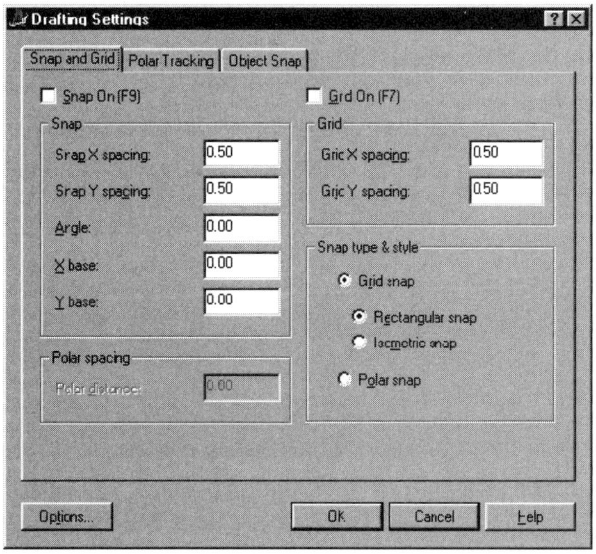

Figure 3–5
Drafting Settings dialog box.

Grid points should appear that are spaced 0.5 unit apart. Repeat the activity and set the Grid to various values. Try setting the Grid to a value of 0.0625. What message did you get at the command prompt?

SNAP

The **Snap** command limits cursor movement to specific intervals. If drawing objects can be drawn based on snap points, it is much easier to edit and position them. The toggle key for turning the snap on/off is F9. The snap can also be turned on/off by double clicking on the SNAP button located at the bottom of the drawing editor. Any points you enter can be locked into alignment by the snap setting if the snap setting is set to accommodate the incremental measurements. Typically, snap increments are of a lesser value than the grid spacing setting. Also, the snap grid can be rotated with different settings for the X and Y spacing. Any change in the snap grid affects only the coordinates of new points. AutoCAD ignores snap mode in perspective views.

At the command prompt, enter snap. The command prompt line should then change and appear as follows:

Snap spacing or ON/OFF/Aspect/Rotate/Style <current>:

Specify a distance, enter an option, or press <Enter> (see Figure 3–6).

Snap increments also can be set in the Drafting Settings dialog box.

TRY THIS

Practice setting the Snap values to different increments to view their effect on cursor movement and object creation.

1. Open the AutoCAD software program.
2. In the Startup dialog box, select **Start from Scratch**.
3. Make sure that you are in **Model space**.
4. From the Tools pull-down menu, select **Drafting Settings**.
5. Select the Snap On box to turn the snap on.
6. Set the Snap X spacing to .25.
7. Set the Snap Y spacing to .25.
8. Select the Grid On box to turn the grid on.
9. Set the Grid X Spacing to .5.
10. Set the Grid Y Spacing to .5.
11. Select **OK** to exit the Drafting Settings dialog box.

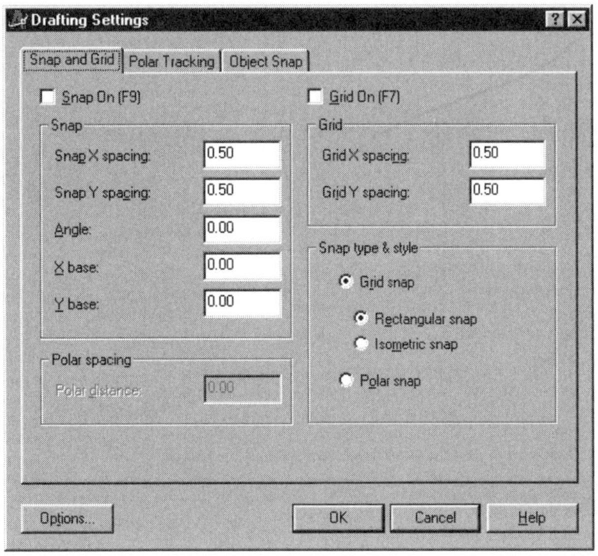

Figure 3–6
Setting snap values.

12. Move the cursor around on the screen. It should move at .25 intervals. Make sure the coordinate readout display located at the bottom is turned on. As you move the cursor around the drawing editor the readout values in the coordinate display should also change at .25 intervals.
13. Create a rectangle that is 3 × 2 units. Since the snap is set to move at .25 intervals, you should be able to watch the coordinate display or count grid points to determine the correct size.

POLAR TRACKING

Polar tracking is one of the selections included in the AutoTrack™ system. AutoTrack™ helps you draw objects at specific angles or in specific relationships to other objects (Autodesk, Inc., 1999). In order to change or set any of the polar tracking variables, select the Polar Tracking tab in the Drafting Settings dialog box (see Figure 3–7). Polar tracking variables include increment angle, measurement, and object snap tracking settings. Polar tracking can be toggled on/off using the F10 function key.

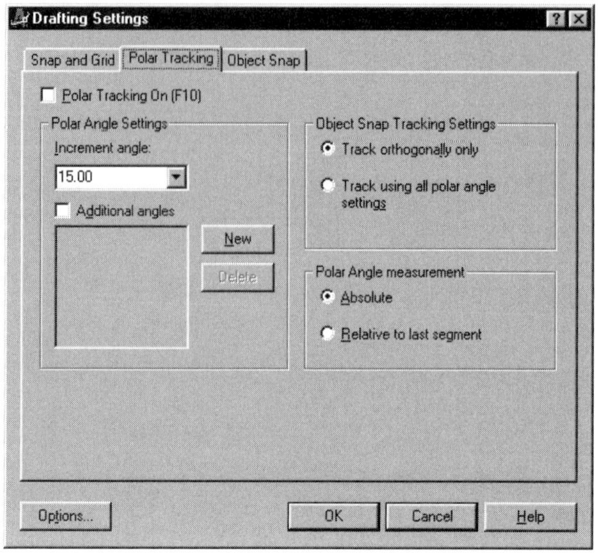

Figure 3–7
Polar Tracking settings.

Chapter 3 ■ Activity

Activity 3–1

Use the Help Menu to Learn How to Use the Grid and Snap Variables

Open the AutoCAD 2000 software program. From the Help pull-down menu select Contents. Scroll down to Chapter 7 Drawing with Precision and click on it. A listing of topics in Chapter 7 should now appear. Select the Adjusting Snap and Grid alignment option, and then select the Display button at the bottom of the dialog box. Read through the information on how to use the snap and grid variables.

CHAPTER

4

Screen Display Commands

AFTER READING THIS CHAPTER, YOU WILL BE ABLE TO:

- Execute commands that affect the visual display.

KEY CONCEPTS:

Aerial View
Pan (p)
Redraw(r)
Regen
Zoom (z)

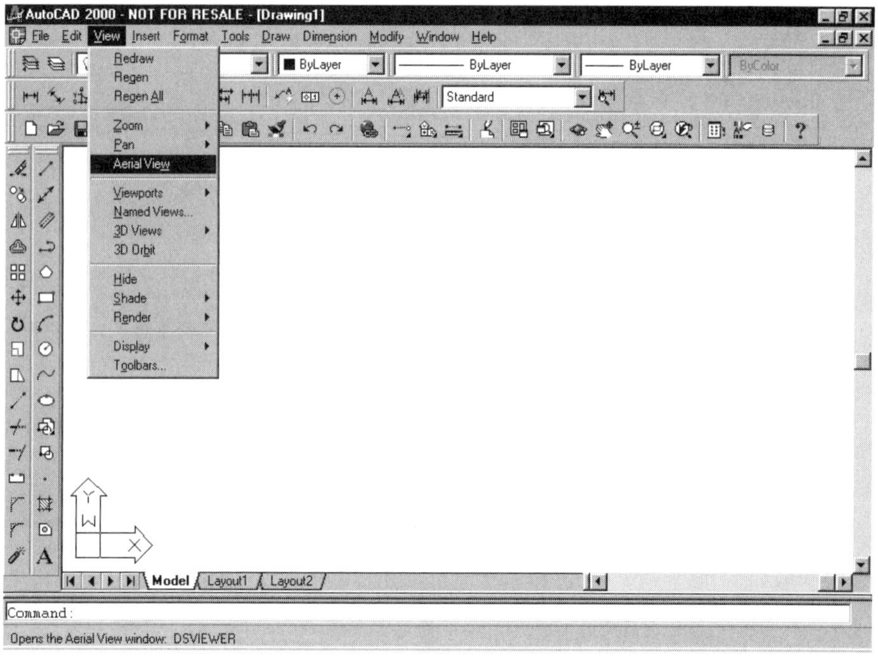

Figure 4–1
View pull-down menu.

To edit a drawing effectively, it is sometimes necessary to enhance or change the visual display of the drawing screen. AutoCAD has several commands that affect the visual display of the drawing editor, namely, Zoom, Pan, Aerial View, Redraw, and Regen.

These commands can be selected from the View pull-down menu, with toolbar icons, or from the screen menu (see Figure 4–1). The English-word equivalent of the command can also be typed at the command prompt line.

ZOOM

The **Zoom** command magnifies or shrinks the drawing on the display screen. Zoom can be selected from the View pull-down menu, or z can be entered at the command prompt. Three zoom icons are also located in the top toolbar. These icons represent Zoom Realtime, Zoom Window, and Zoom Previous (see Figure 4–2).

Figure 4–2
Zoom toolbar icons.

When zoom is entered at the command prompt or Zoom is selected from the View pull-down menu, the following submenu options become available: All/Center/Dynamic/Extents/Previous/Scale(X/XP)/Window/<Realtime>:. Enter an option, specify a zoom window, enter a scale value, or press <Enter> to turn on real-time zooming. Descriptions of the command options follow:

All	Displays entire drawing limits (whichever is larger).
Center	Specifies center point and new display magnification.
Dynamic	Permits you to pan a box representing the viewing screen around the entire generated portion of the drawing and enlarge or shrink it in a dynamic, graphic manner.

Extents	Displays current drawing content as large as possible.
Previous	Restores previous view.
Window	Designates rectangular area to be drawn as large as possible. (This is the default option.)
numberX	Sets scale relative to current display (1×).
numberXP	Sets scale relative to paper space units (1×P).
Realtime	zoom in or out of the drawing by moving the cursor vertically up or down.

The Zoom command is used extensively to view objects and details in a complex drawing. It is much easier to add objects and details to a drawing if you zoom in on the area where they are to be placed.

PAN

The **Pan** command gives you the option of moving the display window in any direction, without changing its magnification. The effect of the pan is similar to using either a vertical or horizontal scroll bar (see Figure 4–3). When either the down arrow or the up arrow is selected in the vertical scroll bar, the screen shifts in the direction of the arrow. Moving the arrow in a horizontal scroll bar would move the view to either the left or the right of its current place.

Portions of entities that are not fully displayed on the drawing screen can be displayed with the Pan command. AutoCAD 2000 uses the realtime pan option. A hand icon appears when the Pan command is used (see Figure 4-4). In order to use pan, you must select (hold the mouse button down

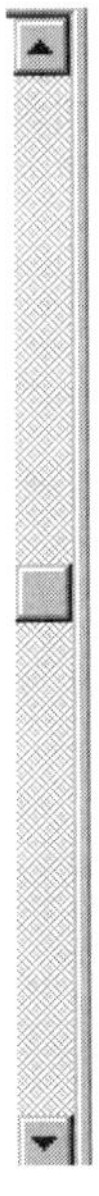

Figure 4–3
Vertical scroll bar.

Figure 4–4
Pan icon.

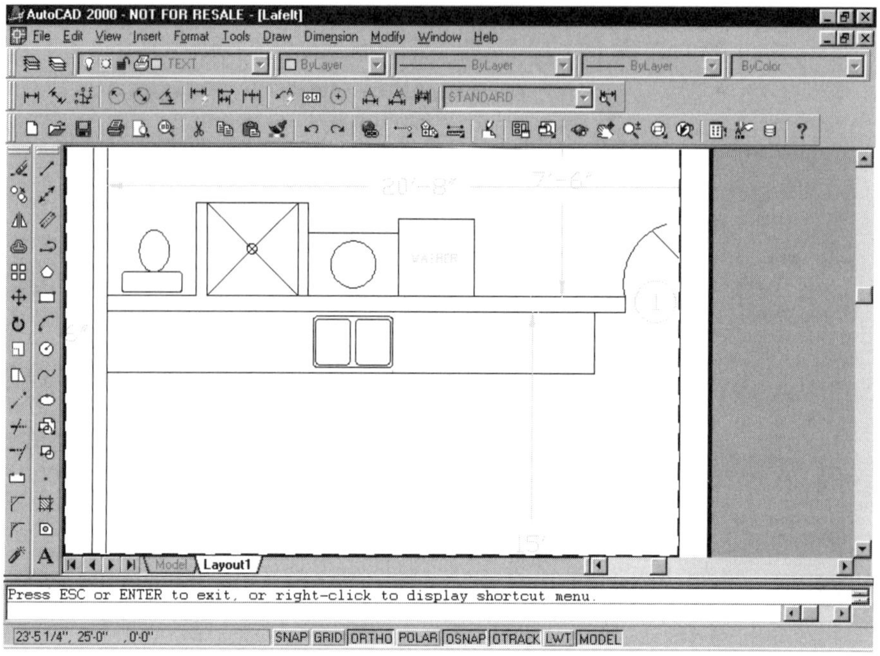

Figure 4–5
Exiting the Pan command.

on) a point in the drawing editor, move the hand icon to a new position, and release the mouse button. To exit the pan, press Esc or Enter, as indicated at the command prompt in Figure 4–5.

Figure 4–6 shows two partial circles being displayed in the drawing editor. The Pan command was used to adjust the screen to show all parts of the circles (see Figure 4–7).

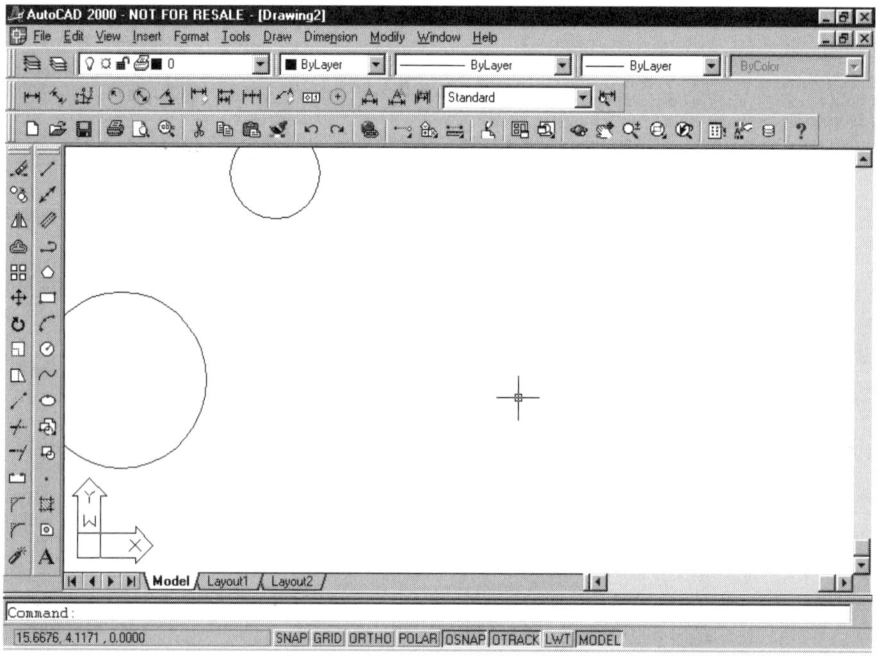

Figure 4–6
Pan command.

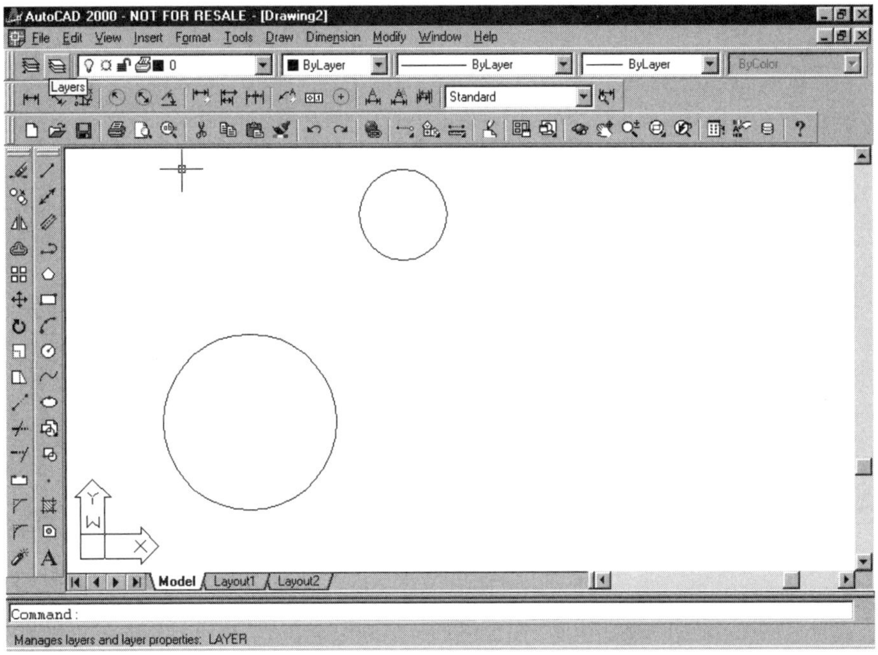

Figure 4–7
Using Pan to adjust the view.

TRY THIS

Open the drawing file oceanarium.dwg from the AutoCAD/Samples subdirectory and use the realtime pan mode to move about the drawing.

1. Open the existing drawing file **oceanarium.dwg.**
2. From the View pull-down menu select **Zoom**. Use the Window command to zoom in anywhere on the drawing.
3. Type **Pan**, then press **<Enter>**.
4. Click and move the hand icon around the drawing to view different parts of the drawing.

AERIAL VIEW

Aerial view is a navigation tool that displays the drawing in a separate window (see Figure 4–8). To access the aerial view, select Aerial View from the View pull-down menu. If you keep the Aerial View window open, you can zoom and pan without choosing a menu option or entering a command by selecting and moving the pointing device inside the Aerial View window. The pan or zoom view in the drawing responds to the direction of movement of the input device. The three zoom icons found in the toolbar icon menu of the Aerial View window are zoom in, zoom out, and global zoom (see Figure 4–9). Once you have determined the magnification level of the zoom, a realtime window allows you to pan to different portions of the drawing.

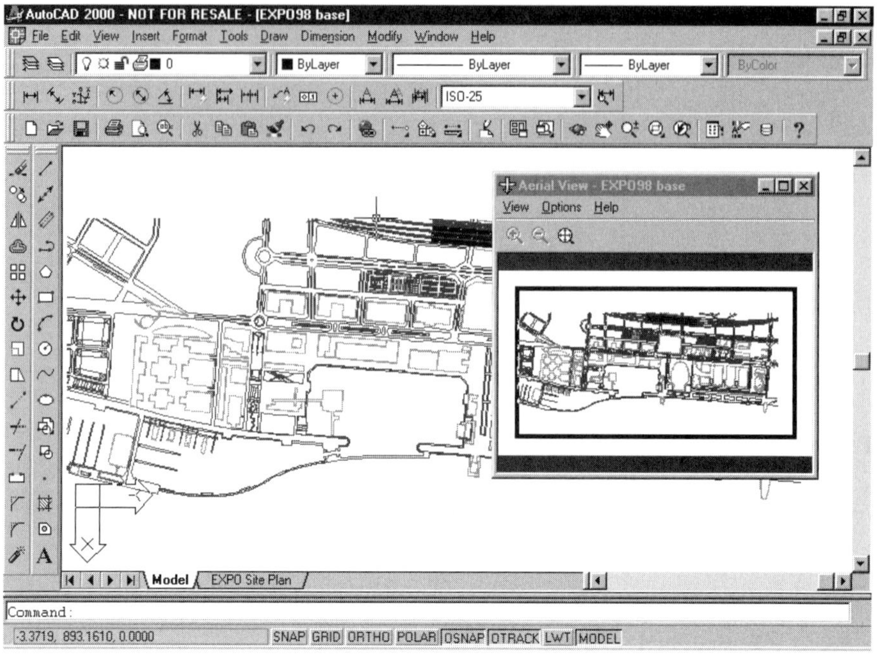

Figure 4–8
Aerial View window.

Figure 4–9
Zoom icons in Aerial View window.

REDRAW

Any time you create or edit an entity, blip marks appear on the screen if the blipmode command is on. Often the clutter from these blip marks hides part of the drawing entity or creates excess clutter on the screen. The **Redraw** command redraws the current active display screen. When the redraw (r) command is selected, any point entry blips are removed from the screen display. The Redraw command affects only what is seen on the screen; it does not affect any information in the drawing database.

To activate the redraw, choose Redraw from the View pull-down menu, or type r (redraw) at the prompt.

TRY THIS

See the effects of the Redraw command on the drawing screen.

1. Open AutoCAD and start a drawing from scratch.
2. At the command prompt, type **Blipmode**, then **<Enter>**, **On**.

3. From the Draw pull-down menu select **Polygon**.
4. Draw an eight-sided polygon.
5. Use the erase command to delete the polygon and then press **<Enter>**.
6. There should be three blip marks on the screen.
7. Type **r** (redraw).
8. The blip marks should disappear from the screen.

REGEN

The **Regen** command regenerates the drawing in the active display by recalculating all the entities in the drawing database for optimum display and object selection. Any entities that have been edited, erased, or purged are affected by the Regen command. Regeneration occurs automatically when you change the display of your drawing with some of the zoom or pan operations.

To activate regeneration, choose Regen from the View pull-down menu, or type regen at the command prompt.

ACTIVITY 4–1

Real-time Zooming and Panning

Open the AutoCAD software program. Select the Start from Scratch option to open the drawing editor. From the Help pull-down menu, select Auto-CAD help. Select the Index tab, and type real time in the space provided. A list of options should appear. From the list double click on real-time zooming and panning. A dialog box should appear with information on real-time zooming and panning. Read the information to gain a better understanding of the Real time Pan and Zoom options.

ACTIVITY 4–2

Practice Using the Aerial View Option

Open the AutoCAD software program. Select the Open a Drawing option, find the Oceanarium drawing in the AutoCAD Samples directory, and open it. From the View pulldown menu, select Aerial View. Practice zooming in on various parts of the drawing by moving the window in the Aerial View dialog box (see Figure 4–10).

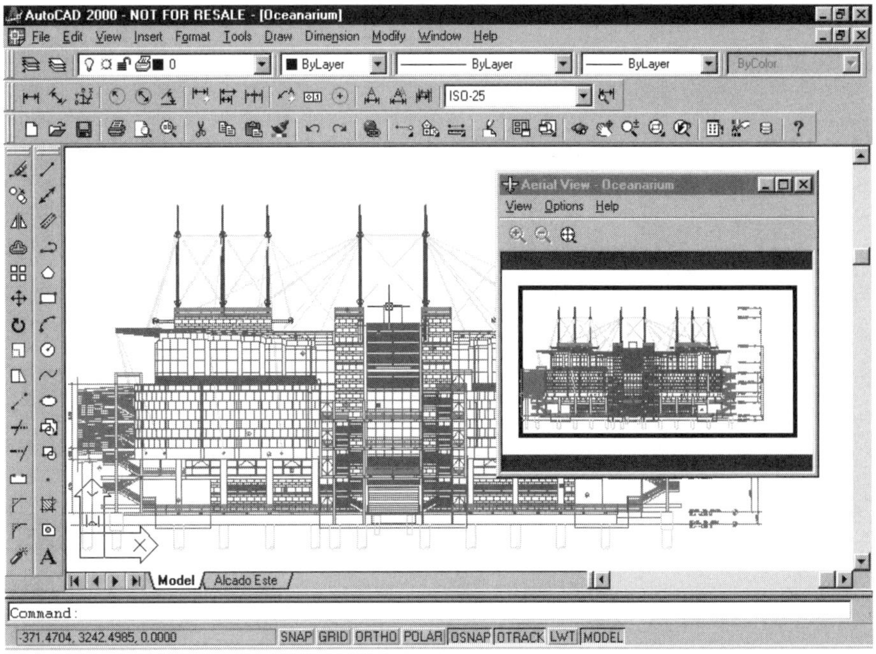

Figure 4–10
Aerial view.

CHAPTER

5

Object Snaps

AFTER READING THIS CHAPTER, YOU WILL BE ABLE TO:

- Use Osnap (object snaps) for locating objects.

KEY CONCEPTS:

Apparent Intersection (appint)
Center (cen)
Endpoint (endp)
Extension
Insertion (ins)
Intersection (int)
Midpoint (mid)
Nearest (nea)
Node
Parallel
Perpendicular (per)
Quadrant (qua)
Quick
Tangent (tan)

INTRODUCTION

Object snaps are functions that help locate objects by snapping exactly to specific points on an existing object.

AutoCAD has several drawing aids that have been built into the program to help you create accurate, precise drawings. One group of functions that is extremely valuable for creating accurate drawings is the **Osnap** (object snaps) functions. These are functions that help locate objects by snapping exactly to specific points on existing objects. For example, you can snap to the center point of a circle, the midpoint of a line, or the intersection of two lines. The various Osnap functions are listed in the Key Concepts. The object snaps are an easy way to locate the exact position of an object without knowing coordinate points.

The object snaps functions can be typed in at the command prompt, selected from the toolbar, or selected from the screen menu on the right side of the drawing editor. Right clicking on the OSNAP button on the status bar also allows you access to the OSNAP dialog box. Typically, the OSNAP toolbar is not displayed. In order to display the OSNAP toolbar, go to the View pull-down menu and select Toolbars. The dialog box for the various toolbars that can be displayed appears. Selecting the OSNAP toolbar produces the screen shown in Figure 5–1.

Object Snap Functions

Endpoint (endp)	Snaps to the closest endpoint of an object such as a line or arc.
Midpoint (mid)	Snaps to midpoint of a line or arc.
Intersection (int)	Snaps to the intersection of objects such as lines, circles, arcs, and splines.
App Int (appint or app)	Snaps to the intersection of two objects that do not intersect each other in 3D space but might appear to on the screen.
Center (cen)	Snaps to the center of an arc, circle, or ellipse.
Quadrant (qua)	Snaps to the closest quadrant of an arc, circle, or ellipse—another way to say it will snap to the 0°, 90°, 180°, and 270° points.
Node (node)	Snaps to a point drawn with the Point command.
Insert (ins)	Snaps to the insertion point of a block, shape, text, attribute, or attribute definition.
Perpend (per)	Snaps to a point that forms a perpendicular alignment with another object. Used with lines, circles, ellipses, splines, and arcs.
Tangent (tan)	Snaps to the point on a circle or arc that when is connected, forms a line tangent to that point (Autodesk, Inc., 1997).
Nearest (nea)	Snaps to a point that is closest to the specified point.
Quick (qui)	Snaps to the nearest point it can find.

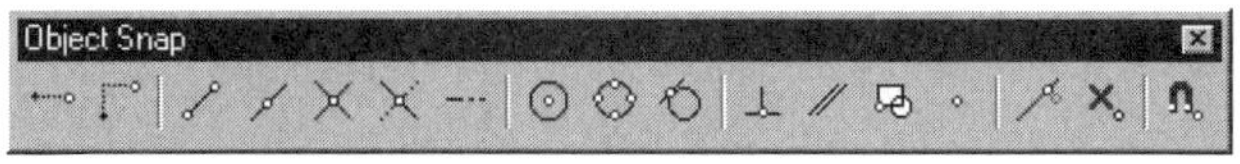

Figure 5–1
Osnap toolbar.

Extension (ext)	Used to extend a line or an arc.
Parallel (par)	Snaps to an extension in parallel with an object.
None (none)	Turns off the object snap mode.

Running object snap–One or more object snaps that are on continuously.

An object snap that is on continuously is called a **running object snap**. More than one object snap can be turned on at one time. In order to turn a running object snap on, go to the Tools pull-down menu and select Drafting Settings. Select the Object Snap tab, and a dialog box similar to the one in Figure 5–2 should appear. Click in each blank box in order to turn on that particular OSNAP. Pressing the F3 function key will toggle the Running Object Snap on/off. If you select to have Object Tracking on, both distance and angle will be displayed as seen in Figure 5–3.

The symbols located next to each of the Osnap modes are graphical representations of the Osnap settings.

ENDPOINT

It is often necessary to find exact points after you have edited a drawing or created entities. In the example in Figure 5–3, an arc was to be drawn from the endpoint of two parallel lines. The easiest way to find the start and endpoint of the arc is to use the **Endpoint** Osnap function, using the following procedure.

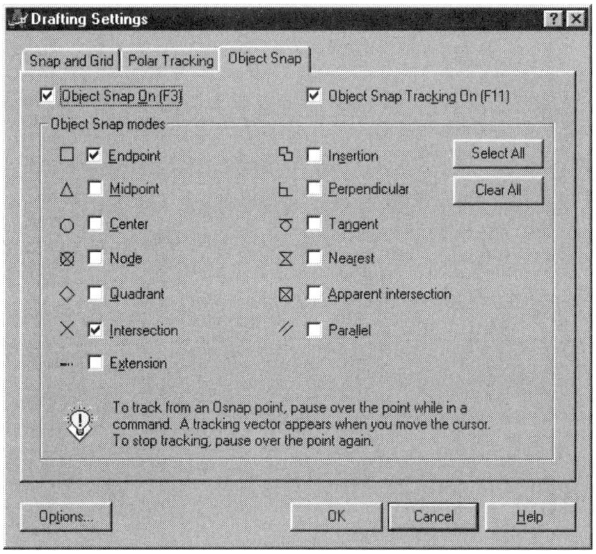

Figure 5–2
Object snap settings dialog box.

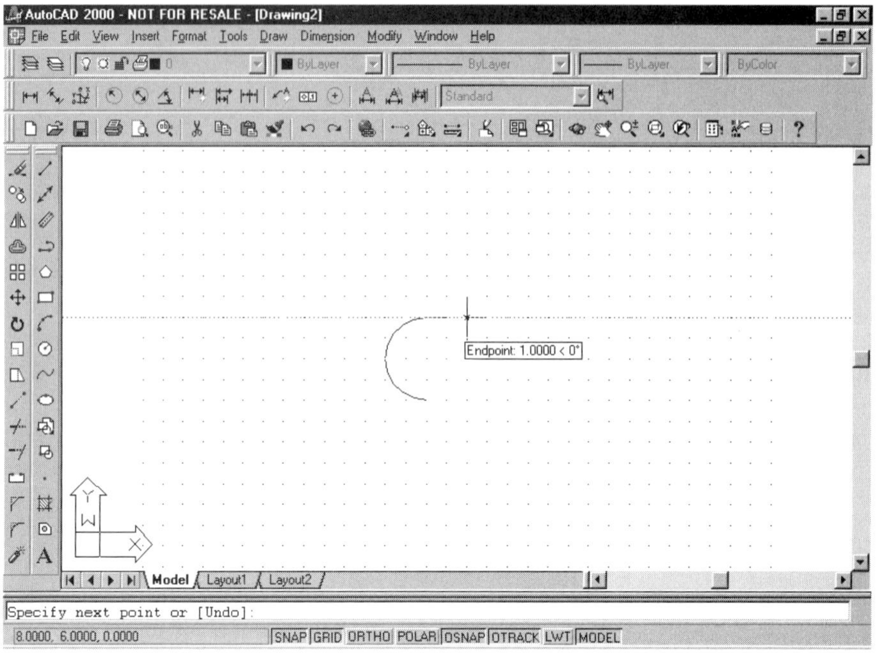

Figure 5–3
Using Osnap Endpoint to connect an arc to two lines.

Command: Arc (a)	
Center/(Start Point):	endp (When the cursor is moved near the endpoint of each line, it is easy to select where the arc will start and end.)
Center/End/(Second Point):	endp
End Point:	Select a point with the pointing device.

TRY THIS

Create an arc of any size, and draw two lines from the endpoints of the arc.

1. Use the **Advanced Setup** wizard.
2. In Step 5 make sure you set your paper size to **15.5** × **10**.
3. Using the Arc toolbar icon, create an arc near the center of the drawing editor.
4. Draw two lines, each 1″ long, from each endpoint of the arc. Locate the endpoints of each arc with the **endp Osnap** command.

EXTENSION

Use the Extension object snap to extend a line or an arc. To use Extension, pause over the endpoint of a line or arc. A small plus sign (+) should appear signifying that the line or arc has been selected. Move the cursor along the extension path to display a temporary extension path. If Intersection or Apparent Intersection is on, you can find the extended intersection of a line or arc with another object.

MIDPOINT

The **Midpoint (mid)** object snap command is used to snap to the middle of objects such as arcs and lines. It is used when you want to create a line or other object from the midpoint of an existing arc or line. In Figure 5–5 a horizontal line was to be drawn across the middle of the rectangle. Osnap Midpoint (mid) was used to find the starting point of the line as well as the endpoint of the line. When the cursor was placed at any point on the line, the midpoint was automatically located. The midpoint was indicated by a yellow triangle-shaped icon.

The command sequence for creating the horizontal line in the rectangle in Figure 5–5 was as follows:

Command:	l (line)
LINE From point:	mid (midpoint) Select any point on the right vertical line.

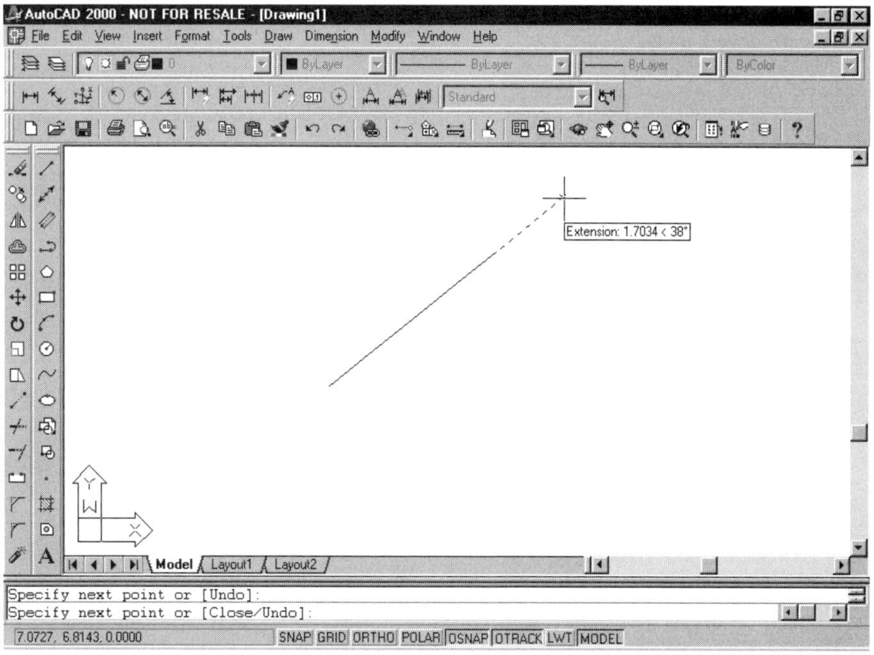

Figure 5–4
Extension object snap.

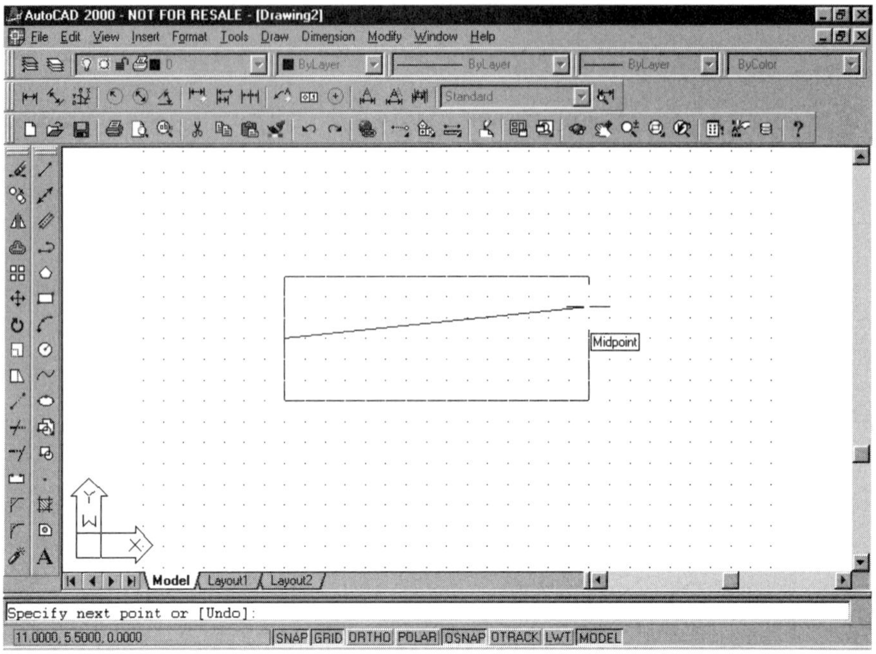

Figure 5–5
Using Osnap Midpoint.

To point:	mid (midpoint) Select any point on the left vertical line.
To point:	<Enter>

Try This

Create two horizontal lines 2.75″ long and draw a vertical line from the midpoint of each line. Draw the horizontal lines from two different X plane coordinates.

1. Use the **Advanced Setup** wizard to create a drawing with paper size set to 15.5 × 10.
2. Set the grid spacing to **0.5.**
3. Set the snap to **0.25.**
4. Select the line icon.
5. At the From point: command, enter **3,3.**
6. At the To point: command, type **5.75, 3.**
7. Press **<Enter>** twice (once to cancel the command and once to restart the command).
8. At the From point: command, enter **5,5.**
9. At the To point: command, type **7.75, 5.**
10. Press **<Enter>** twice (once to cancel the command and once to restart the command).
11. At the From point: command, type **mid** and select any point on the lower line.

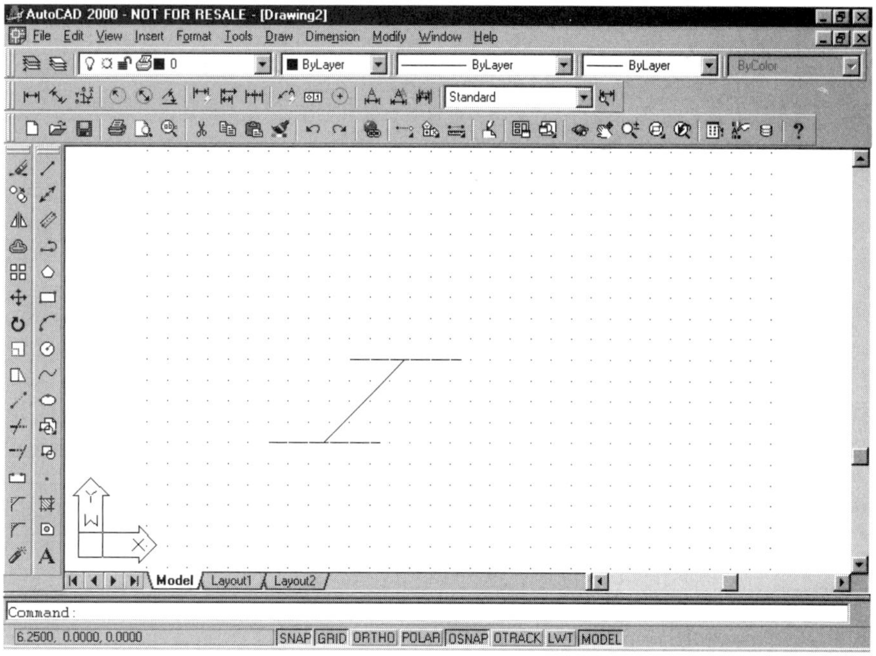

Figure 5–6
Using Osnap Midpoint to draw a line between two parallel lines.

12. At the To point: command, type **mid** and select any point on the upper line.

Your drawing should look similar to Figure 5–6.

CENTER

The **Center (cen)** object snap command is useful for locating the centers of arcs, circles, or true ellipses. In order to snap to the center of an object, you must select some part of the visible entity. In Figure 5–7, the center (cen) object snap is being used to locate a smaller circle inside a larger circle. Both circles will have the same center.

INTERSECTION

The **Intersection (int)** object snap command snaps to the intersections of objects such as lines, circles, arcs, and splines. If you want to create an entity from the point where two objects intersect, the intersection (int) object snap will automatically find the intersection. In Figure 5–8, a diagonal line was drawn from the intersection of the horizontal and perpendicular. Osnap Intersection (int) was used to locate the point where the two objects crossed each other.

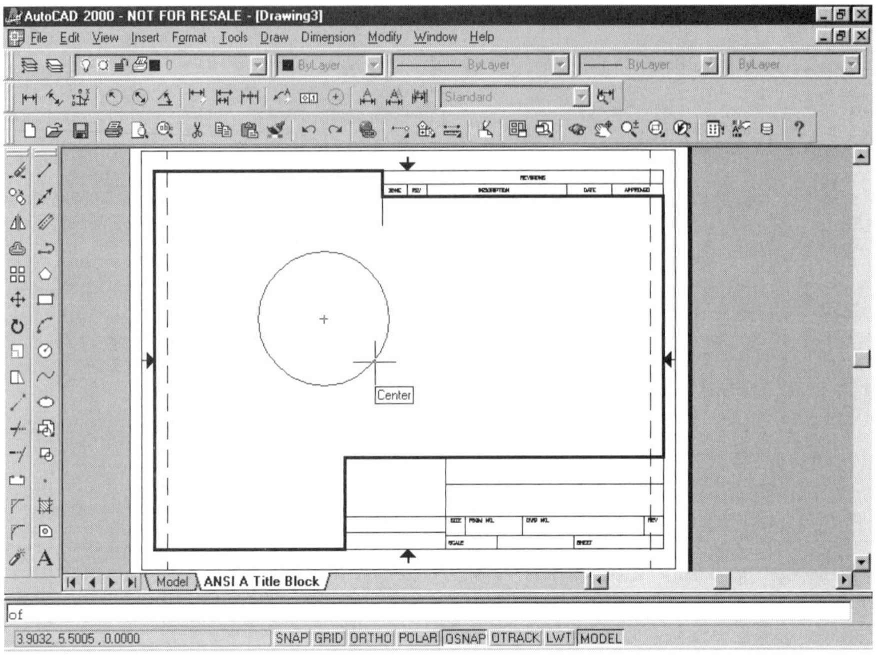

Figure 5–7
Locating the center of the circle with Osnap Center..

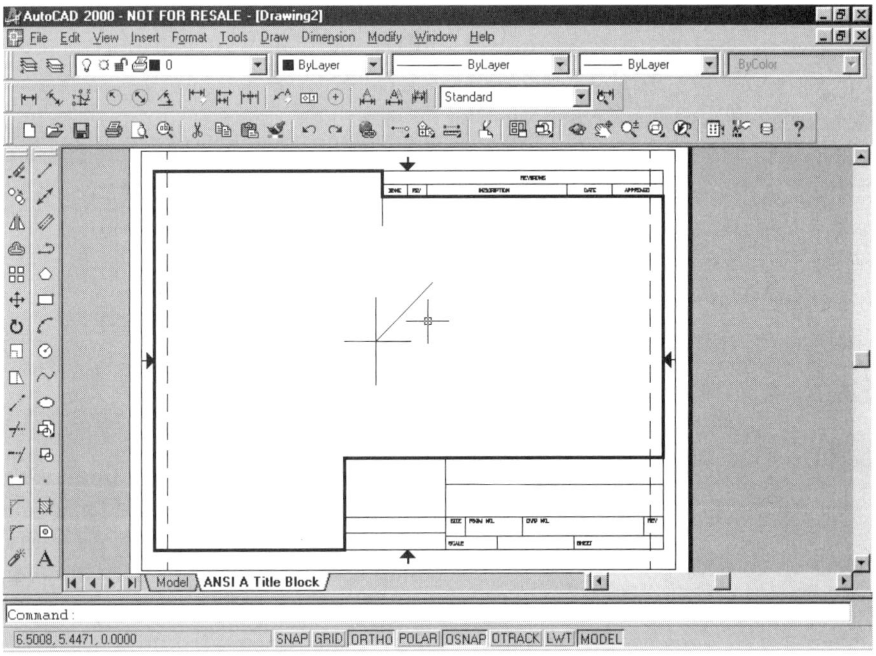

Figure 5–8
Intersection osnap.

TRY THIS

Draw four diagonal lines from the intersection of two 6″ lines that are perpendicular to each other.

1. Use the **Advanced Setup** wizard to create a drawing with the paper size set to **10** × **7.7**.
2. Set the grid spacing to **0.5**.

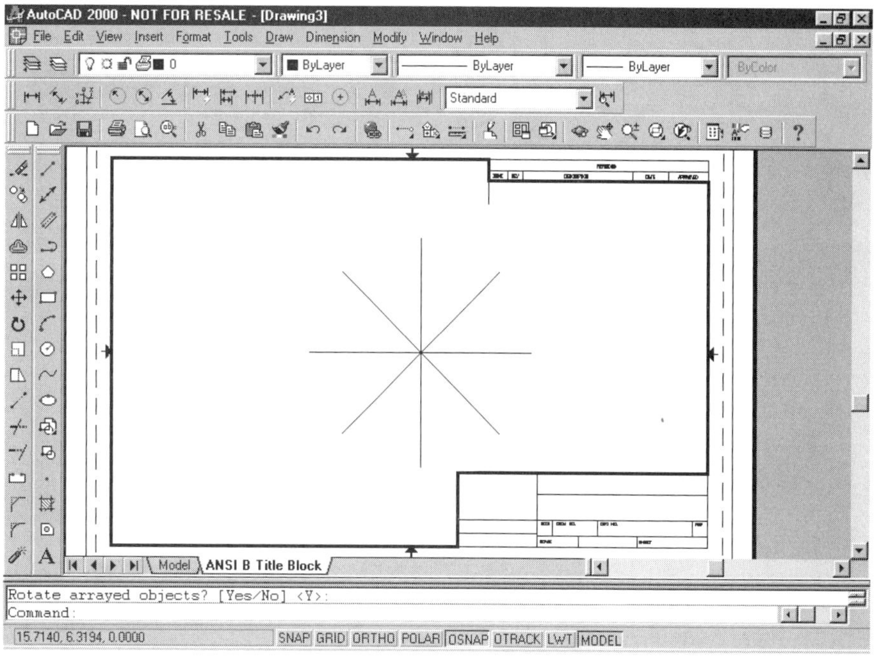

Figure 5–9
Using Intersect Osnap to create multiple lines from an intersection.

3. Set the snap to **0.25.**
4. Create two 4″ lines whose intersection is **8,5.**
5. Use **intersec** object snap to draw four 3″ diagonal lines that bisect each quadrant and whose common endpoint is the intersection of the original horizontal and perpendicular lines.

Your object should look similar to Figure 5–9.

PARALLEL

The **Parallel (par)** object snap command can be used for straight line segments. The parallel alignment path is based on the object and the command's From point: (AutoDesk, Inc., 1999). In Figure 5–10 the lower line was drawn parallel to the preexisting line using the Parallel Osnap command. The command sequence was as follows

Command:	l (line)
LINE Specify first point:	(Pick any point.)
Specify next point or [Undo]: parallel to	(Move cursor to a position over existing line and pause, then go and pick the other ending point.)

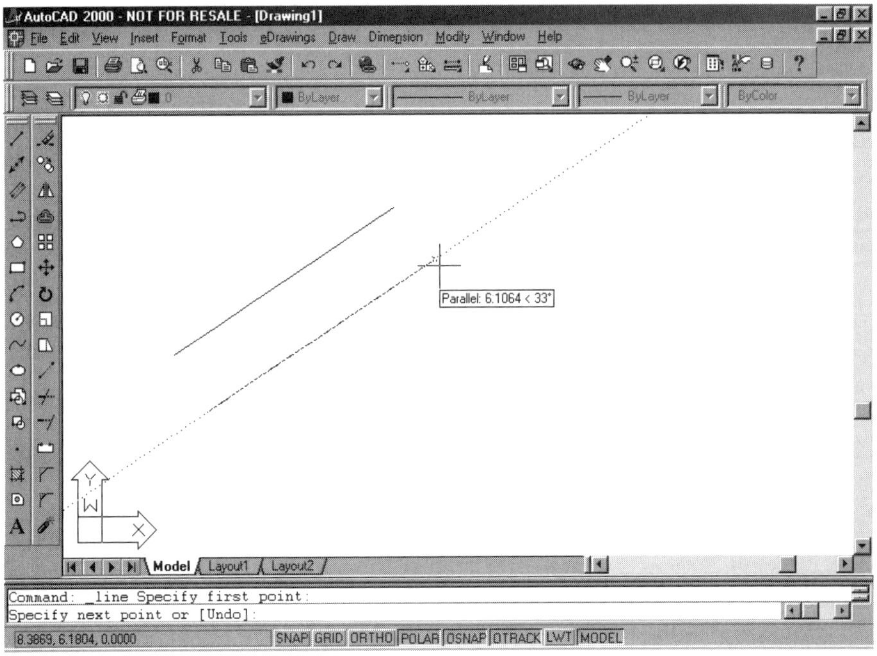

Figure 5–10
The Parallel Osnap command.

PERPENDICULAR

The **Perpend (per)** object snap command snaps to a point that is perpendicular (90°) to another object or to an imaginary extension of that object. The perpendicular object snap can be used to find a starting point or an ending point.

TRY THIS

Use the Perpend object snap to intersect a line at a 90° angle.

1. Start the AutoCAD software program.
2. Select **Start from Scratch** at the Startup dialog box.
3. Draw a line 3″ long at a 45° angle. Start the line at **4,4**.
4. Draw another line with the starting point of **6.5,4.**
5. Use the Perpendicular (per) object snap to connect to the original line.

The drawing should look similar to Figure 5–11.

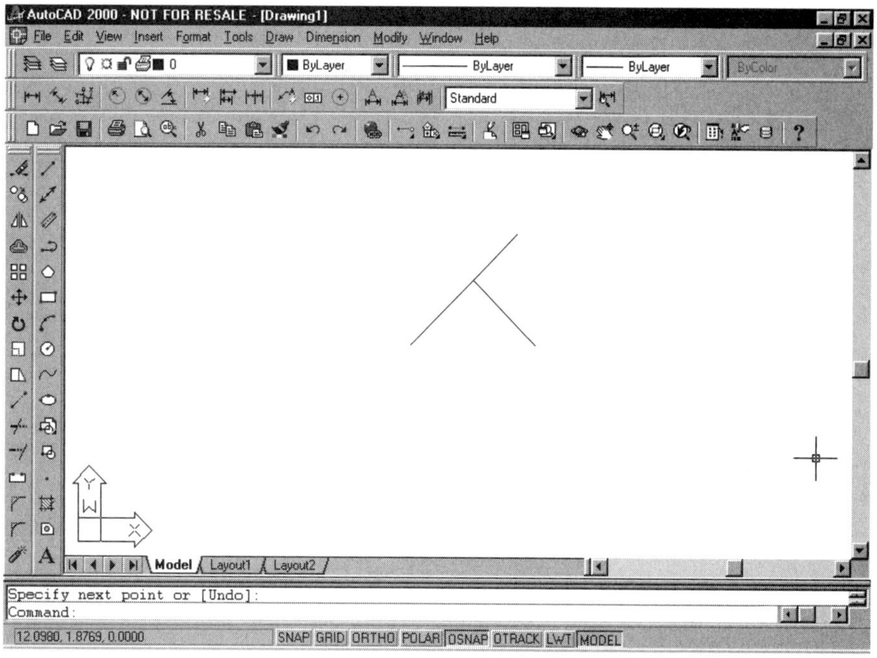

Figure 5–11
Using Osnap Perpend to create a perpendicular line.

QUADRANT

The **Quadrant (qua)** object snap command is used to snap to the closest point of an arc, circle, or ellipse. There are four quadrants, thus four quadrant points: 0, 90, 180, and 270.

TRY THIS

Create two circles of dissimilar sizes and draw lines connecting the circles using quadrant object snap.

1. Start the AutoCAD software program.
2. Select **Start from Scratch** from the Startup dialog box.
3. Create two circles. Place the center point of one circle at 2.5,3 with a radius of 1. Place the center of the second circle at 6,3 with a radius of .5.
4. Using the quadrant object snap command, draw a line from the 90° quadrant point of each circle.
5. Using the quadrant object snap command, draw a line from the 270° quadrant point of each circle.

The drawing should look similar to Figure 5–12.

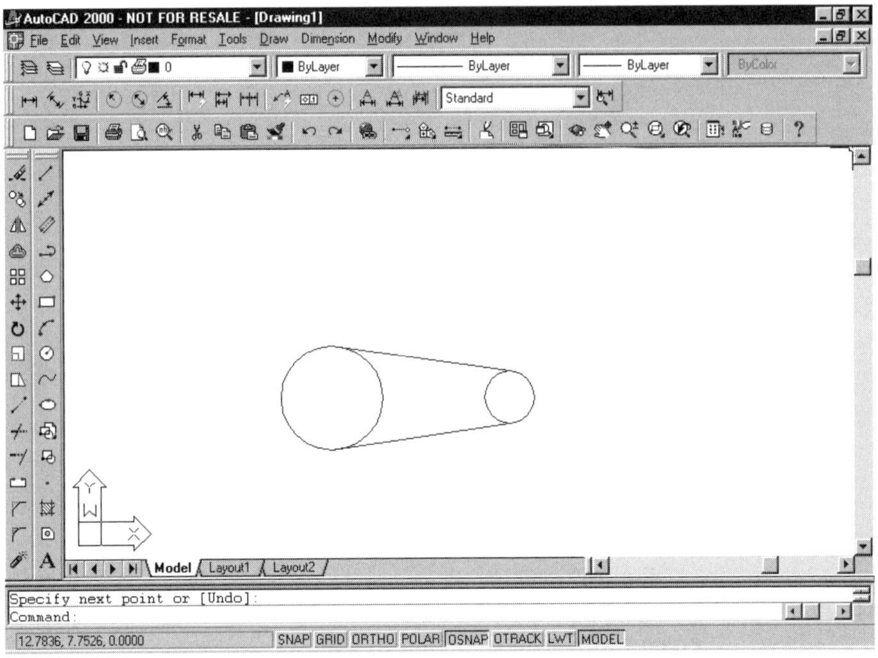

Figure 5–12
Using Osnap Quadrant to draw lines between two circles.

TANGENT

The **Tangent (tan)** object snap command snaps to the point of a circle or arc, that when connected to the last point creates a line tangent to that object (AutoDesk, Inc., 1997). For instance, if you want to draw a line tangent to a circle from a point, use the tangent object snap when selecting the circle or arc to which you want to connect. In Figure 5–13, two lines tangent to a circle were drawn from a single point.

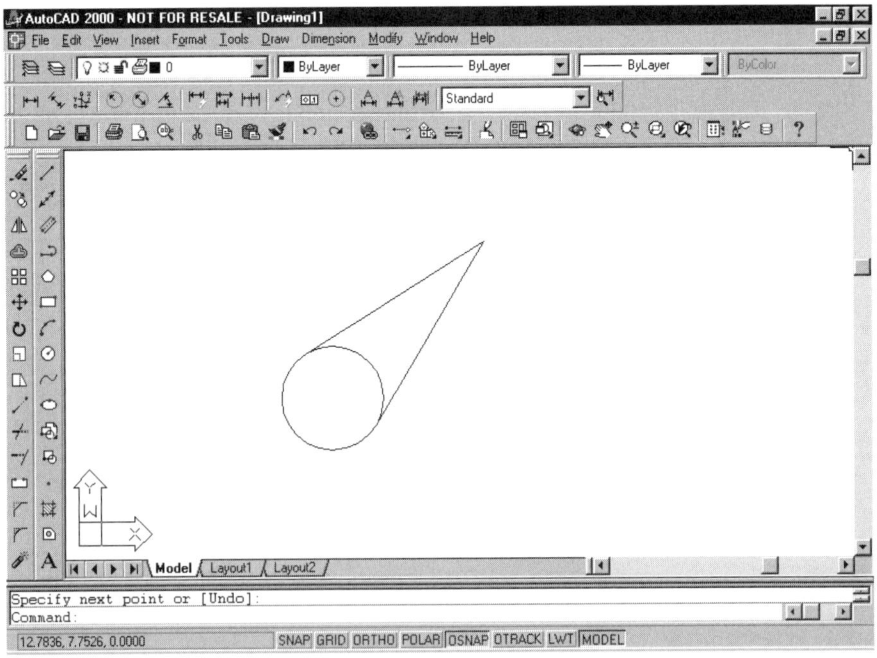

Figure 5–13
Using Osnap Tangent to draw lines tangent to a circle from a point.

ACTIVITY 5–1

Review Tutorial on Use of Object Snaps

Open the AutoCAD software program and select Start from Scratch. Select Learning Assistance from the Help pull-down menu, then select Tutorials. From the list of tutorials select Creating and Editing Objects More Efficiently. Then click on the underlined blue text "Object Snaps and Auto-Track." Select Using Object Snaps, AutoSnap™, and Direct Distance Entry to Select Points underlined text. Click on the Play Video option to review the multimedia presentation.

ACTIVITY 5–2

Practice Using Object Snaps

This activity was designed for you to practice your use of object snaps. The drawing in Figure 5–14 on page 81 provides you with a sample that you are to replicate. Be sure to label all entities. Use the following procedure:

1. Start the AutoCAD software program, and at the Startup dialog box, select Use a Template.
2. Select the A-size template you created in Chapter 2.
3. Check your layer settings to be sure they are set correctly.
4. Draw all entities in Model space.
5. Place all geometric figures on the OBJ layer.
6. Place all text on the TXT layer.
7. When you have finished drawing, save the activity as Act5-1.

Plotter Paper Size:	A	
Suggested Settings:	Grid	0.50″
	Snap	0.125″

Layers (7) **0** (default border)
Cen, Linetype center, Color: cyan
Dim, Linetype continuous, Color: green
Hid, Linetype hidden, Color: magenta
Object, Linetype continuous, Color: black
Tbk, Linetype continuous, Color: red
Text, Linetype continuous, Color: green

Hints:

1. Open your border template file for an A-size drawing. After it has loaded, use the Saveas command to rename the drawing file ACT5-1.
2. Make sure you are in Model space before you begin drawing the objects.
3. Be sure to check layer settings before you begin to draw or enter text.
4. Use the Osnap commands to create the entities.
5. Remember to save the drawing.

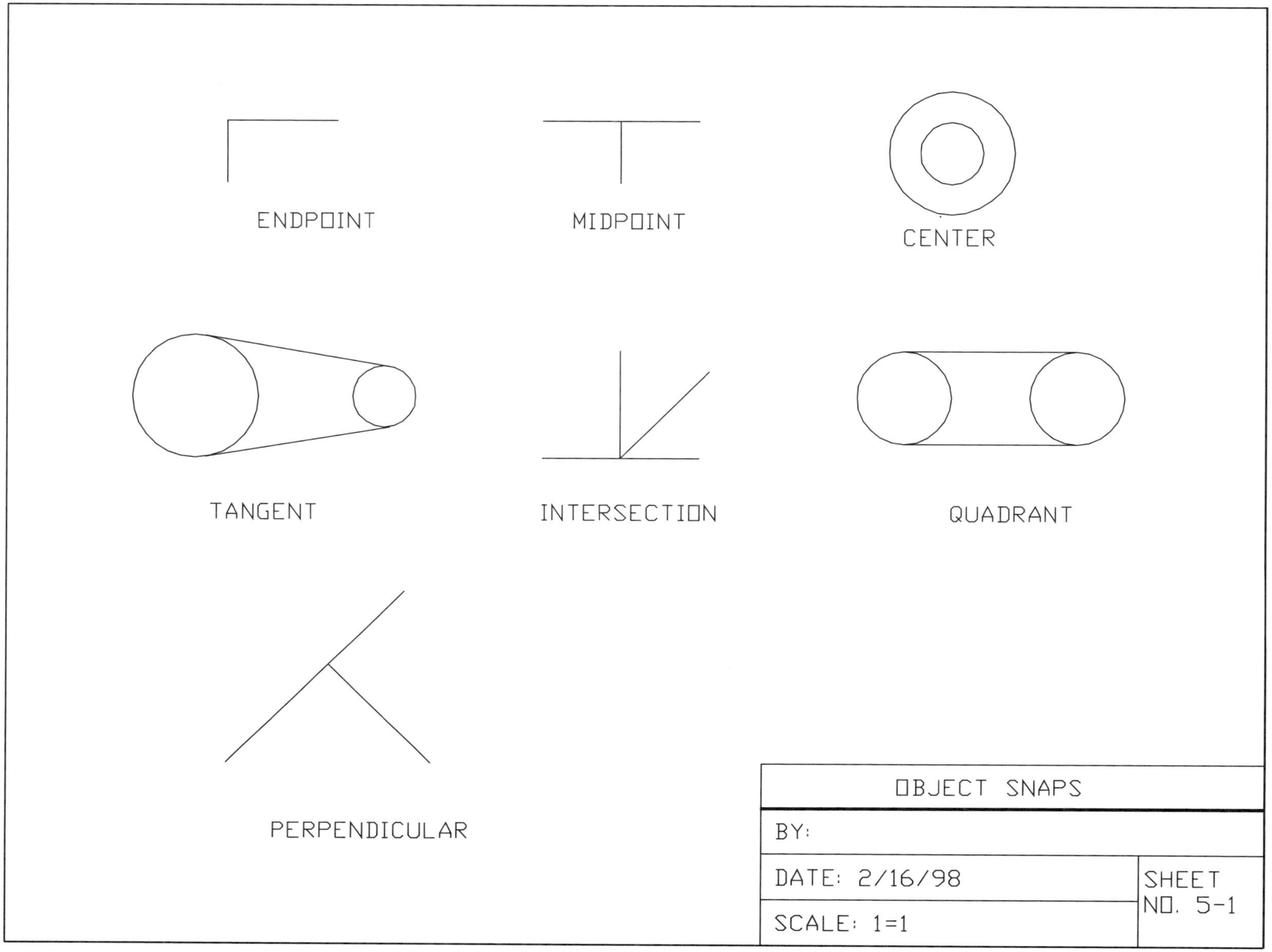

Figure 5–14
Activity 5–2

CHAPTER

6

Edit Commands

AFTER READING THIS CHAPTER, YOU WILL BE ABLE TO:

- Understand and use various editing commands to make changes to your drawing(s).

KEY CONCEPTS:

Array
Break
Chamfer
Copy (Co)
Ddedit
Erase (E)
Explode
Extend
Fillet
Mirror
Move (M)
Offset
Oops
Pedit
Rotate
Scale
Stretch
Trim

EDITING ENTITIES

In the design phase of creating a drawing, it is sometimes necessary to edit the objects created. There are several commands in AutoCAD for editing. Common editing commands include Break, Ddedit, Erase, Explode, Extend, Move, Oops, Pedit, Rotate, Scale, Stretch, and Trim. Edit commands can be selected from the Modify pull-down menu (see Figure 6–1) or from the modify toolbar (see Figure 6–2).

SELECTION SETS

Before objects can be edited, a selection set needs to be created. A selection set may be a single object or a group of objects. A variety of selection modes are available for creating a selection set, as described in the following list:

All	Selects all entities on thawed layers. To use the filter list, you must define Point1 and Point2 as dummy arguments.
Crossing	Selects objects within and crossing a rectangular area whose corners are defined by Point1 and Point2.
CrossingPolygon	Selects objects within and crossing an area defined by an array of points in Point1. To use the filter list, you must define Point2 as a dummy argument.

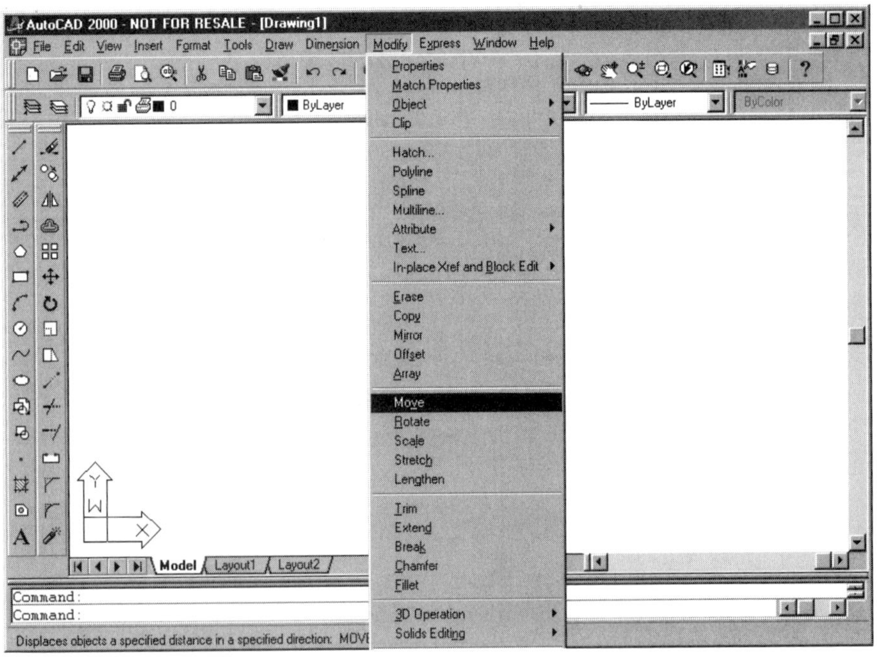

Figure 6–1
Modify pull-down menu.

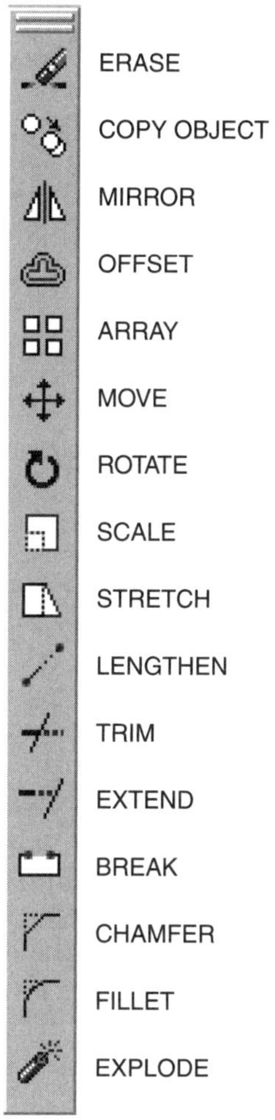

Figure 6–2
Modify toolbar icons.

Fence	Selects all entities crossing a selection fence. Point1 contains an array of points defining the fence. To use the filter list, you must define Point2 as a dummy argument.
Last	Selects the most recently created visible entity. To use the filter list, you must define Point1 and Point2 as dummy arguments.
Previous	Selects the most recent selection set. This mode is ignored if you switch between paper and model space and attempt to use the selection set. To use the filter list, you must define Point1 and Point2 as dummy arguments.
Window	Selects all entities completely inside a rectangular area whose corners are defined by Point1 and Point2.
WindowPolygon	Selects objects within a polygon defined by an array of points in Point1. To use the filter list, you must define Point2 as a dummy argument.

The two most common methods for selecting objects are to use the pickbox (see Figure 6–3) or to use a window that is created when an edit command is selected.

A **selection window** is rectangular in shape, and the objects within the window are defined by picking two opposing corners. Typically the entire object must be enclosed within the window for it to be selected. However, various window options affect how objects will be selected within a window. For example, in Figure 6–4 we wanted to erase some of the smaller interior rectangles, so we used the following sequence:

Command: E (erase)

Select Objects: pick point (The lower left corner of the window was selected.)

Select Objects: Other corner: pick point (The upper right corner was selected.)

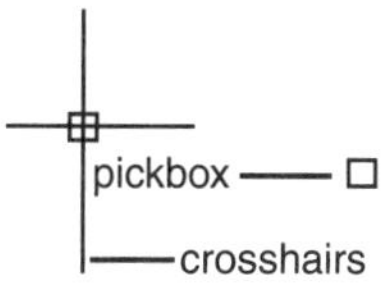

When you choose an editing command, AutoCAD prompts you to select objects and replaces the crosshairs with a pickbox. You select individual objects with the pointing device or by using the methods described in this section.

Figure 6–3
Crosshairs and pickbox symbol.

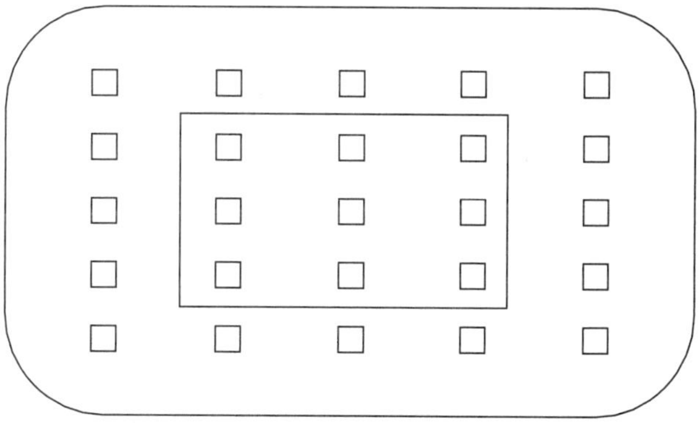

Figure 6–4
Using a window to select objects.

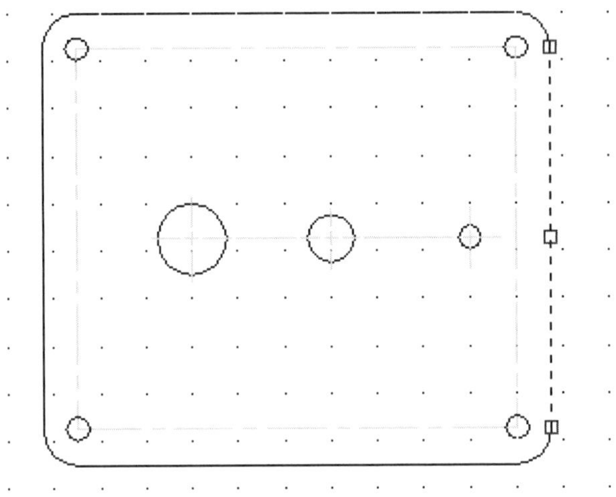

Figure 6–5
Grips.

All the entities located within the rectangular box would be erased when the commands were executed.

If a **crossing window (c)** is used, any part of an object that is located within the rectangular window set is selected. This means that even if part of the object is outside the window set, it will still be selected. The **pickbox** is used to select single entities.

If objects are selected before the editing command is used, **grips** (blue boxes that indicate control points) appear on the entity selected. In Figure 6–5 there are three blue grip boxes. The line on which the boxes appear was selected prior to the selection of an editing command. Grips mark control locations on a selected object. Once the object has been selected, you can select the editing command that you want to use. To control grips go to the Tools pull-down menu, select Options, and then click on the Selection tab. Options for turning grips on or off can be selected.

EDIT COMMANDS

Break

To **break** an entity means to remove a portion of the entity between two points.

To **break** an entity means to remove a portion of the entity between two points. If the Break command is used to remove a portion of a circle, the order in which points are picked will determine what part of the entity remains. Figure 6–6 illustrates the difference that direction makes in the selection of break points. If you break a circle, it changes to an arc by deleting the portion from the first point to the second, going counterclockwise. In order to break an object, select the object by pointing to it. The break begins at the selection point and ends at the second point selected.

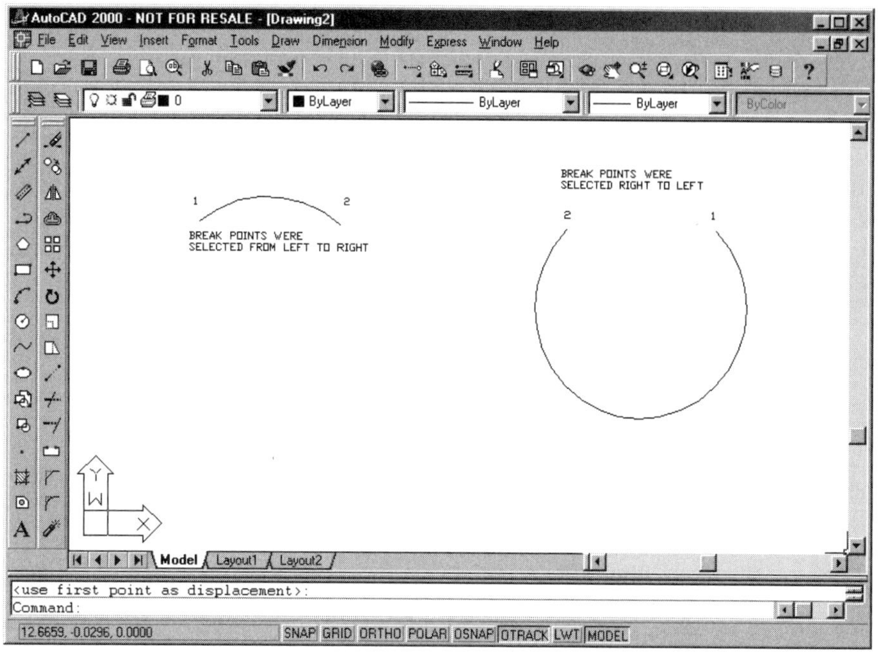

Figure 6–6
Using the Break command to break a circle.

TRY THIS

Break two circles, one in a clockwise direction and the other in a counterclockwise direction.

1. Open a new AutoCAD drawing, using **Start from Scratch**.
2. Create two circles 2″ in diameter. Position them like those shown in Figure 6–6.
3. From the Modify pull-down menu, select **Break**.
4. Break the circle on the left using a clockwise motion, left to right.
5. Break the circle on the right using a counterclockwise motion, right to left.

Erase/Oops

The **Erase** command deletes objects. If erase is used to delete an object drawn with the line command, single lines of the object will be deleted. However, an object drawn with a polyline or a form thereof is considered a group and if it is selected, all parts of the object disappear (see Figure 6–7). The shortcut key for erase is (E).

The opposite of the erase command is **Oops**. If an object or portion of an object is mistakenly erased, the Erase command can be undone by typing oops. The Oops command can be used only immediately after the Erase command. As seen in Figure 6–7, the Oops command is found in the screen menu with the erase command.

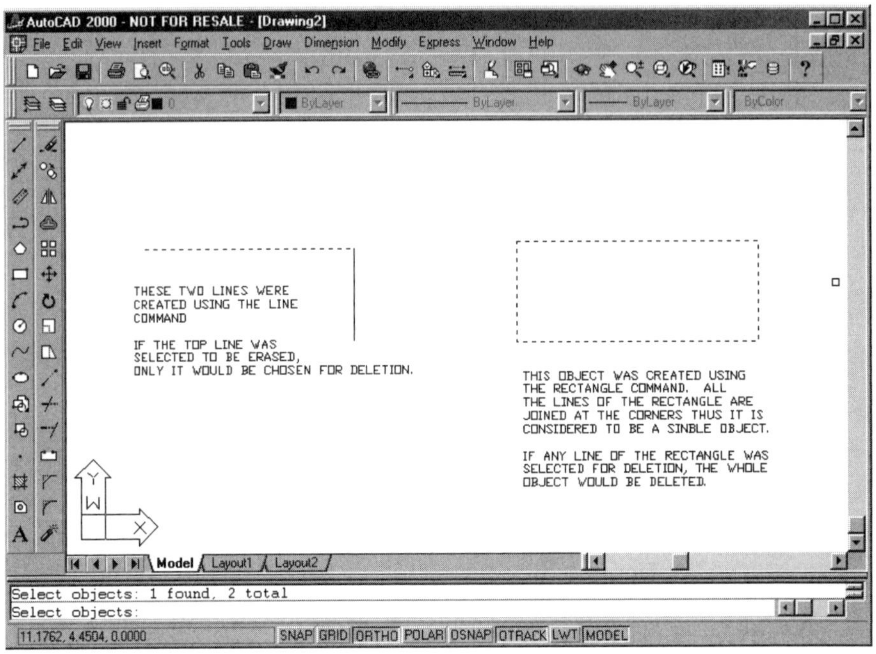

Figure 6–7
Erasing a single line and a rectangle that is a polyline.

Try This

Use the Erase command to delete objects, and use the Oops command to undo the Erase command.

1. Open a new AutoCAD drawing, using **Start from Scratch**.
2. Draw two lines perpendicular to each other.
3. Draw a rectangle using the **Rectangle** command.
4. From the Modify pull-down menu, select **Erase**.
5. Using the pixel box that represents the cursor, select either the horizontal or the perpendicular line to delete it.
6. Also pick one line on the rectangle to erase the whole object.
7. Press **<Enter>** to complete the command.

Depending on the line that you selected, it should disappear, as should the rectangle when you press **<Enter>** to finish the command.

Explode

Explode separates a compound object into individual objects.

The **Explode** command is used to edit a compound object. A compound object comprises more than one AutoCAD object. For example, an object that is created with a polyline is a compound object. Common 2D objects that are exploded for editing purposes include solids, blocks, dimensions, multilines, and polylines. In the previous example a rectangle was erased when one line of the rectangle was selected. If the rectangle was exploded instead, then it would comprise four separate lines, not a polyline.

TRY THIS

Explode a rectangle.

1. Open a new AutoCAD drawing, using **Start from Scratch.**
2. From the pull-down Draw menu, select **Rectangle**.
3. Create a rectangle that has a lower left corner at 1,1 and an upper right corner of 5,4.
4. From the Modify pull-down menu, select **Explode**.
5. Using the pixel box, pick one line of the rectangle.
6. From the Modify pull-down menu, select **Erase**.
7. Using the pixel box, pick on any line of the rectangle. Only that line should be erased, not the whole rectangle.

Extend

Extend lengthens one object to join another.

The **Extend** command allows an object to be lengthened to join another. Extend is used when one object falls short of another and the objects need to be joined. Executing the command requires the selection of a boundary edge first (see Figure 6–8) and then an object or portion of an object (see Figure 6–9) that will intersect the boundary selected.

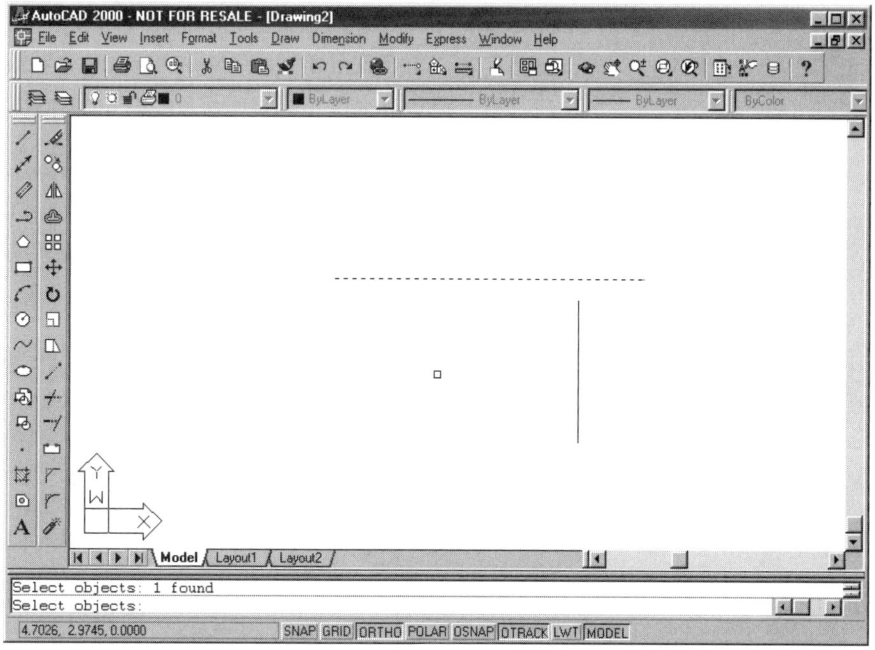

Figure 6–8
Selecting a boundary edge for the Extend command.

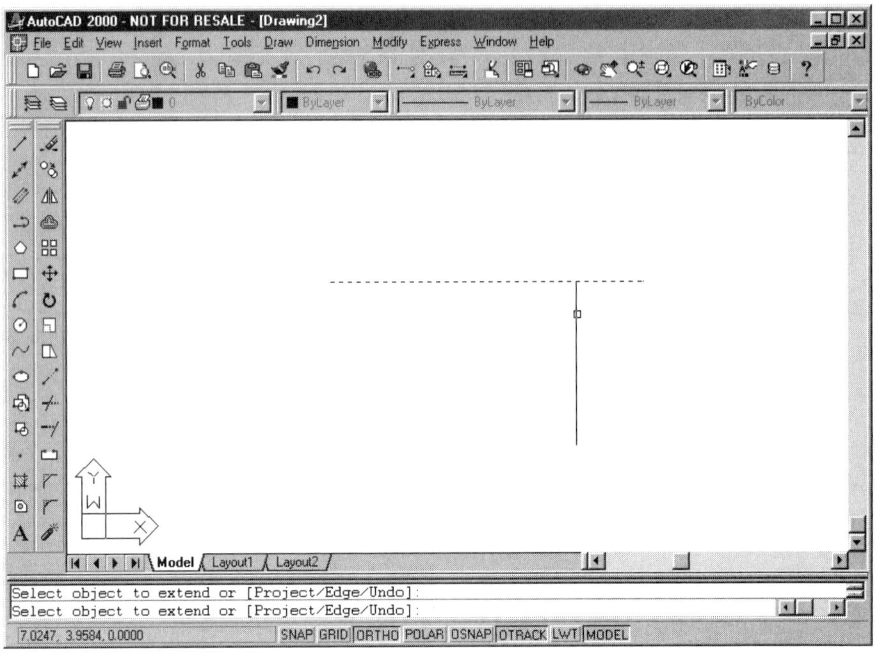

Figure 6–9
Extending a line to intersect the boundary edge.

TRY THIS

Draw two lines that do not touch or do not close an object.

1. Open a new AutoCAD drawing, using **Start from Scratch.**
2. From the Draw pull-down menu, select **Line** to create two lines. Make sure the lines do not intersect or touch one another, as in Figure 6–8.
3. From the Modify pull-down menu, select **Extend**.
4. In Figure 6–8, the horizonital line is the boundary line, and the vertical line would be the entity extended to meet the horizonital line.
5. Select the horizontal line as the boundary edge.
6. Select the vertical line as the line to extend.

After completion of the command, the vertical line should be touching the horizontal line.

Trim

The **Trim** command is used for editing objects in a drawing so they end precisely at a "cutting edge." One or more other objects in the drawing define a cutting edge. The Trim command is often used where portions of an object extend past a boundary edge. The command sequence for trim is as follows:

Command: Trim <Enter>

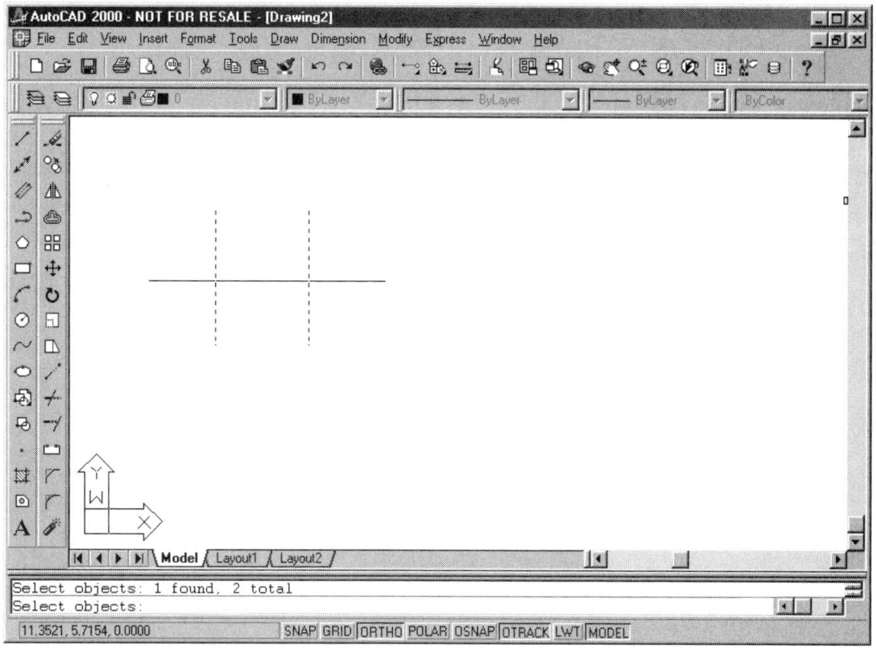

Figure 6–10
Selecting cutting-plane lines.

Select Objects: Pick a cutting edge (entity that acts as a boundary line). <Enter>

<Select object to trim>/Project/Edge/Undo: Select that portion of the entity you want to trim. <Enter>

In Figure 6–10 the two vertical parallel lines were chosen as the cutting edges or planes. Since it was determined that the horizontal line between the two vertical lines was to be removed, that portion of the line between the two vertical lines was selected. The result is depicted in Figure 6–11.

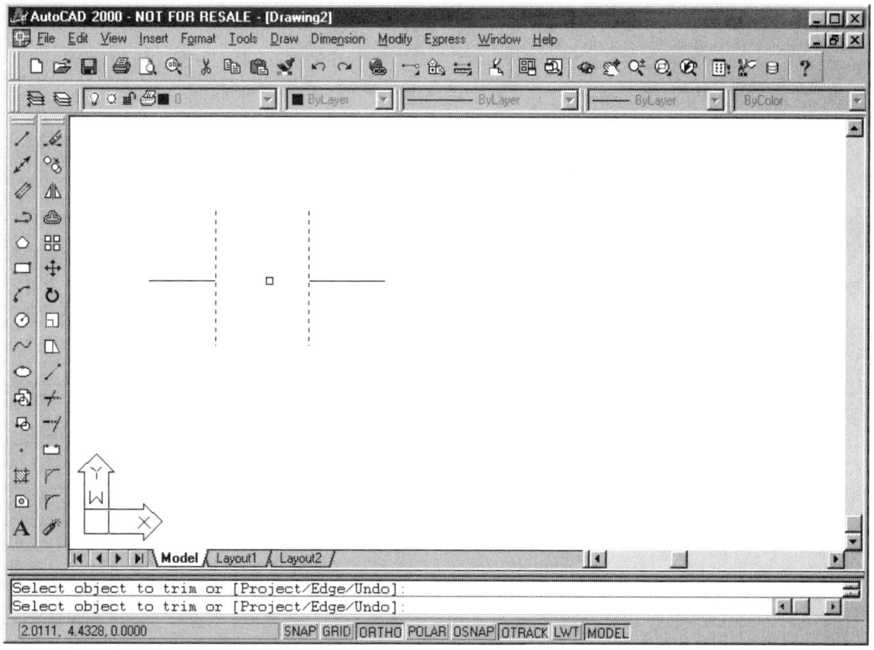

Figure 6–11
Using the Trim command to remove lines between two cutting planes.

TRY THIS

Create a tic-tac-toe pattern and trim it so that all you have left is a rectangle.

1. Open a new AutoCAD drawing, using **Start from Scratch.**
2. From the pull-down Draw menu, select **Line** or **Multiline** to create the tic-tac-toe pattern.
3. After the pattern has been created, go to the Modify pull-down menu and select **Trim.**
4. Select the appropriate cutting planes and trim lines to end up with a rectangle.

Move

The **Move** command is used to move one or more objects to a new location. A single keystroke **(m)** activates the move command. At the command prompt, enter move or select Move from the Modify pull-down menu. The command sequence is as follows:

Command: m

Select objects: Use an object selection method.

Base point or displacement: Specify a base point (1).

Second point of displacement: Specify a point (2), or type movement displacement using polar coordinates.

The two points you specify define a displacement direction that indicates how far the selected objects are to be moved and in what direction (see Figure 6–12).

TRY THIS

Move an object a certain distance.

1. Open a new AutoCAD drawing, using **Start from Scratch**.
2. Draw a 2″-diameter circle with a center point at **3,3**.
3. From the Modify pull-down menu, select **Move**.
4. Pick the circle and move it a distance of 1″ using a polar coordinate reading of **@1″<0**.

The circle should move 1″ to the right of its original position.

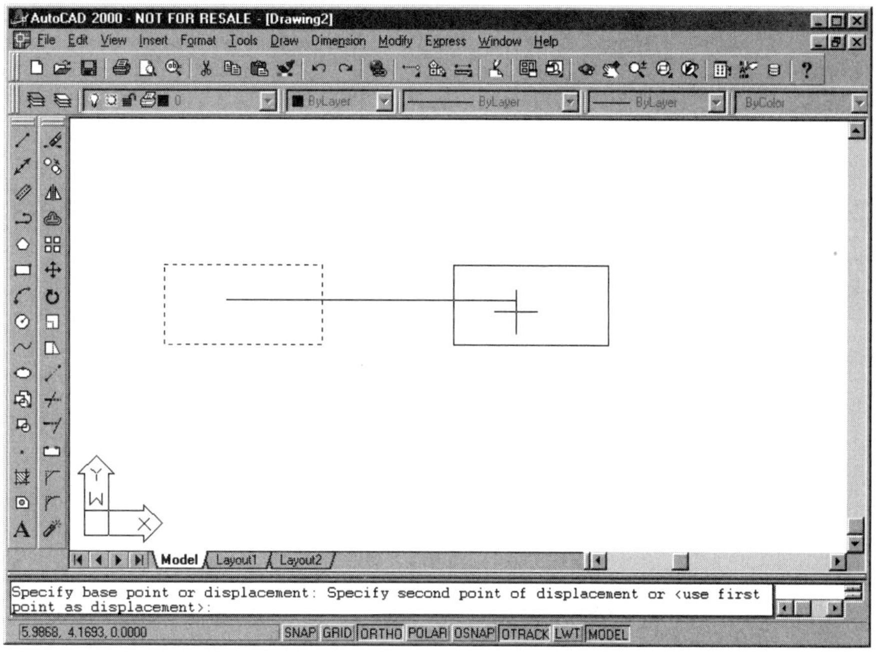

Figure 6–12
Move command.

Rotate

Objects or parts of objects often have to be repositioned based on a certain point. The **Rotate** command rotates an object around a selected point (base point).

> Select Rotate from the Modify pull-down menu or at the command prompt, type rotate.
>
> Command: Rotate
>
> Select objects: Use an object selection method.
>
> Base point: Specify a point (1).
>
> <Rotation angle>/Reference: Specify an angle or press <Enter> return.

After selection of the second point, the object should rotate to its new position (see Figure 6–13).

TRY THIS

Create a square and rotate it 45°.

1. Open a new AutoCAD drawing, using **Start from Scratch.**
2. From the icon toolbar on the left side of the drawing editor, select **Rectangle**.
3. Create a square with an origin point at 1.5,1.5 that is 3″ × 3″.
4. Select the rotate icon.
5. Click on any line of the rectangle.

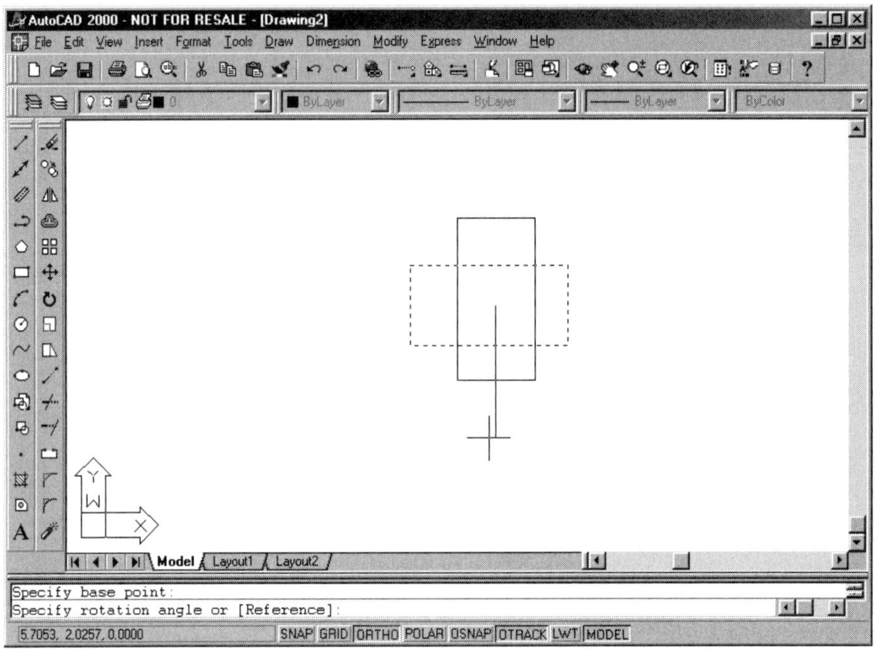

Figure 6–13
Rotating a rectangle.

6. Press **<Enter>** at the Select object: prompt after you have selected the object.
7. At the Base point: prompt, pick near the center of the square.
8. At the Rotation angle: prompt, type **45** then **<Enter>**.

The square should now appear on the screen rotated at a 45° angle.

Scale

Often it is necessary to resize an object. Rather than redrawing an object to meet specifications, you can use the **Scale** command to change object size. From the Modify pull-down menu, select Scale, or at the command prompt, type scale.

Command: Scale

Select objects: Use an object selection method.

Base point: Specify a point (1) around which the object will be scaled.

<Scale factor> / Reference: Specify a numerical value or <Enter>.

The image in Figure 6–14 was scaled by dragging the mouse to a certain point and then picking at a point that was close to the appropriate size. In most instances, to get an accurate size, you would type in a scale value at the command prompt.

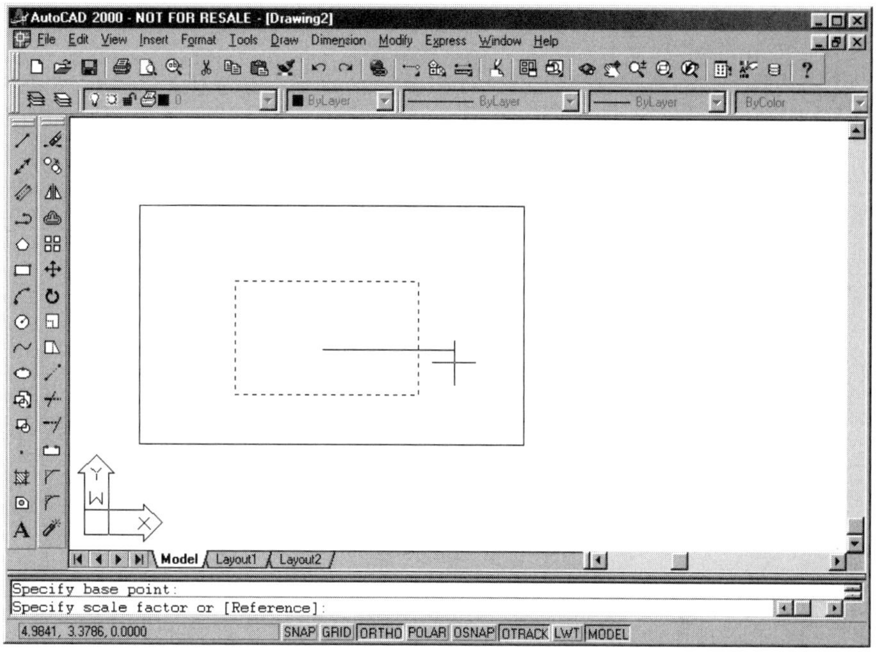

Figure 6–14
The Scale command.

TRY THIS

Create a circle that is 3″ in diameter and scale it by a factor of 0.75.

1. Open a new AutoCAD drawing, using **Start from Scratch.**
2. Select **Circle** from the icon toolbar on the left side of the drawing editor.
3. Type **4,4** as the center point of the circle.
4. Enter **1.5** as the radius of the circle.
5. Select the **scale** icon.
6. At the Select object: prompt, pick on the circle at any point.
7. Press **<Enter>**.
8. Type **cen** at the **Specify** base point: prompt.
9. Pick any point of the circle.
10. At the Scale/Reference point: prompt, type **0.75**.

The circle should shrink in size to 75% of its original size.

Stretch

To **stretch** an object is to enlarge or shrink a portion of a drawing. The Stretch command is used with lines, arcs, traces, solids, polylines, and 3D Faces. Portions of an object to stretch are typically selected with a crossing window. Parts of the object called anchor points are left in place and are not within the selection set of the crossing window. The command sequence for stretch is as follows:

Command: Stretch

Select object: Select the object parts of the object to be stretched by using a crossing window to leave unselected points anchored.

Base point: Pick a base point.

Pick a new point that you want object stretched to, or type in direction and distance (see Figure 6–15).

Figure 6–15 depicts how the object would be stretched. Since this was a rectangle (as such, a polyline) only the right side of the object was selected using a crossing window. A base point was selected, and the object was then stretched to the desired size.

TRY THIS

Draw a line that is 2″ long, then stretch it and make it 4″ longer.

1. Open a new AutoCAD drawing, using **Start from Scratch.**

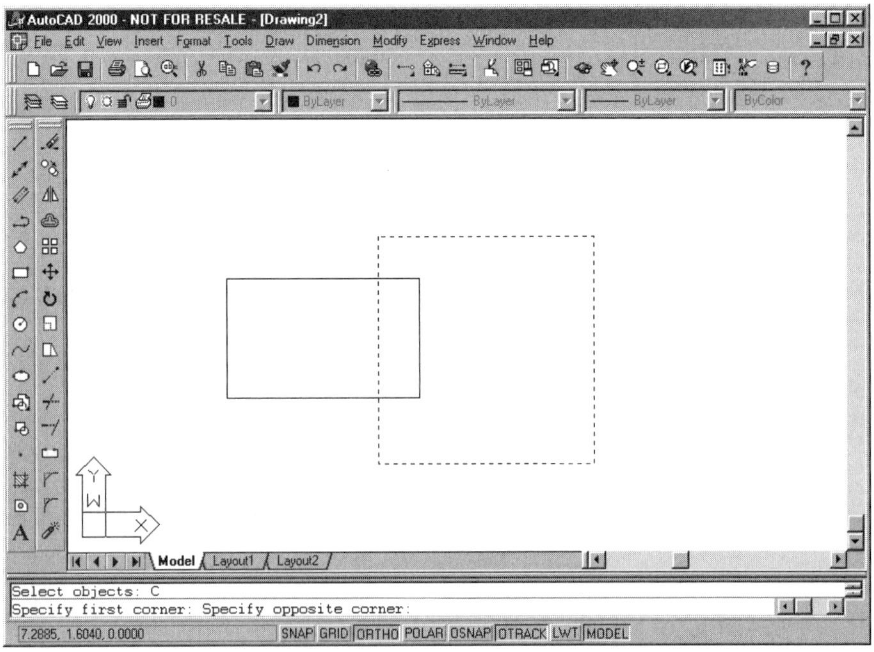

Figure 6–15
Stretching a rectangle.

2. From the toolbar icon menu, click on the **line** icon.
3. At the Starting point: prompt, type **1,1**.
4. At the To Point: prompt, type **@2<0**.
5. Press **<Enter>** to exit the command.
6. From the Modify pull-down menu, select **Stretch**.
7. Type **c** (stands for crossing window), press **<Enter>**.
8. At the First point: prompt, use the input device to pick a point near the right endpoint of the line.
9. At the Second point: prompt, use the input device to pick a point beyond the right endpoint.
10. Press **<Enter>** at the Select object: prompt.
11. At the Base point: prompt, pick near the right endpoint of the line.
12. At the Second point: prompt, type **@2<0**.

Copy

To **copy** objects in a drawing means to create entities that have the same characteristics as the object being copied.

The **Copy** command is used to copy objects in a drawing or to copy objects from one drawing to another. The Copy command is found in the Modify pull-down menu. When you copy an object within a drawing, you will be asked to specify a starting point and an endpoint for the copy. These points are called the **base point** and the **second point of displacement**. Single or multiple copies can be made.

Select Copy from the Modify pull-down menu or at the command prompt, type copy.

Command: Copy

Select objects: to copy, and press <Enter>.

Base point: Any point on the drawing.

<Rotation angle>/Reference: Specify the point of displacement (where you want the copy object to appear on the drawing).

To copy an object several times (see Figure 6–16):

1. From the Modify pull-down menu, select Copy.
2. Select the objects to copy, and press <Enter>.
3. Enter m (multiple).
4. Specify the base point.
5. Specify the second point of displacement.
6. Specify the next point of displacement.
7. Press <Enter> to end the command after placing all the copies that you need.

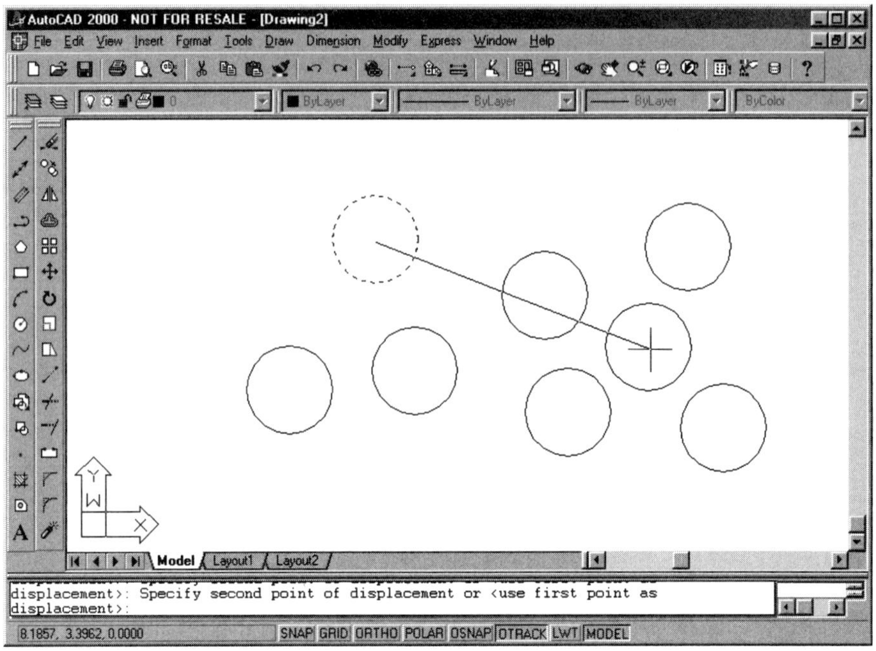

Figure 6–16
Using the Copy command to create multiple copies of an object.

TRY THIS

Create multiple copies of a circle.

1. Open a new AutoCAD drawing, using **Start from Scratch.**
2. Create a circle that is 2″ in diameter and place it on the drawing.
3. From the Modify pull-down menu, select **Copy.**
4. At the Select object: prompt, select the circle.
5. Press **<Enter>** to exit the Select object: prompt.
6. Type **m** at the Base point/Multiple: prompt.
7. At the Base point: prompt, pick near the center of the circle.
8. Place six more circles in the drawing at random locations.

Objects from an AutoCAD drawing can be copied and placed in another drawing file or application. In order to copy drawing objects, use the copy from the Edit menu or type Ctrl+C (hold down the Ctrl key and type C). Objects are copied to the Clipboard, from which they can be placed in other drawings or applications, as is common with other programs that are used in Windows applications.

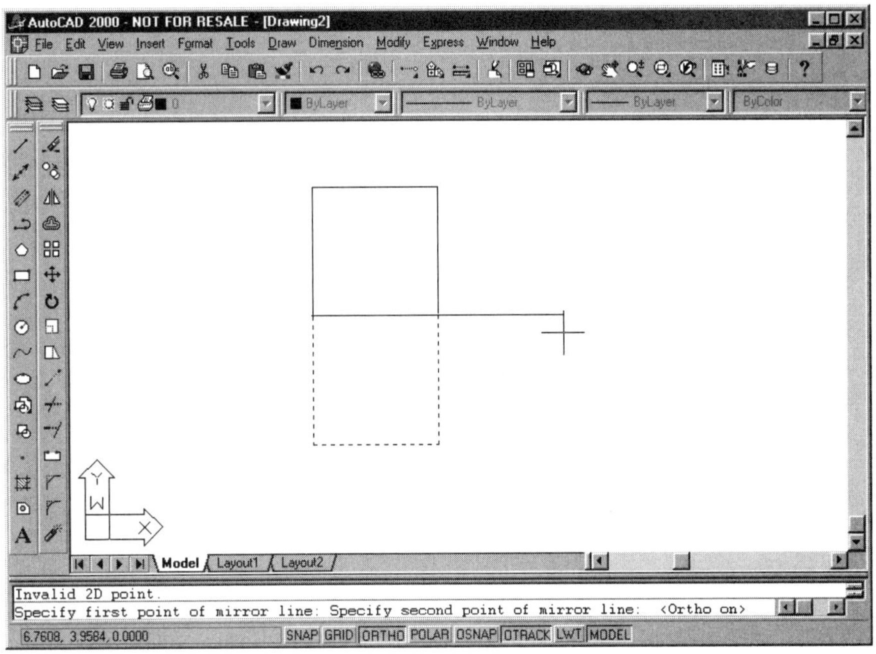

Figure 6–17
Using the Mirror command to mirror a rectangle.

Mirror

Drawing objects are typically **mirrored** when half the object is drawn, and the second half is created by mirroring the first half (see Figure 6–17). If an object is symmetrical, it makes sense to draw half the object and mirror it to create the second half. Objects are mirrored around a mirror line that is defined by picking two points. The original mirrored object can be deleted or retained. The Mirror command is most commonly used in the XY plane. The sequence of commands to mirror objects is:

Select the mirror icon from the Modify toolbar.

Select objects: To be mirrored with a window. Command: Mirror

Base point: Specify the first point of the mirror line. Specify the second point of the mirror line.

<Rotation angle>/Reference: Press <Enter> to retain the original object(s).

TRY THIS

Create half of a rectangle, and use the Mirror command to create the other half.

1. Open a new AutoCAD drawing, using **Start from Scratch.**
2. Use the **Line** command to create half of a rectangle. Be sure two legs of the rectangle are equal.

3. From the toolbar, select the **mirror** icon.
4. Using a window for creating the selection set, select the three lines to be mirrored.
5. Press **<Enter>** to exit the Select objects: prompt.
6. Use **Osnap endp** to establish the first point of the mirror line. Select the endpoint of the line about which the object will be mirrored.
7. Move the mouse or other input device in the direction that provides the correct mirror results. Select the appropriate point.

Fillet

The **Fillet** command rounds or fillets the edges of two objects.

The **Fillet** command is used to connect two objects (lines) with an arc. Figure 6–18 depicts two perpendicular lines that have a 0.5″ fillet (rounded corner). AutoCAD treats both inside and outside corners as fillets. Common entities that can be filleted include line segments, polyline line segments, circles, arcs, and true ellipses. The fillet radius is the arc radius that connects filleted objects. If a rectangle or polygon is filleted, all corners are filleted the same. Fillet options at the prompt include the following:

Polyline/Radius/Trim/<Select first object>:

The default setting of the fillet radius is (0).

To set the fillet radius and use the fillet command, select Fillet from the Modify pull-down menu.

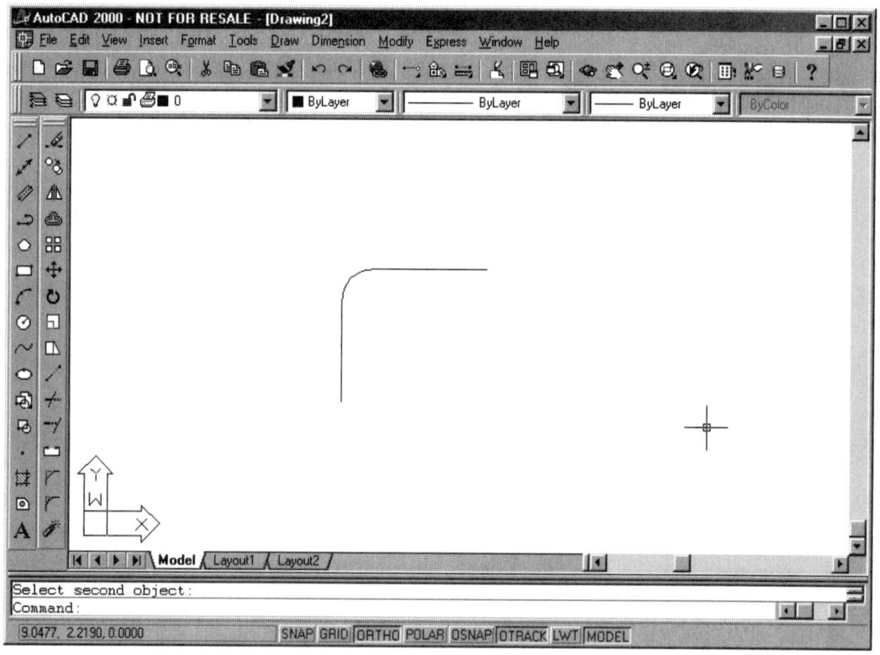

Figure 6–18
Fillet command used to round a corner.

Command: Fillet

Select object: Type the letter r (to set radius value) and press <Enter>.

Base point: Enter the numerical value for the radius.

<Rotation angle>/Reference: Press <Enter> twice to reactivate the fillet command. Select the objects to be filleted.

TRY THIS

Create a fillet with a radius of 0.375″ on four corners of a rectangle.

1. Open a new AutoCAD drawing, using **Start from Scratch.**
2. Draw a rectangle that measures 2″ × 3″.
3. From the toolbar, select the **fillet** icon.
4. Change the radius value to **0.375**″.
5. Pick near the endpoint of each line to be filleted. Repeat the command for each corner.

Chamfer

The **Chamfer** command creates a beveled corner or edge.

The **Chamfer** command creates a beveled line between two nonparallel objects (see Figure 6–19). However, if the chamfer distance is left at zero, a perpendicular corner is created. Lines and polylines are common objects that are chamfered.

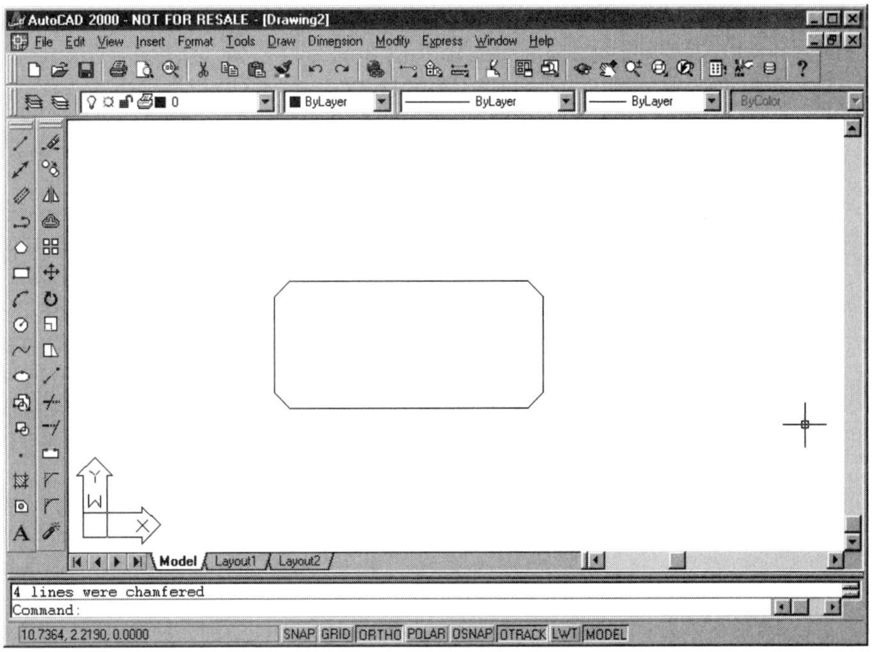

Figure 6–19
A rectangle with chamfered corners.

Chamfer options at the prompt include the following: Polyline/Distance/Angle/Trim/Method:. If a polyline is chamfered, all corners are beveled the same. The chamfer Distance prompt lets you determine the length of each line to be chamfered. Similarly, the chamfer Angle option allows you to determine the angle of each beveled line.

TRY THIS

Create a 2″ × 3″ rectangle using the Rectangle command.

1. Open a new AutoCAD drawing, using **Start from Scratch.**
2. Create a 2″ × 3″ rectangle using the **Rectangle** command.
3. From the Modify pull-down menu, select **Chamfer**.
4. Type **D**, then **<Enter>**.
5. At the Enter first chamfer distance: prompt, type **0.25**; press **<Enter>**.
6. At the Enter second chamfer distance: prompt, type **0.25**; press **<Enter>**.
7. Press **<Enter>** to restart the Chamfer command.
8. Select **polyline**; press **<Enter>**.

All corners of the rectangle should be chamfered the same.

Array

The **Array** command allows you to copy an object numerous times at set increments in both the vertical and horizontal directions or around an imaginary circle.

There are two array options, polar and rectangular, that can be used to replicate objects. The Array command allows you to copy an object numerous times at set increments in both the vertical and horizontal directions or around an imaginary circle. The Array command can be activated through the Modify pull-down menu, typed at the command prompt, or selected from either the screen menu or the toolbar. Rectangular arrays are used to array objects in rows (horizontal) and columns (vertical). Both positive and negative values can be entered. A positive value will create copies up and to the right of the original. Negative values will copy down or to the left of the original. Polar arrays are used to array items in a circular pattern. Often, it is more efficient to use the Array command rather than the Copy command when you have multiple objects to create.

If you use the rectangular array, you must specify the number of rows, columns, and the distance between each. If you select a polar array, you must designate the number of objects and the angle through which you want the objects arrayed, and you must specify if the objects are to be rotated.

Figure 6-20 is a drawing in which both a polar and rectangular array were used. A polar array was used to array the four 0.25″-diameter circles. A rectangular array was used to create the text box that identifies the circles and circle diameters.

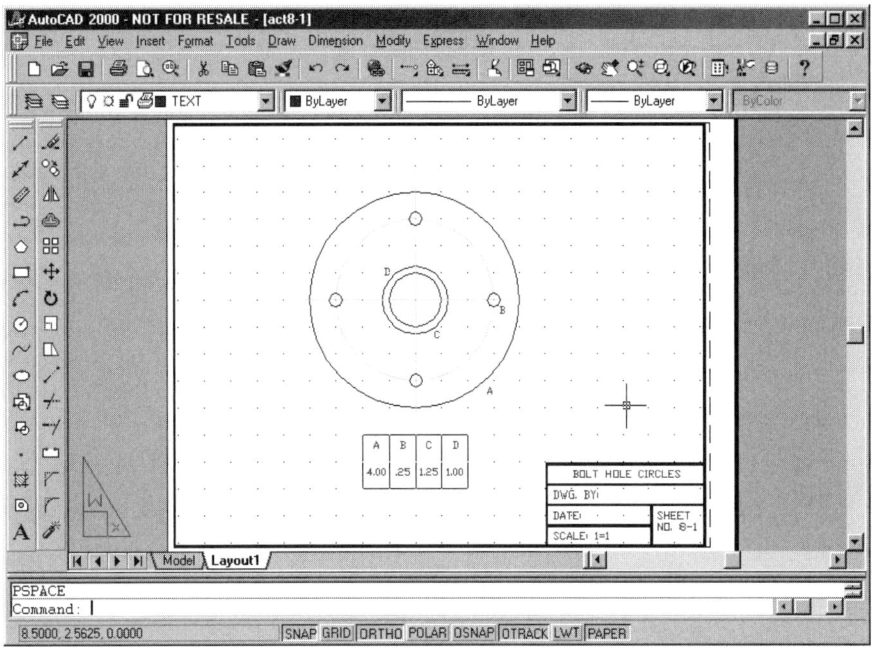

Figure 6–20
A polar and a rectangular array.

TRY THIS

Use polar array to array a line within a circle.

1. Start the AutoCAD software program.
2. Select **Use a Template** and select the **A-size template** file you created in Chapter 2.
3. Make sure you are in model space, and create a circle with a center point of 5,5 and a radius of 2.
4. Create a line that has one endpoint of 5,5 and another endpoint that intersects the circle.
5. From the Modify pull-down menu, select **Array**.
6. Select the line to array it.
7. When prompted to respond to Rectangular/Polar:, enter **P**.
8. For the center point select the center of the circle. Use the object snap **cen** to find the circle center.
9. At the Number of items: prompt, enter **30**.
10. At the Angle to fill: prompt, accept the default of 360.
11. Respond **yes** to the prompt asking if the objects are to be rotated.
12. The line should then be arrayed 30 times in the circle.

TRY THIS

Use rectangular array to array a square.

1. Start the AutoCAD software program.
2. Select **Use a Template** and select the **A-size template** file you created in Chapter 2.
3. Make sure you are in model space, and use the rectangle command to draw a square that is 1 × 1.
4. Select the **array** icon from the toolbar.
5. Select the rectangle at the Select Object: prompt.
6. Enter **r** for rectangular.
7. At the Number of rows: prompt, enter **2**.
8. At the Number of columns: prompt, enter **4**.
9. Distance between rows is **2**.
10. Distance between columns is **2**.

Two rows of squares should appear on the screen (see Figure 6–21). There should also be four columns. The spacing between the rows and columns is 1. In a rectangular array, AutoCAD always reads the lower left point of the entity as the origin point. That is why we entered 2 for the spacing.

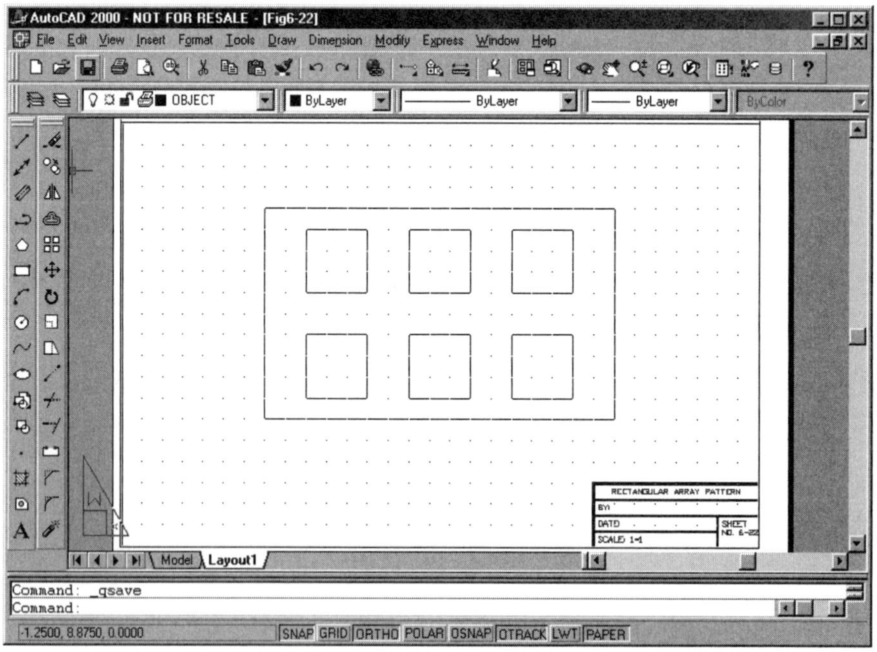

Figure 6–21
Rectangular array of squares.

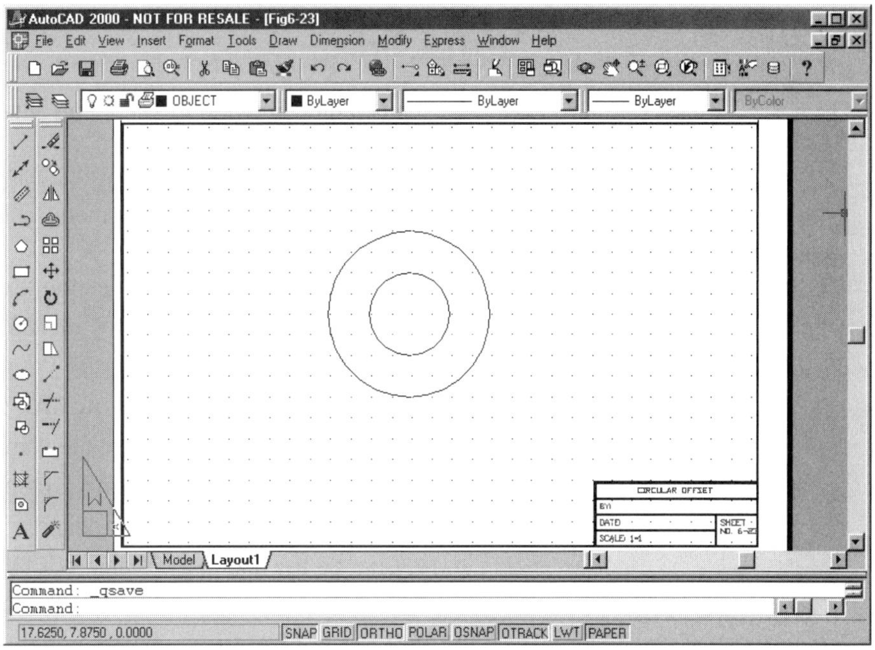

Figure 6–22
Offset of a circle.

Offset

When an object is **offset**, a new object is created that is similar to the selected object.

Offset is another command located in the Modify pull-down meu. When an object is offset, a new object is created that is similar to the selected object. Many objects can be offset, including lines, arcs, circles, 2D polylines, and ellipses. When you offset an object, you need to enter a distance and a side of an object to offset. In the example in Figure 6–22, a 4″-diameter circle was offset to the inside 1″ to create a 2″-diameter circle.

Ddedit

The **Ddedit** command is used to edit text.

The editing command for editing text is **Ddedit**. This command is used for editing text that was created with the Text command. It is commonly used to correct misspelled words or text information in the drawing. To execute the command, either select it from the Modify pull-down menu, or type ddedit at the command prompt. Click on the text to be edited. When a dialog box appears with the highlighted text (see Figure 6–23), enter the new text, and press <Enter> when you are finished. The dialog box will close, and the selected text will automatically be changed in the drawing.

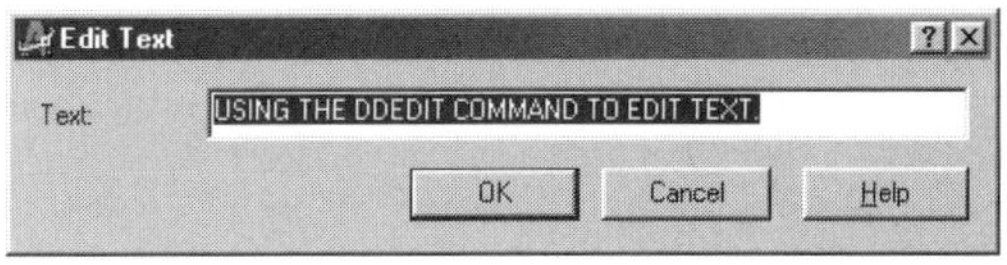

Figure 6–23
Ddedit dialog box.

TRY THIS

Use the Ddedit command to edit a line of text.

1. Open a new AutoCAD drawing, using **Start from Scratch.**
2. From the **Draw** pull-down menu, select **Text**, then select **Single line text**.
3. Using your input device, pick the text starting point.
4. Change the size of the text to **0.125**″.
5. Leave the rotation angle at (0).
6. At the text prompt type **"AutoCAD 2000 is fun to use".**
7. Press **<Enter>** twice to exit the command.
8. Type **ddedit** at the command prompt.
9. Select the line of text to be edited.
10. Change the text in the dialog box to read, **"AutoCAD is fun"**.
11. Click **OK** to change the text in the drawing.
12. Press **<Enter>** to exit the command.

Pedit (polyedit)

The **Pedit** command is used to edit objects that were made with a polyline.

Objects that are created with polylines require a special editing command, **pedit**. The following options are included in the Pedit command:

Close/Join/Width/Edit vertex/Fit/Spline/Decurve/Ltype gen/Undo/eXit<X>:

Close	Closes a polyline entity; can add a segment to close entity.
Join	Connects dissimilar entities to make one continuous polyline.
Width	Changes the default width of the polyline.
Edit vertex	Edits individual vertices.
Fit	Creates smooth curves that pass between vertices.
Spline	Creates a curve that passes through the first and last vertices. Uses other vertices to pull the curve in one direction or the other.

Figure 6–24
Screen menu display of Pedit options.

```
PEDIT Select polyline:
Enter an option [Open/Join/Width/Edit vertex/Fit/Spline/Decurve/Ltype gen/Undo]:
```

Decurve	Returns the polyline to its original state.
Ltype gen	Changes the linetype application.
Undo	Reverses the last Pedit command.
eXit	Exits the Pedit command.

Figure 6–24 displays a listing of the pedit commands in the screen menu.

If the object that you select is not created with a polyline, you will be asked if you want to convert the line to a polyline.

TRY THIS

Create a rectangle and change its line width to 0.05″ using the pedit command.

1. Open a new AutoCAD drawing, using **Start from Scratch.**
2. From the Draw pull-down menu, select **Rectangle.**
3. Create a rectangle that has an origin point at 2,2 and an upper right corner point of 6,5.
4. From the Modify pull-down menu select **polyline**.
5. Select any line of the rectangle.
6. Type **w** (width).
7. Type **0.05**″ as the width for all line segments.

Activity 6–1

Draw a Rotated Square

In this activity you will use the Copy and Rotate commands to create a rotated square. Make the suggested settings, and create the necessary layers as listed. (To learn how to add layers to a drawing, go to the Help menu and select AutoCAD Help Topics. Click on the Index tab and type the word layers where indicated. Find the add/deleting layers to/from option, and select it. A dialog box should appear with information on how to create layers.) A likeness of the drawing appears in Figure 6–25.

Plotter Paper Size: A

Suggested Settings:	Grid	0.50″
	Snap	0.125″
	Layers (7)	**0** (default border)
		Center (cen), Linetype center, Color: cyan
		Object (obj), Linetype continuous, Color: black
		Hidden (hid), Linetype hidden, Color: magenta
		Tbk (title block), Linetype continuous, Color: red
		Txt (text), Linetype continuous, Color: green
		Dim (dimensions), Linetype continuous, Color: green
	Units	Decimal

Hints:

1. Open your border template file for an A-size drawing. After it has completed loading, use the Saveas command to rename the drawing file ACT6-1.
2. The star consists of 2″ squares drawn in model space. Be sure the snap and grid are set and are On before drawing. Draw one square using the line, rectangle, or polygon command. Copy the original square and rotate it 45°. Move the rotated copy so that it overlays the original square. Now copy both squares and rotate them 22.5°. Move the copied object back so that they overlay the original entity.

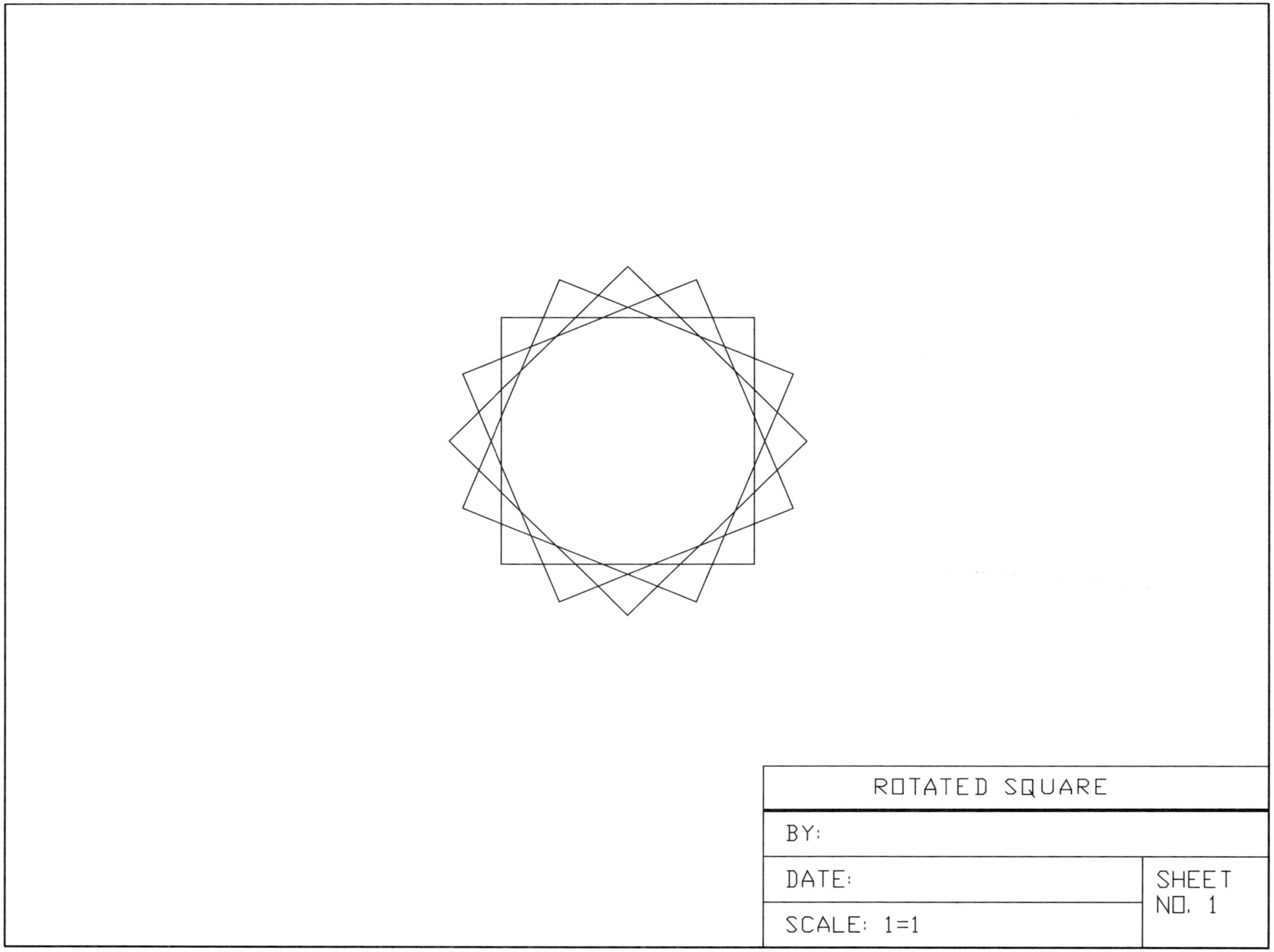

Figure 6–25
Activity 6–1

ACTIVITY 6–2

Draw a Slider Bracket

In this activity you will use the Chamfer and Fillet commands to create two separate objects. Make your settings and create the necessary layers as listed. A likeness of the drawing appears in Figure 6–26.

Plotter Paper Size: A

Suggested Settings:	Grid	0.50″
	Snap	0.125″
	Layers (7)	**0** (default border)
		Center (cen), Linetype center, Color: cyan
		Object (obj), Linetype continuous, Color: black
		Hidden (hid), Linetype hidden, Color: magenta
		Tbk (title block), Linetype continuous, Color: red
		Txt (text), Linetype continuous, Color: green
		Dim (dimensions), Linetype continuous, Color: green
	Units	Decimal

Hints:

1. Open your border template file for an A-size drawing. After it has completed loading, use the Saveas command to rename the drawing file ACT6-2.
2. Make sure you are in model space before you begin drawing the object.
3. In this activity you will draw three views: top, front, and right side. The three views are spaced 1.5″ apart. Dimensions of the object are provided in Figure 6–26.
4. Depending on the layers you created in your A-size template, you may have to add new layers in this object. The linetypes of hidden and center will have to be loaded and assigned to the Hidden and Center layers, respectively. (To load a linetype, type linetype at the command prompt and press <Enter>. The LineType Manager dialog box should appear. Select the Linetype tab and click on Load. Select the linetype you want loaded and click OK. Click on the Layer tab. Select the layer to which you want to assign a linetype and click on the linetype that currently is assigned to that layer. A dialog box should appear that lets you select a different linetype for that layer. Select the linetype you want to use for that layer and click OK.)
5. The easiest method for creating the centerlines for the circles is to use Cen in the Dimension pull-down menu. The Dimension menu has several variables that can be changed. In order to create the centerlines in the circle, use the following procedure:

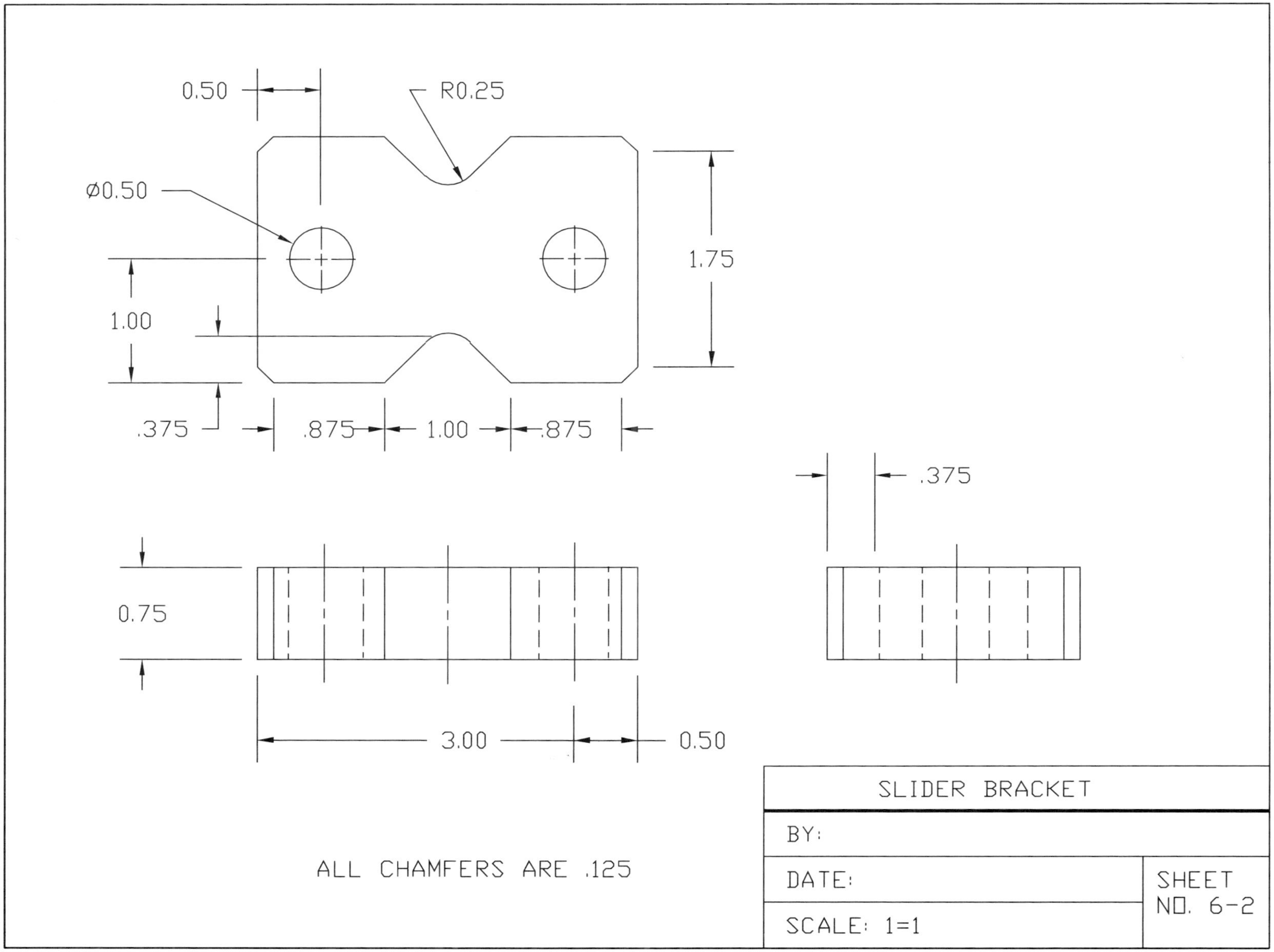

Figure 6–26
Activity 6–2

- At the command prompt, enter Dim
- At the Dim command, enter dimcen
- Enter a value of -0.0625 and press <Enter>
- At the Dim command, enter cen
- Select the circle
- The centerline complete with the crosshairs should appear.

6. **Do not** include the dimensions on the drawing.

ACTIVITY 6–3

Draw a Baseplate

In this activity you will use the polar array drawing command to array a series of circles within a larger circle. Make your settings and create the necessary layers as listed. A likeness of the drawing appears in Figure 6–27.

Plotter Paper Size: B

Suggested Settings:	Grid	0.50″
	Snap	0.125″
	Layers (7)	**0** (default border)
		Center (cen), Linetype center, Color: cyan
		Object (obj), Linetype continuous, Color: black
		Hidden (hid), Linetype hidden, Color: magenta
		Tbk (title block), Linetype continuous, Color: red
		Txt (text), Linetype continuous, Color: green
		Dim (dimensions), Linetype continuous, Color: green
	Units	Decimal

Hints:

1. Open your border template file for a B-size drawing. After it has completed loading, use the Saveas command to rename the drawing file ACT6-3.
2. Create the baseplate drawing. See Figure 6–27 for all dimensions.
3. **Do not** include dimensions on the drawing.

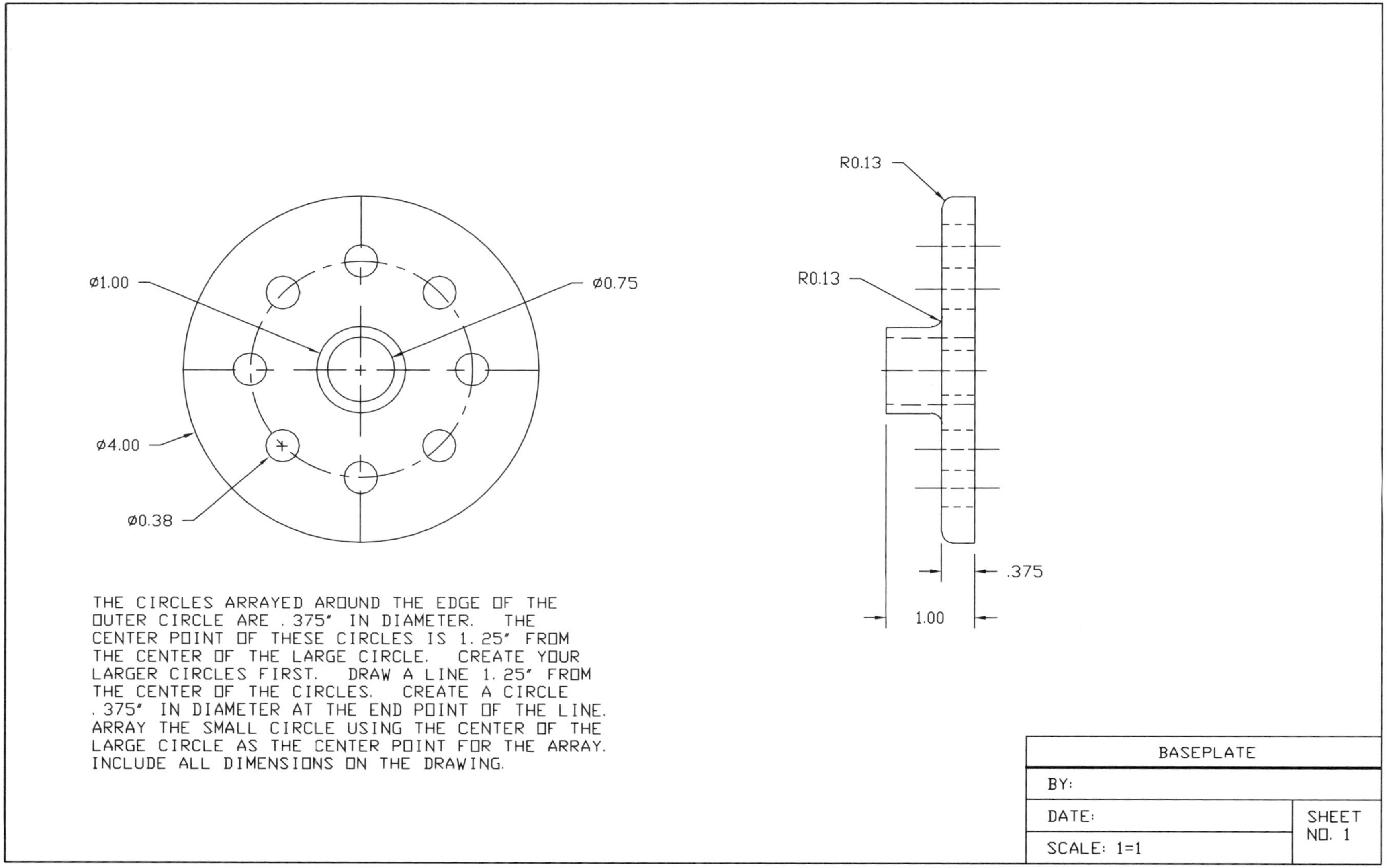

Figure 6–27
Activity 6–3

ACTIVITY 6–4

Draw a Grate

In this activity you will use the rectangular array drawing command to array a series of objects in rows and columns. Make your settings and create the necessary layers as listed. A likeness of the drawing appears in Figure 6–28.

Plotter Paper Size: A

Suggested Settings:	Grid	0.50″
	Snap	0.125″
	Layers (7)	**0** (default border)
		Center (cen), Linetype center, Color: cyan
		Object (obj), Linetype continuous, Color: black
		Hidden (hid), Linetype hidden, Color: magenta
		Tbk (title block), Linetype continuous, Color: red
		Txt (text), Linetype continuous, Color: green
		Dim (dimensions), Linetype continuous, Color: green
	Units	Decimal

Hints:

1. Open your A-size drawing template file. After it has completed loading, use the Saveas command to rename the drawing file ACT6-4.
2. Create the grate drawing. See Figure 6–28 for all dimensions.
3. **Do not** include dimensions on the drawing.

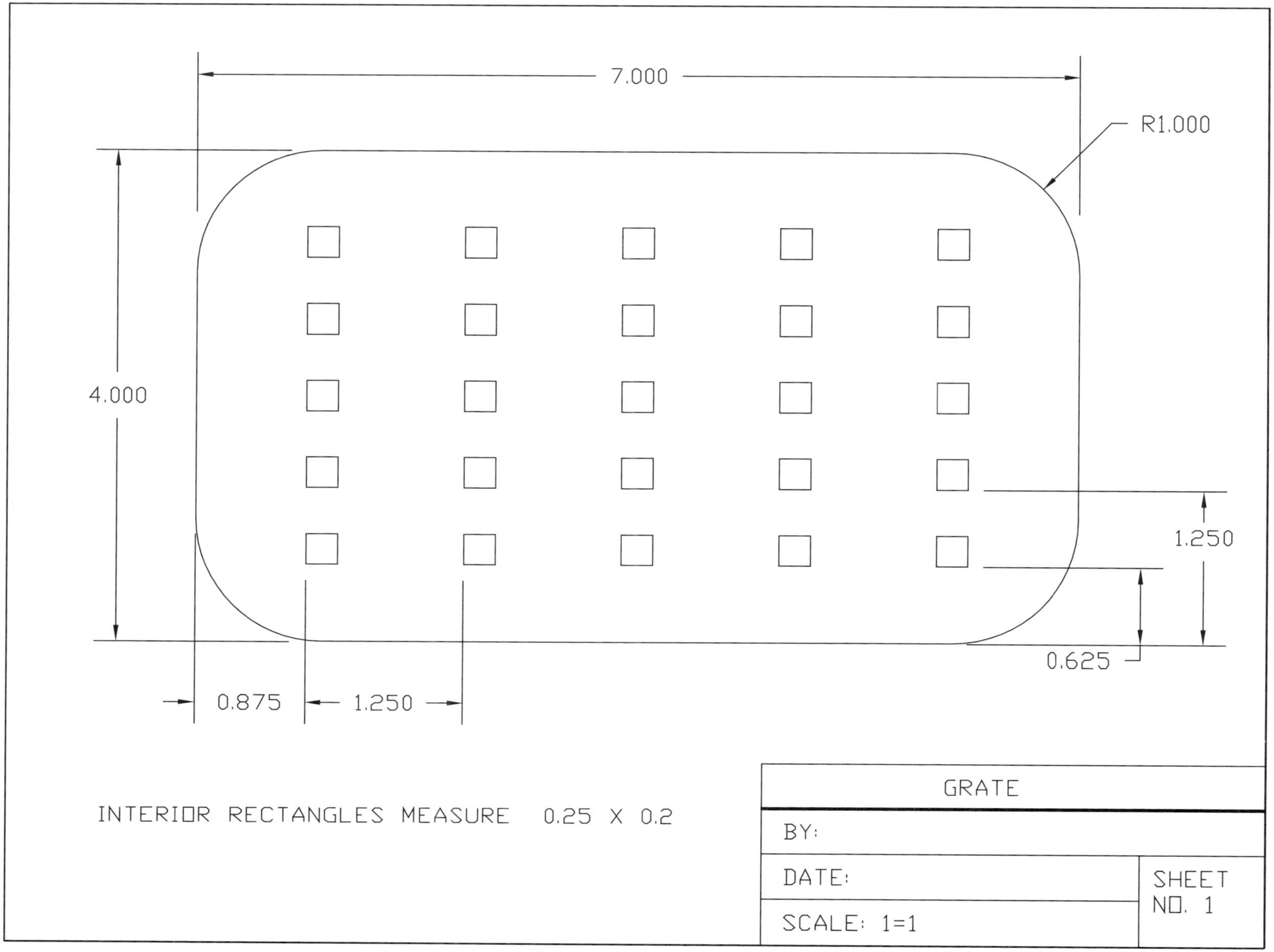

Figure 6–28
Activity 6–4

CHAPTER

7

Using and Creating Template Files

AFTER READING THIS CHAPTER, YOU WILL BE ABLE TO:

- Use template drawing files.
- Use those options associated with layer control.
- Identify typical drawing scales.

KEY CONCEPTS

Drawing Scales
Layers
Template Files

Whenever AutoCAD is opened from the desktop, the Startup dialog box is displayed. This dialog box contains four options for starting the software, namely, Use a Wizard, Use a Template, Start from Scratch, or Open a Drawing.

If you select Start from Scratch to make a prototype drawing, you will be able to specify the drawing parameters that you want, which may include grid, limits, snap, and units. It makes sense to establish drawing parameters in a prototype drawing, since it can continually be reused. Title blocks, borders, and layers are a few of the other items that can be set in a template or prototype drawing so that this information is consistent from drawing to drawing. Because drawings are printed/plotted on standard sizes of paper, prototype or template drawings can be created for each size of paper used for printing and/or plotting.

USING A TEMPLATE DRAWING FILE

New drawings are based on a template, one created by you or, in some instances, one created by AutoCAD. Any drawing can be used as a template. When templates are used, any changes that are made to the template are saved under a different file name. Template files include settings that are consistent with your particular office standards. These may include:

- Unit type and precision
- Drawing limits
- Snap and grid
- Layer organization
- Title blocks, borders, and logos
- Dimension and text styles
- Linetypes

TRY THIS

Open up a template file to review title block styles.

1. Open the AutoCAD software program.
2. From the startup menu select **Use a Template.**
3. Open the **ANSI_anamedplotstyles.dwt** template file.
4. Type **ps** to change to paper space.
5. Zoom in on the Title Block.
6. Above DWG NO, type your name, and set the text height to **0.25″.**
7. Fill in the rest of the information in the title block, changing text size as needed.
8. Save the drawing file under a new name.

In Figure 7–1 the Find File option was used from the Open Existing dialog box window. All template files (.dwt), rather than drawing files (.dwg), were sought. Figure 7–1 displays a partial listing of the template files that exist. The style and size of each template file is determined by the template file name. For example, ANSI_a.dwg is a standard template file established by the American National Standards Institute that fits A-size drawing paper. ISO is the acronym for International Standards Organization.

TRY THIS

Open up a template file to review title block styles.

1. Open the AutoCAD software program.
2. From the startup menu select **Use a Template**.
3. Open the **ISO_A1.dwt** template file. This is a metric title block.
4. Switch to model space and check the limits of the drawing. What do they read?
5. How would you scale this drawing to fit A-size paper?

When you use a template file, remember to save the drawing file with a name that is different from the given template file name.

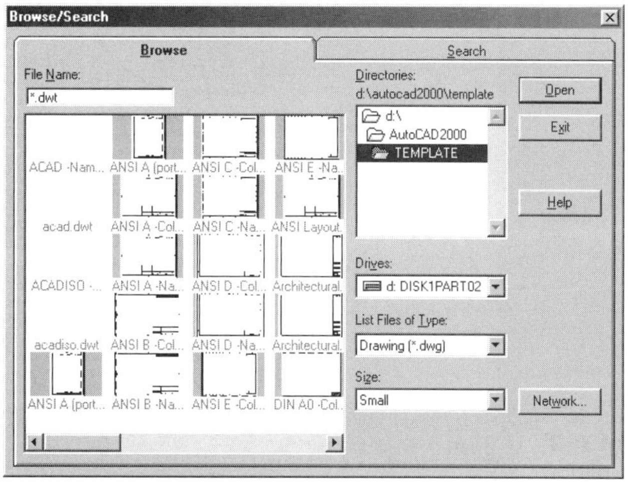

Figure 7–1
AutoCAD 2000 template drawing files.

LAYER ORGANIZATION

Layers are primarily an organizational tool in AutoCAD. Each layer has an associated color lineweight, plot style, and linetype. Layers group information by function, and in AutoCAD, layers are sorted alphabetically by name. In any template, any number of layers can be created and saved with the template file. However, certain standards have been created by business and industry for the naming of layers and assigning of layer characteristics. These standards have been developed for manufacturing, architectural/residential, and architectural/mechanical commercial drawings.

Layer characteristics are assigned in the Layer Properties Manager dialog box (see Figure 7–2). Color and linetype are the two most common characteristics assigned to a layer. The dialog box appears when you type la at the command prompt or if you select the Layers icon on the Object Properties toolbar.

The status of the layer you are currently working on is displayed in this toolbar, which is displayed at the top of the drawing editor screen (see Figure 7–3). The various options associated with the Object Properties toolbar are described next.

Make Object's Layer Current	Gives you the option of selecting a layer based on the selection of the object.
Layers	Activates the Layer Properties Manager dialog box.

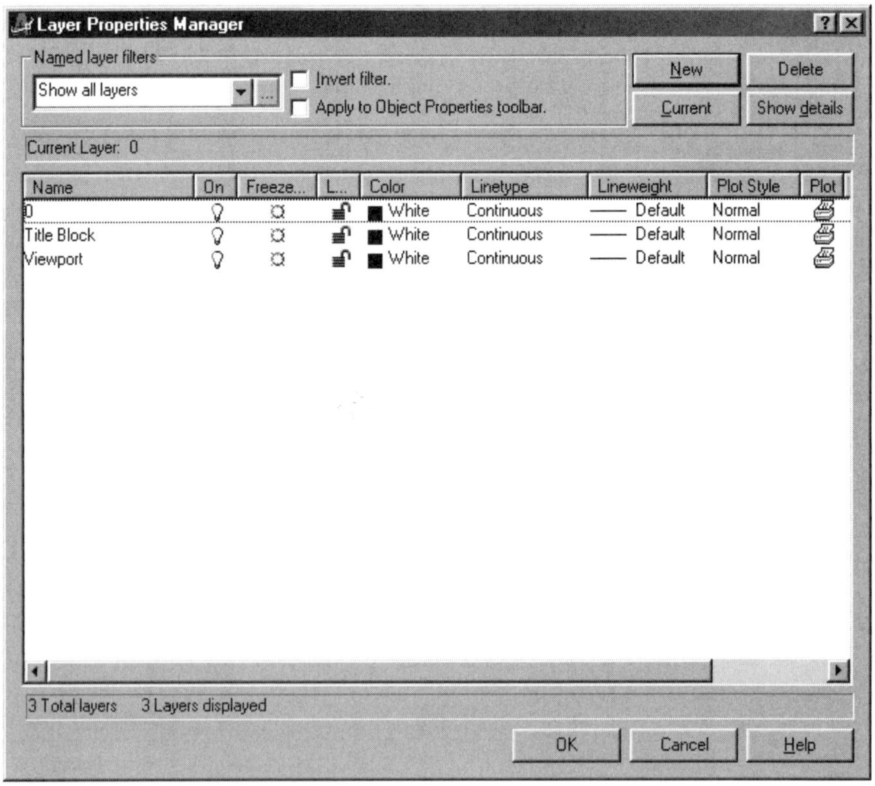

Figure 7–2
Layer Properties Manager dialog box.

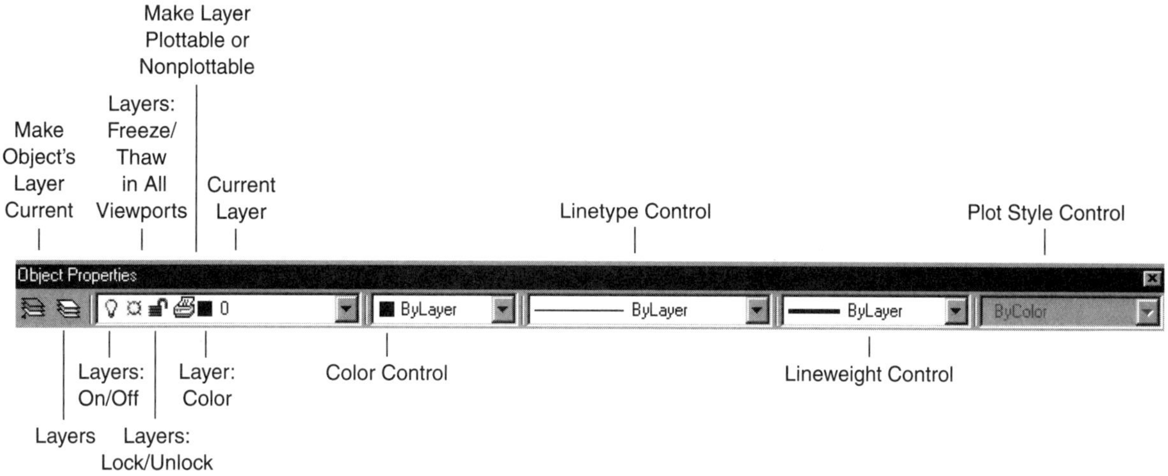

Figure 7–3
Object Properties toolbar.

Layers On/Off	Used to turn layers on or off. If the light bulb icon is yellow, the layer is on. If the light bulb icon is grayed out, the layer is off.
Layers: Freeze/Thaw in All Viewports	Layer will not show in current viewport if it is frozen in that viewport.
Layers: Lock/Unlock	If a layer is locked, it will be displayed, but any objects located on that layer cannot be edited.
Layers: Lock/Unlock	Make layer plottable or nonplottable.
Layers: Color	Depicts the color assigned to that layer. All objects drawn on that layer will be displayed based on the color assigned to the layer.
Color Control	Allows you to change how colors are assigned to a layer. Specific colors can be assigned or specific objects, which enables you to have multiple colors appear on a single layer.
Linetype Control	Similar to color control. Linetypes can be singularly assigned to objects that are on the same layer.
Lineweight Control	Individual lines can be assigned a lineweight.
Plot Style Control	There are two plot style modes: either color-dependent or named. Existing object characteristics can be overridden depending on the mode selected. (Use the AutoCAD Help Index to find out more about plot styles.)

Table 7–1

Standard Layer Names for a Manufacturing Drawing

LAYER NAME	COLOR	LINETYPE	DESCRIPTION
CEN	Cyan	Center	Centerlines
DIM	Green	Continuous	Dimensions
HID	Magenta	Hidden	Hidden features
OBJ	Black	Continuous	Solid object lines
TBK	Red	Continuous	Title block and borderlines
TXT	Green	Continuous	Text

As we mentioned previously, industry has tried to set standards or guidelines for layer names. Tables 7–1 through 7–6 provide an overview of different layers used based on these standards.

If there are several parts on a drawing, add the prefix **P** and a numerical value that indicates there are several parts, for example, P3-hat, which stands for part 3 hatch lines.

Table 7–2

Standard Layer Names for an Architectural Residential Drawing

LAYER NAME	COLOR	LINETYPE	DESCRIPTION
APP	White	Continuous	Appliances
CAB	Blue	Continuous	Cabinetry
DIM	Green	Continuous	Dimensions
DOR	Cyan	Continuous	Doors
ELC	Magenta	Continuous	Electrical
FIX	White	Continuous	Fixtures (plumbing)
FUR	Green	Continuous	Furniture
STR	Blue	Continuous	Stairs
TBK	Red	Continuous	Title block and border
WAL	Yellow	Continuous	Walls
WIN	Cyan	Continuous	Windows

Table 7–3

Standard Layer Names for an Architectural Commercial Drawing

Layer Name	Description
A00WALPN	Walls on a plan view
A00WALEL	Walls on an elevation view
A00WALSC	Walls on a sectional view
A00DORPN	Door symbols on a plan view
A00WINPN	Window symbols on a plan view
A00FIXON	Fixtures (plumbing) on a plan view
A00CABPN	Cabinetry on a plan view
A00DIMON	Dimensions on a plan view
A00TXTPN	Text on a plan view

Table 7–4

Standard Layer Names for a Mechanical Commercial Drawing

Layer Name	Description
M00ARHPN	Air-handling units on a plan view
M00SUPPN	Supply air on a plan view
M00RETPN	Return air on a plan view
M00VENPN	Ventilation on a plan view
M00CONON	Condensing system on a plan view
M00CTRPN	Controls on a plan view
M00DIMPN	Dimensions on a plan view
M00TXTPN	Text on a plan view

Table 7–5

Standard Layer Names for a Plumbing Commercial Drawing

Layer Name	Description
P00CWSPN	Cold-water supply on a plan view
P00DHWPN	Domestic hot water on a plan view
P00HWSPN	Hot-water supply on a plan view
P00WRPN	Hot-water return on a plan view
P00SANPN	Sanitary waste on a plan view
P00VENPN	Vents on a plan view
P00TEMPN	Tempered water on a plan view
P00STMPN	Storm drain on a plan view

TRY THIS

Add the standard layer names, linetypes, and colors to a drawing.

1. From the AutoCAD Startup dialog box, select **Use a Template**.
2. Open your A-size border template.
3. Enter **la** at the command prompt.
4. Create the standard mechanical layer names with the correct colors and linetypes as indicated in Table 7-1.
5. To change the color of a layer, select the colored square of the corresponding layer.
6. To change the linetype, click on the linetype showing, and a linetype dialog box will appear. If the linetype is not listed, select **Load**, and a linetype dialog box will appear from which you can load the linetype you need.

Repeat the procedure for the B-size template that you created at the end of Chapter 2.

Architectural layers can be further defined by adding the prefix F to indicate floor level.

Numerous types of layers also are used in the construction industry. These include architectural, structural, mechanical, and landscape layers. Layer names are defined with a prefix letter to identify the discipline to which they are related. Disciplines include the following:

A for Architecture	S for Structural
M for Mechanical	P for Plumbing
F for Fire Protection	E for Electrical
C for Civil Engineering	L for Landscape

The layer name is then followed by a floor designation and a category designation (see Tables 7–3 through 7–6).

Table 7-6

Standard Layer Names for an Electrical Commercial Drawing

LAYER NAME	DESCRIPTION
E00PWRPN	Power on a plan view
E00HETPN	Heat on a plan view
E00LITPN	Lighting on a plan view
E00CGDPN	Ceiling grid on a plan view
E00COMPN	Communications on a plan view
E00CTRPN	Controls on a plan view
E00ALMPN	Alarm systems on a plan view

Third-party software add-ons to AutoCAD may also have specific layer name conventions that are used with particular applications.

DRAWING SCALES

Just as there are layer name conventions, so are there standard scale conventions. Standard scales that have been established include metric, engineer, and architect scales (see Table 7–7).

Scaling enables you to place drawing entities on different sizes of papers. Standard paper sizes are listed:

SIZE	ENGLISH MEASUREMENT	METRIC MEASUREMENT
A	8.5 × 11	256 × 196
B	11 × 17	394 × 251
C	17 × 22	525 × 396
D	22 × 34	829 × 524
E	34 × 44	1089 × 835

The actual paper surface area that can be used for plotting varies depending on the type of output device used. Each plotter or printer has physical devices that determines the amount of surface area that can be used for either plotting or printing. Check with the manufacturer to determine the largest parameters available for printing and/or plotting.

Table 7–7

METRIC	MECHANICAL ENGINEER	ARCHITECT
1:1	1″ = 1″	1″ = 1′
1:20	$\frac{1}{2}$″ = 1″	$\frac{3}{4}$″ = 1′
1:125	$\frac{1}{4}$″ = 1″	$\frac{1}{2}$″ = 1′
1:250	$\frac{1}{8}$″ = 1″	$\frac{3}{8}$″ = 1′
1:300		$\frac{1}{4}$″ = 1′
1:500		$\frac{3}{16}$″ = 1′
1:1000		$\frac{1}{8}$″ = 1′
1:8000		$\frac{3}{32}$″ = 1′

ACTIVITY 7–1

Use the What's New Option to Learn More about Layers

This activity was developed by AutoDesk to provide you with information on how to manage layers.

ACTIVITY STEPS

1. Start the AutoCAD 2000 software program.
2. Select Start from Scratch in the Startup dialog box.
3. Select the Learning Assistance option from the Help pull-down menu.
4. Select Tutorials. From the Tutorials menu select Organizing Your Project.
5. From the Organizing Your Project option select Organizing Your Objects with Layers and Properties. Select the Play Video option to view the tutorial. Complete the Try It! activity after watching the video.
6. After watching the video, click on the Contents tab above the video screen.
7. Select the Using Layers to Reduce Drawing Maintenance tutorial. Select the Play Video option to view the tutorial. Complete the Try It! activity after watching the video.
8. After watching the video, click on the Contents tab above the video screen.
9. Select the Managing Layers with the AutoCAD Express Tools tutorial. Select the Play Video option to view the tutorial. Complete the Try It! activity after watching the video.

ACTIVITY 7–2

Create New Layers on a Template Drawing

This activity was designed to give you practice in adding layer names and assigning linetypes and color to template drawings.

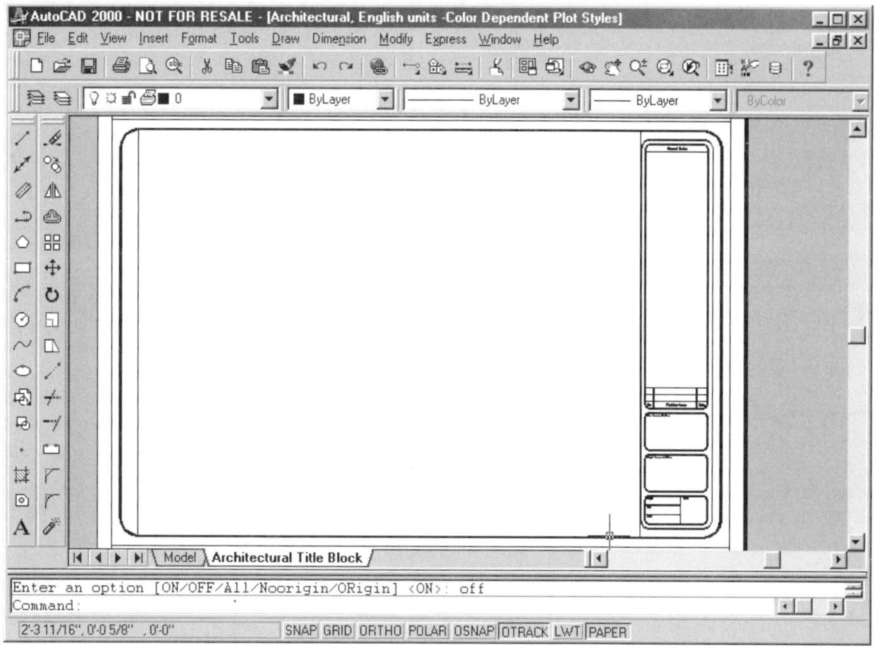

Figure 7–4
Architectural title block.

ACTIVITY STEPS

1. Start the AutoCAD 2000 software program.
2. Select Use a Template in the Startup dialog box.
3. Select Architectural, Color Dependent Plot Style (see Figure 7–4). It is for architectural drawings that are to be printed/plotted on 36″ × 24″ paper.
4. Type la at the command prompt.
5. Two layers, 0 and Title_block, should show up in the Layer Properties Manager dialog box. Change the color to red for the Title_block layer.
6. Select New to create new layers.
7. Refer to Table 7–2 and add the layers with linetypes and colors as listed in the table.
8. Save the file using a different name.

CHAPTER

8

Dimension Variables

AFTER READING THIS CHAPTER, YOU WILL BE ABLE TO:

- Understand the syntax used with setting dimension variables.
- Use dimension commands to correctly place dimensions on a drawing.

KEY CONCEPTS

- Dimension drawing commands (Linear, Aligned, Ordinate, Radius, Diameter, Angular, Baseline, Continue, Leader, Tolerance, and Center Mark)
- Dimension editing commands (Dimedit and Dimtedit)
- Dimension line
- Dimension style commands
- Dimension text
- Dimension utility commands (dimension variables)
- Extension line

ELEMENTS OF A DIMENSION

The horizontal line that is broken by the text is called the **dimension line**.

Extension lines are located at the end of dimension lines.

Before discussing dimensions, let's look at what makes up a dimension. There are three basic parts: an **extension line**, a **dimension line**, and **dimension text**. In Figure 8–1 the horizontal line that is broken by the text is called the **dimension line**. Dimension lines are terminated by extension lines. Dimension lines typically have an arrowhead, tick mark, or some other symbol that designates the termination point of the line. The vertical lines in Figure 8–1 represent extension lines. These are the boundary lines of the dimension. The dimension text appears with the dimension line. The default setting for the dimension text is to appear at the middle point of the dimension line, but it can be repositioned at different points along the line. AutoCAD does dimensioning semiautomatically. It will construct the dimension lines and measure the distances for you.

To begin dimensioning, select the Dimension pull-down menu or select DIMNSION from the screen menu (see Figure 8–2), or enter DIM at the command prompt. Dimension commands also can be started from the Dimension toolbar (see Figure 8–3).

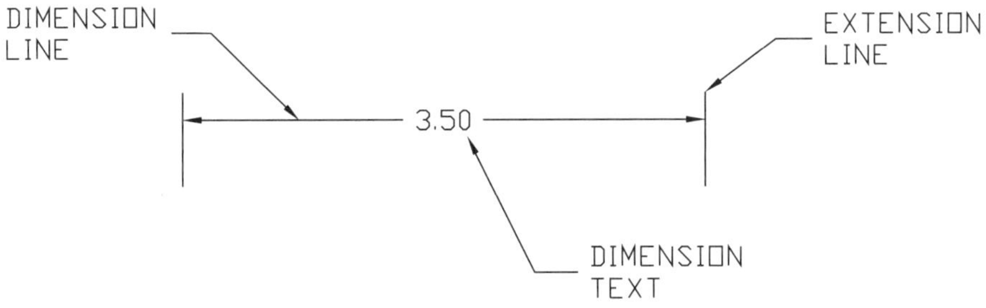

Figure 8–1
Dimension elements.

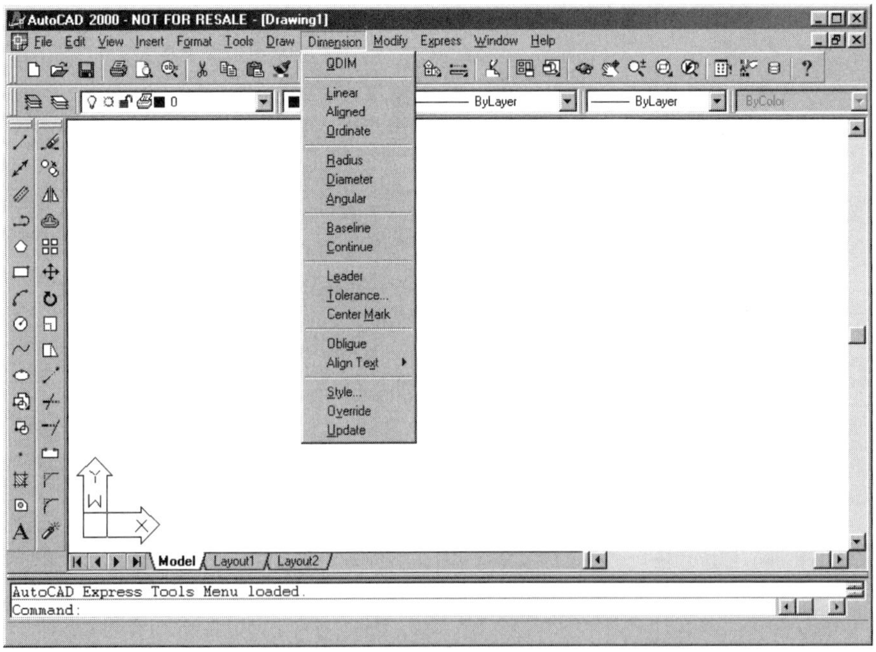

Figure 8–2
Dimension pull-down menu.

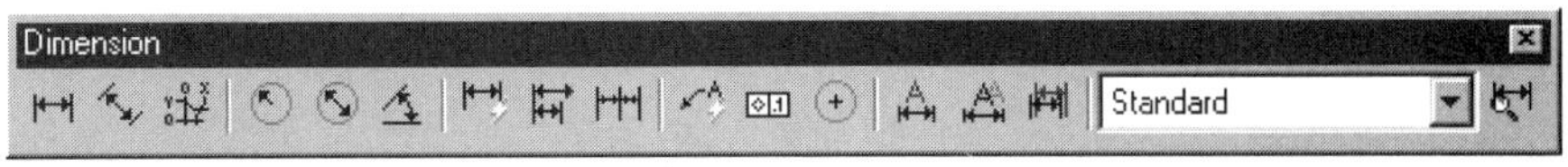

Figure 8–3
Dimension toolbar.

AutoCAD dimensioning commands can be grouped into three basic types of AutoCAD dimension drawing commands that include dimension editing commands, dimension utility commands, and dimension style.

DIMENSION DRAWING COMMANDS

Dimension drawing commands are used to create various types of dimensions. The following table lists the dimension drawing commands.

Dimension Drawing Commands

Linear	Draws horizontal, vertical, or rotated dimensions.
Aligned	Creates a dimension parallel to an object or extension line origins you pick.
Ordinate	Dimensions the X or Y coordinate from a specified point.
Radius	Creates a dimension that depicts the radius of an arc or circle.
Diameter	Dimensions the diameter of a circle.
Angular	Creates a dimension between two nonparallel lines.
Baseline	Continues a dimension in reference to the first extension line.
Continue	Continues a dimension from the second extension line of the selected dimension.
Leader	Attaches text to a line and arrowhead.
Tolerance	Allows you to select a tolerance symbol to display with the dimension.
Center Mark	Creates a center mark and/or centerlines at the center point of an arc or circle.

TRY THIS

Dimension a rectangle.

1. Open the AutoCAD software program.
2. From the Startup dialog box, select **Use a Template**. Select the A-size template you created in Chapter 2.
3. Make sure to switch to model space to create the rectangle and the dimensions.
4. Select the **Rectangle icon** from the Draw toolbar.
5. Enter **3,4** as the start point and **7,6** as the other corner.
6. A rectangle should show in the drawing editor.
7. From the **Dimension** pull-down menu, select **Linear.**

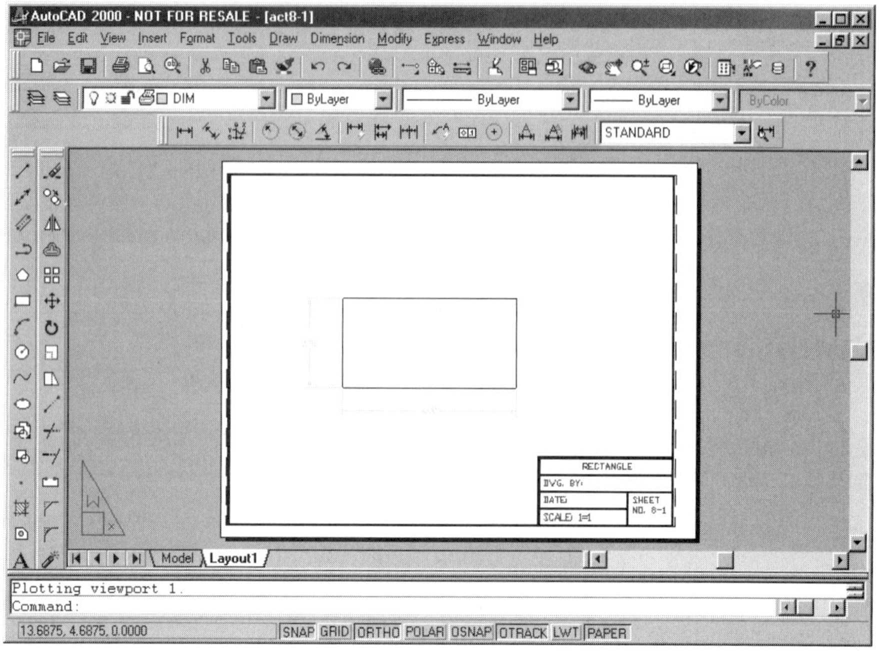

Figure 8–4
Dimensioned rectangle.

8. Create the vertical dimension. Use object snap **Endpoint** to locate the starting and ending points of the dimension.
9. Repeat step 8 and create the horizontal dimension.

The dimensioned rectangle should look similar to Figure 8–4.

Dimensioning Arcs and Circles

Radius dimensions are used with arcs and circles, and diameter dimensions are used with circles. Common methods for dimensioning an arc or a circle are shown in Figure 8–5.

Try This

Dimension two circles using the diameter dimensioning option.

1. Start the AutoCAD software program.
2. Select **Start from Scratch** in the Startup dialog box.
3. From the Draw pull-down menu, select **Circle**.
4. Draw two circles, one 5″ in diameter and the other 1″ in diameter.
5. Dimension the 5″ circle with the **Diameter** option in the Dim menu.

The resulting drawings should be similar to those in Figure 8–6.

If your dimensions do not appear exactly as seen in Figure 8–6, you may need to change some of your dimension variables.

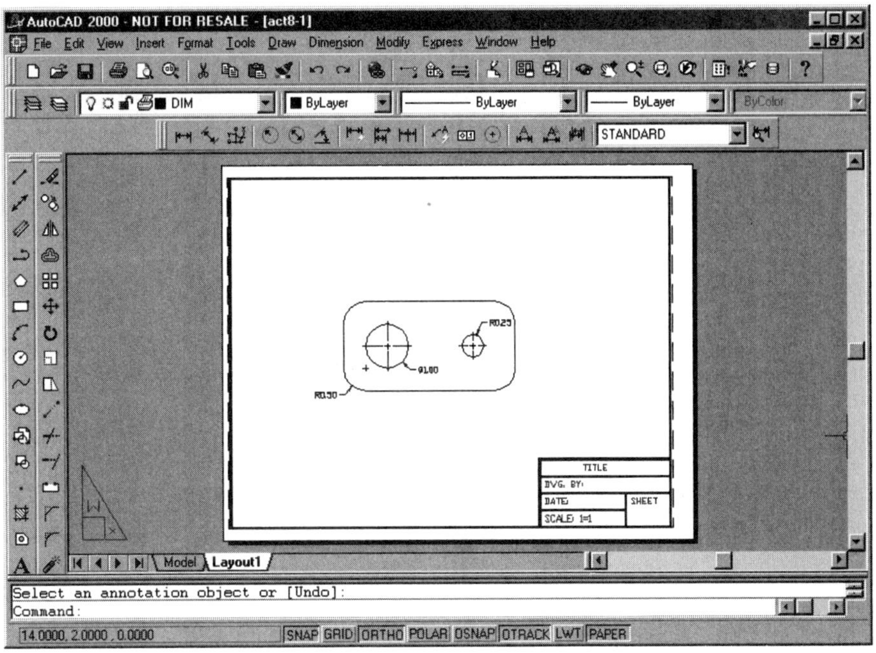

Figure 8–5
Dimensioned arc and circles.

Dimensioning Angles

The Angular dimensioning option is used to dimension angles. There are four ways (see Figure 8–7) to specify angular dimensions:

- Select two nonparallel lines.
- Select an arc.
- Select a circle.
- Specify vertex.

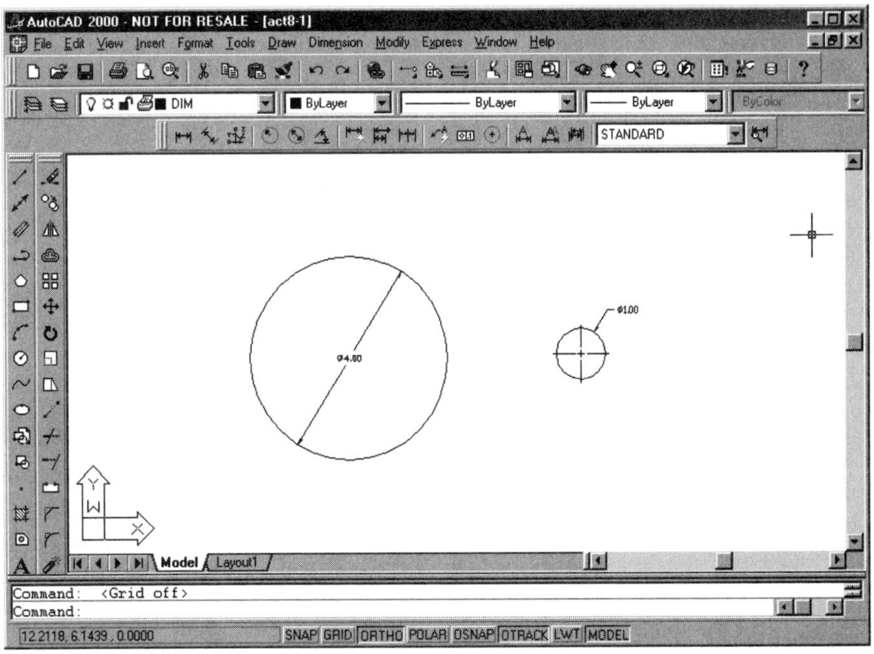

Figure 8–6
Two examples of dimensioned circles.

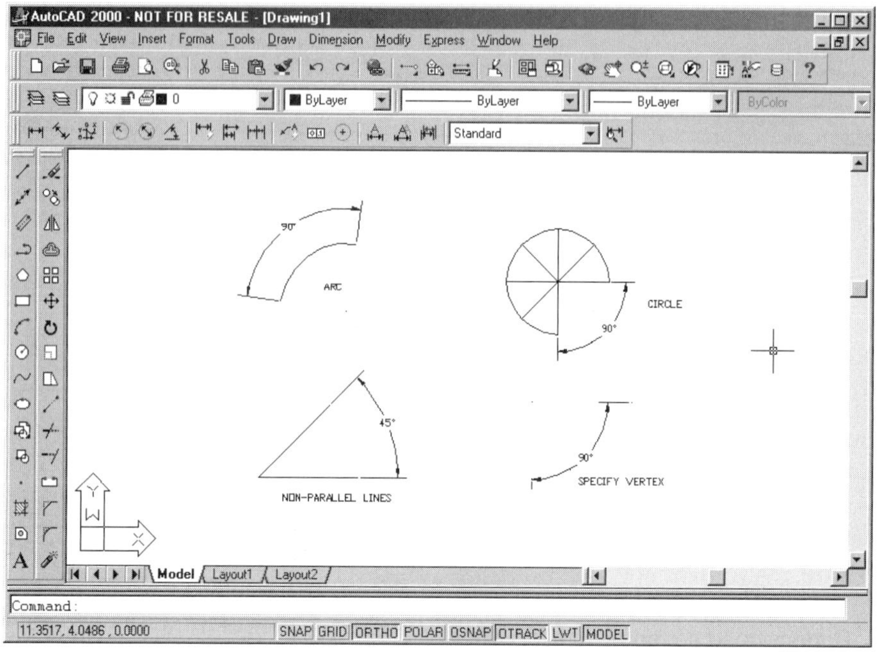

Figure 8–7
Four methods of angular dimensioning.

Try This

Use the angular dimension command to dimension two objects.

1. Open the AutoCAD software program.
2. Select the **Start from Scratch** option from the Startup dialog box.
3. Select the **Line icon** from the Draw toolbar to draw a line.
4. Draw one horizontal line from point 3,3 that is 3 units long.
5. Draw one diagonal line from point 3,3 that is 3 units long and forms a 120° angle with the horizontal line **(3<120)**.
6. Use the **Angular** dimension variable to dimension the angle.
7. Select the **Arc icon** from the Draw toolbar. Draw an arc (SEA) that is 75°.
8. Dimension the arc.

Baseline and Continue Dimension Commands

When you are doing linear dimensions, it is sometimes easier to refer to previous dimensions rather than to choose reference points that have been used by prior dimensions. AutoCAD includes two dimension options that allow you to use previous dimensions, namely, **Baseline** and **Continue**. The Baseline dimension command creates continuous dimensions from the first extension line after you specify an initial dimension (AutoDesk Press 1997, pp. 15–17). Figure 8–8 shows a sample of baseline dimensions. The dimen-

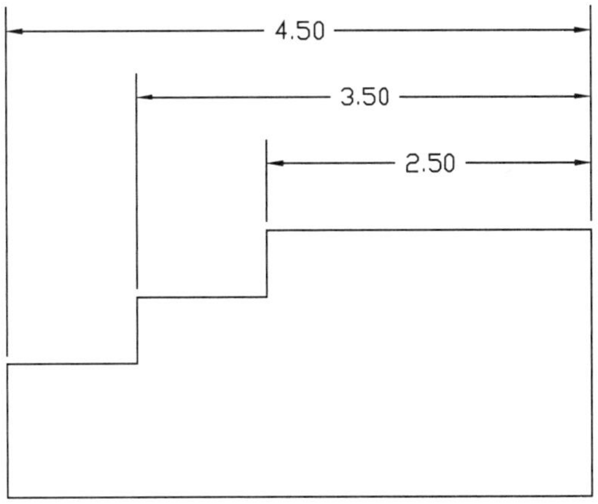

Figure 8-8
Baseline dimensions.

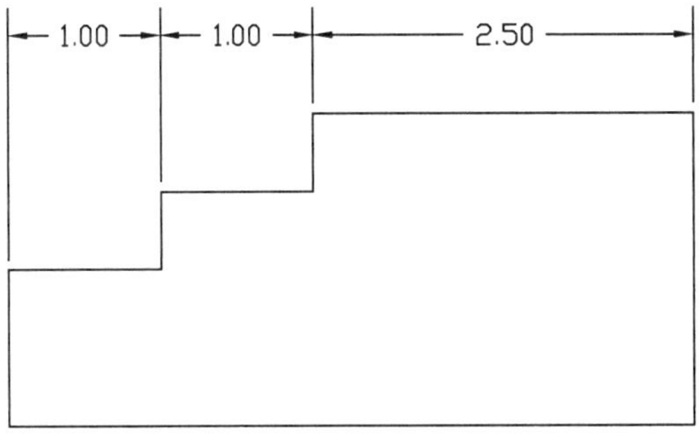

Figure 8-9
Continued dimension.

sion closest to the object (2.50) was the first dimension. All the other dimensions were measured from the *first* extension line of that dimension.

A continued dimension (see Figure 8-9) is different from a baseline dimension in that all measurements are taken from the *second* extension line of the dimension. The continued dimension will usually be collinear with the original dimension.

Center Marks

Center marks can be automatically generated with the **dimcen** command. Dimcen controls the size of the center mark and how it will look. If you enter a negative number for the dimcen value, centerlines along with the center mark will appear. If you enter a positive value, only the center mark will appear. In order to have the center mark appear with a circle or radius, you must set the dimcen variable to the desired value. Use the following sequence to set the size of the center mark:

1. Enter dim at the command prompt.
2. Enter dimcen at the command prompt.
3. Enter a numerical value at the Current value: prompt.
4. At the Dim: command prompt type cen and select the arc or circle in which you want to create the center mark with or without the centerlines.

TRY THIS

Create a center mark in one circle. Create a center mark with centerlines in a second circle .

1. Start the AutoCAD software program.
2. Select **Start from Scratch** at the Startup dialog box.
3. Select the **Circle icon** from the Draw toolbar.
4. Pick any point as the center point.
5. Enter **1.5** as the radius.
6. Copy the first circle and move the second one so that it does not intersect the first circle.
7. At the command prompt, enter **dim**.
8. At the Dim: prompt, enter **dimcen**. Type in a value of **0.0625**. This will generate a 0.125″ center mark.
9. At the Dim: prompt, enter **cen**. Pick one of the circles. A 0.125″ center mark should appear.
10. At the Dim: prompt, enter **dimcen**. Type in a value of −**0.0625**. This will generate a 0.125″ center mark complete with centerlines.
11. At the Dim: prompt, enter **cen.** Pick the other circle. A center mark with centerlines should appear.

DIMENSION EDITING COMMANDS

There are two dimension edit commands in AutoCAD: **Dimedit** and **Dimtedit**. The Dimedit command sets the dimension text to its default position, changes existing text, and forces extension lines to a specified angle. Dimedit options include the following:

H	Home text position.
N	New text position.
R	Rotate text.
O	Set text at an oblique angle.

Dimtedit is used to change text placement as well as text orientation. Dimtedit options include the following:

L	Move text to the left.
R	Move text to the right.
H	Home text position.
A	Angle text.

DIMENSION UTILITY COMMANDS

There are numerous dimension variables that you can set to help you dimension. Sometimes when doing a drawing it is necessary to conform to dimension standards. Knowing dimension variables and how to set them is critical to having a drawing look and be correct. Several of the dimension variables have settings of either ON or OFF, whereas for others you must enter a numerical value. The following are some of the dimension variables that you must check before beginning to draw:

DIMASO	Associative dimension variable. If DIMASO is on, and the dimension changes, each part of the dimension will automatically be updated.
DIMASZ	Indicates the size of the arrowheads.
DIMDEC	Indicates the number of decimal places.
DIMEXE	Determines the distance the extension line will extend past the dimension line.
DIMEXO	Determines the extension line origin offset between where the dimension was selected to start and where the extension line actually begins.
DIMGAP	Sets the distance between the text and the end of the dimension line closest to the text.
DIMSCALE	Sets a universal scale factor for all dimension variables. If you were drawing at a $\frac{1}{4}'' = 1'$ scale, the dimscale factor would be 48. This value would automatically scale every dimension variable by a factor of 48.
DIMTXT	Determines the size of the text used in dimensioning.
DIMTSZ	If this variable has a value greater than zero, it displays a tick mark (/) instead of an arrowhead. For instance, if you enter a value of .0625, a tick mark that measures 0.125 will appear at the end of the dimension line.
DIMTXTSTY	Lets you set the text style that you want to use for dimensioning.
DIMUNIT	This value corresponds to the five options (Decimal, Engineering, Architectural, Fractional, or Scientific) in the Advanced or Quick Setup options. The dimension displayed corresponds to the number selected. For example, for architectural dimensions, this value is 3.

To view the dimension variable settings, type **Status** at the Dim: command prompt. A text box will appear with a listing of all the dim variables. If it is necessary to change a dimension variable, enter the variable name at the command prompt. Any options associated with that variable will then be displayed.

TRY THIS

Change the following dimension variables.

1. Start the AutoCAD software program.
2. Select **Start from Scratch** at the Startup dialog box.
3. From the Draw pull-down menu, select **Rectangle**.
4. Create a rectangle that measures 3 × 4.
5. At the command prompt, enter **dim.**
6. At the Dim: prompt, enter **Status**.
7. Follow the prompts on the text display screen. There should be three pages of dimension variables. At the end of the third page, the Dim: prompt should be displayed.
8. At the Dim: prompt in the text display screen, enter the following variables (you can change only one variable at a time). After entering the variable press the <Enter> key in order to type in a value.

   Dimasz = **0.125** Dimexe = **0.125**
   Dimexo = **0.125** Dimgap = **0.0625**
   Dimtxt = **0.125** Dimdec = **2**

9. Check to be sure Dimaso is on.
10. Close the dimension text window.
11. Dimension the rectangle.

DIMENSION STYLE COMMANDS

If you wish to create a customized dimension style, you can do so through the Dimension Style Manager dialog box. At the command prompt, enter ddim, or go to the Dimension pull-down menu and select Style. The Dimension Style Manager dialog box should appear (see Figure 8–10). This dialog box controls almost all the dimension variables that you can set. After you customize the settings, you can save them by giving them a name. Whenever you want to use these settings simply select the style name under which you saved the settings.

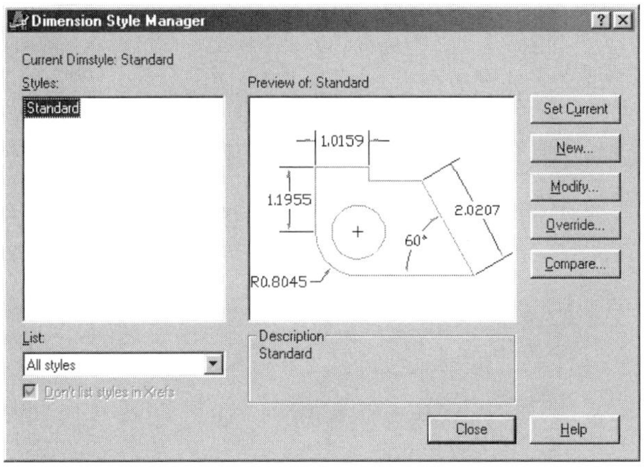

Figure 8–10
Dimension Style Manager dialog box.

Activity 8–1

Draw Bolt Hole Circles

Plotter paper size:	A	
Suggested settings:	Grid	0.50″
	Snap	0.125″
	Layers (7)	**0** (default border)
		Cen, Linetype center, Color: cyan
		Dim, Linetype continuous, Color: green
		Hid, Linetype hidden, Color: magenta
		Obj, Linetype continuous, Color: black
		Tbk, Linetype continuous, Color: red
		Txt, Linetype continuous, Color: green

Hints:

1. Open your border template file for an A-size drawing. After it has loaded, use the Save As command to rename the drawing file ACT8-1. Use Figure 8–11 as the model for the drawing.
2. Make sure you are in model space before you begin drawing the objects.
3. Be sure to check layer settings before you begin to draw or enter text.
4. Use the object snap commands to create the entities.

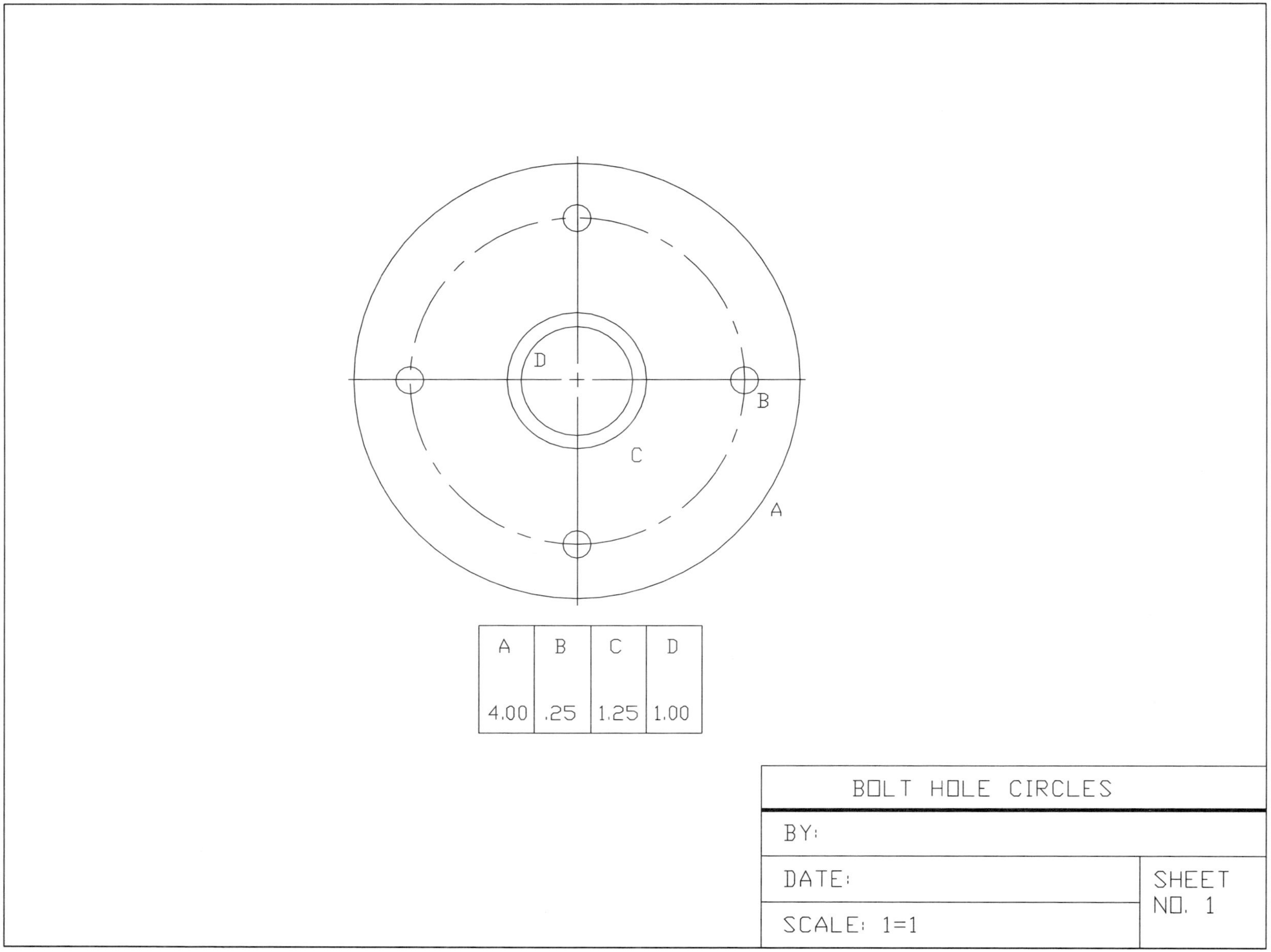

A	B	C	D
4.00	.25	1.25	1.00

Figure 8–11
Activity 8–1

ACTIVITY 8–2

Draw a Flange Bushing

Plotter paper size:	B	
Suggested settings:	Grid	0.50″
	Snap	0.125″
	Layers (7)	**0** (default border)
		Cen, Linetype center, Color: cyan
		Dim, Linetype continuous, Color: green
		Hid, Linetype hidden, Color: magenta
		Obj, Linetype continuous, Color: black
		Tbk, Linetype continuous, Color: red
		Txt, Linetype continuous, Color: green

Hints:

1. Open your border template file for a B-size drawing. After it has loaded, use the SAVEAS command to rename the drawing file ACT8-2. Use Figure 8–12 as the model for the drawing.
2. Make sure you are in model space before you begin drawing the objects.
3. Be sure to check layer settings before you begin to draw or enter text.
4. Use the object snap commands to create the entities.

ACTIVITY 8–3

Draw a Short Shaft

Plotter paper size:	B	
Suggested settings:	Grid	0.50″
	Snap	0.125″
	Layers (7)	**0** (default border)
		Cen, Linetype center, Color: cyan
		Dim, Linetype continuous, Color: green
		Hid, Linetype hidden, Color: magenta
		Obj, Linetype continuous, Color: black
		Tbk, Linetype continuous, Color: red
		Txt, Linetype continuous, Color: green

Hints:

1. Open your border template file for a B-size drawing. After it has loaded, use the SAVEAS command to rename the drawing file ACT8-3. Use Figure 8–13 on p. 144 as the model for the drawing.
2. Make sure you are in model space before you begin drawing the objects.

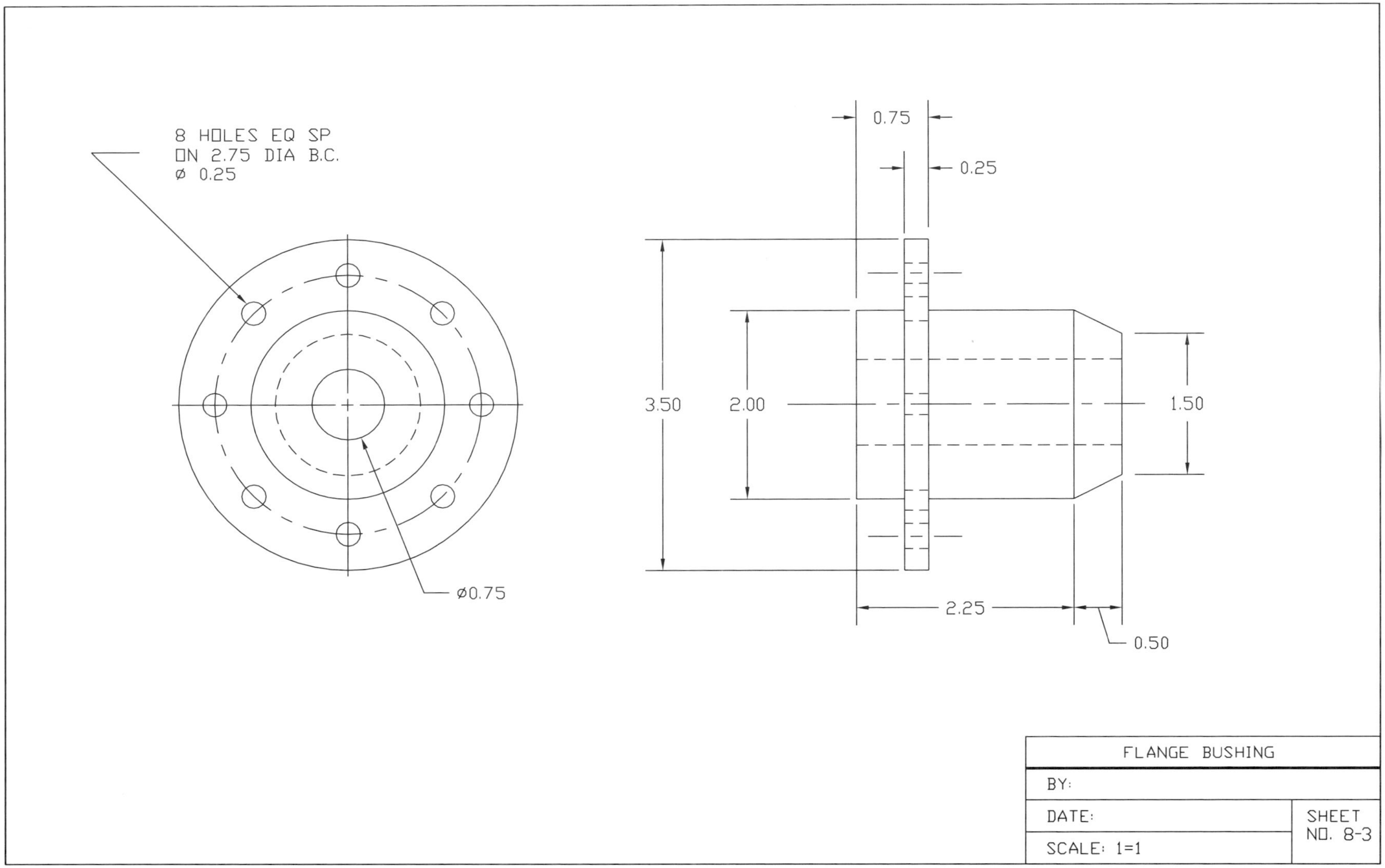

Figure 8–12
Activity 8–2

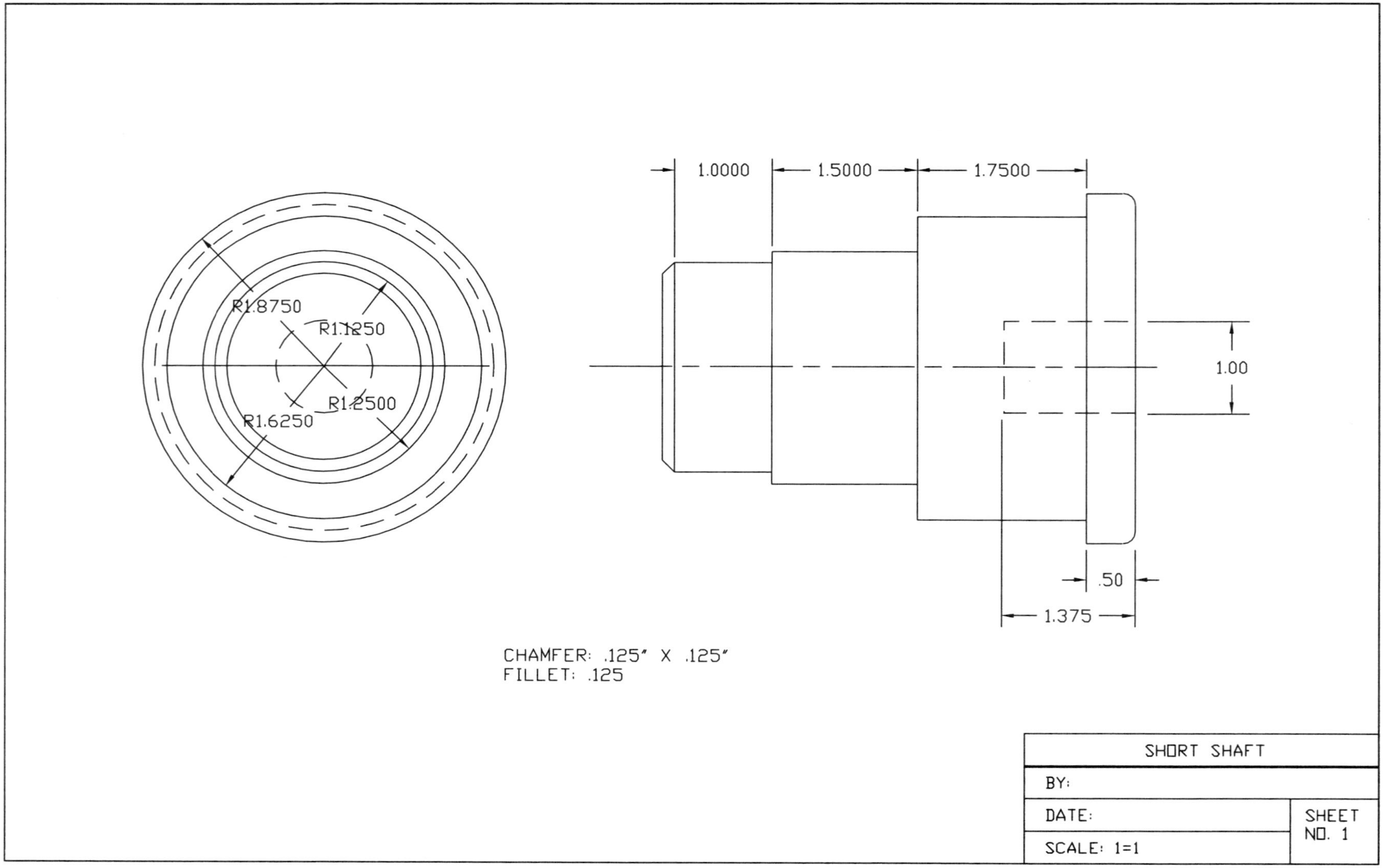

Figure 8–13
Activity 8–3

3. Be sure to check layer settings before you begin to draw or enter text.
4. Use the object snap commands to create the entities and place the dimensions.

ACTIVITY 8–4

Draw a Grate

Plotter paper size:	B	
Suggested settings:	Grid	0.50″
	Snap	0.125″
	Layers (7)	**0** (default border)
		Cen, Linetype center, Color: cyan
		Dim, Linetype continuous, Color: green
		Hid, Linetype hidden, Color: magenta
		Obj, Linetype continuous, Color: black
		Tbk, Linetype continuous, Color: red
		Txt, Linetype continuous, Color: green

Hints:

1. Open your border template file for a B-size drawing. After it has loaded, use the SAVEAS command to rename the drawing file ACT8-4. Use Figure 8–14 on p. 146 as the model for the drawing.
2. Make sure you are in model space before you begin drawing the objects.
3. Be sure to check layer settings before you begin to draw or enter text.
4. Use the object snap commands to create the entities and locate the dimensions.

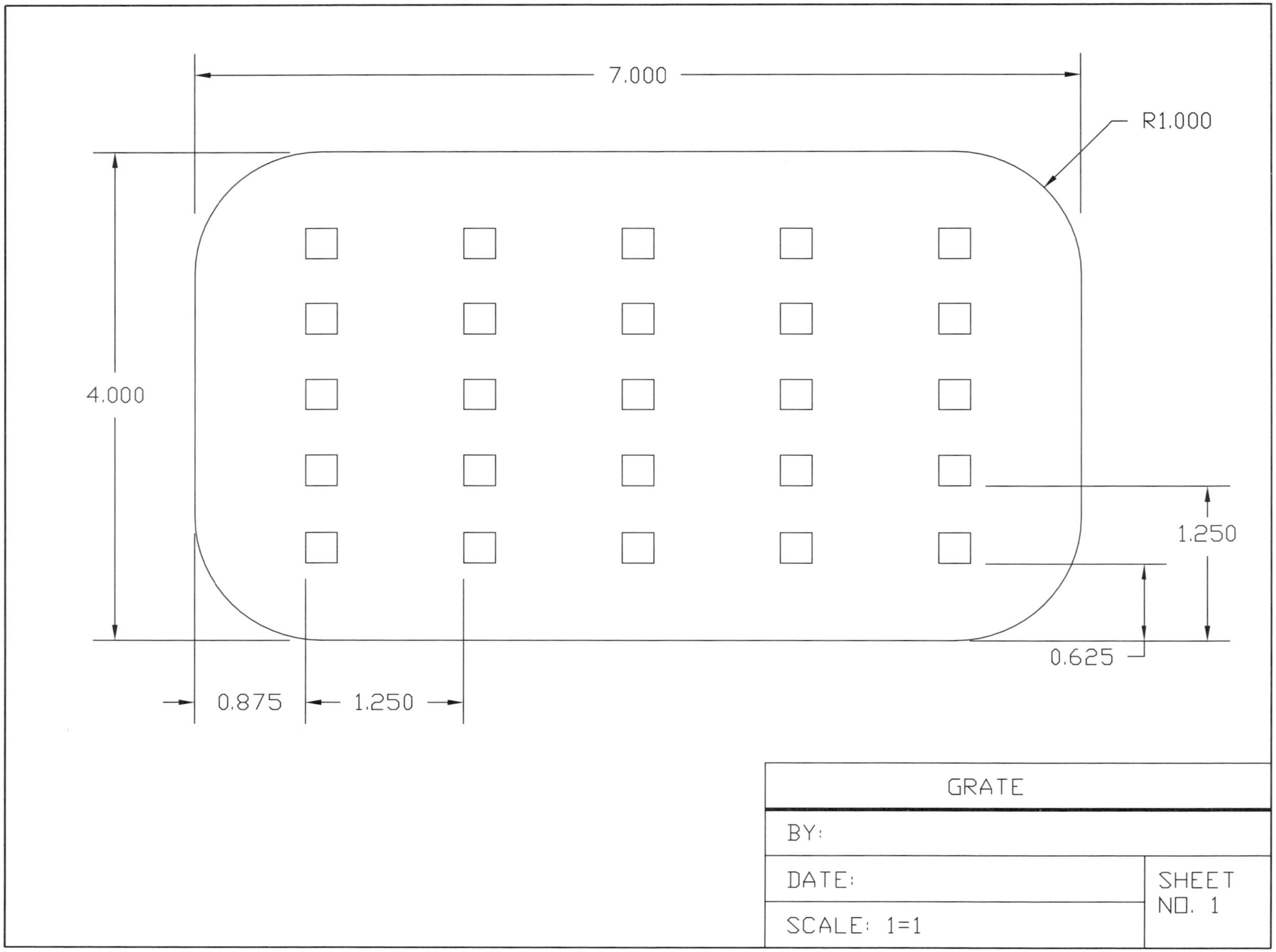

Figure 8–14
Activity 8–4

CHAPTER

9

Printer/Plotter Configuration

AFTER READING THIS CHAPTER, YOU WILL BE ABLE TO:

- Configure a printer or plotter in order to print or plot a drawing.

Before you attempt to plot, you must be sure that the printer or plotter has been configured. Each printer/plotter configuration contains information such as the device name, device model number, output port, and other specific printer/plotter driver settings. A plotter configuration file (PCP file) can also contain information on paper size, orientation, plot scale factors, pen parameters, plot origin, and plot rotation.

To execute the print/plot command, you can use one of four methods: you can click on the printer icon in the Standard toolbar, select Plot from the File pull-down menu (see Figure 9–1), type print or plot at the command prompt, or select Plot, which is in the FILE directory in the screen menu.

Once the plot command is executed, you are presented with a Plot dialog box in which you need to set certain options. You need to remember that the settings in the Plot dialog box can change because each individual who uses the plotter may have different print/plot requirements from yours. Each time you use the plotter/printer, you must check the settings in the Plot dialog box. There are two tabs in the Plot dialog box that list the current settings. These tabs are labeled Plot Device and Plot Settings (see Figure 9–2).

PLOT DEVICE TAB

Plot Device options include Layout name, selection of the output device, pen assignments of output device, plot style table, tab selection for plotting (Model, Layout1, or Layout2), number of copies, page setup name, and an option to save the plot to a file. The Layout name refers to the tab selection (Model, Layout1, or Layout2) of the current drawing. Plotter configuration identifies the currently selected output device. In order to review the properties of the currently selected output device, click on the Properties button. A separate dialog box will appear (see Figure 9–3) in which you can customize settings of the current plotter/printer.

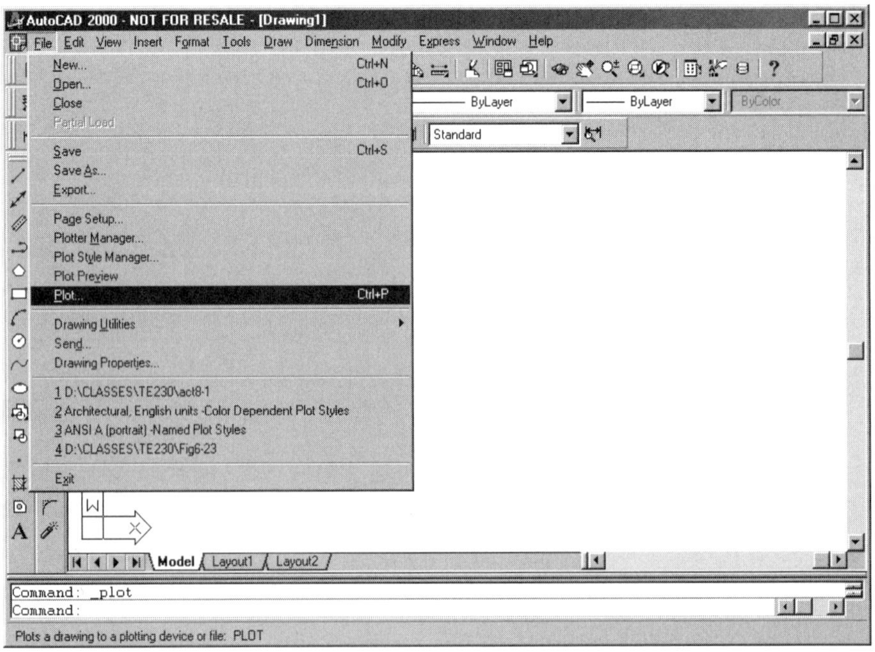

Figure 9–1
File pull-down menu plot command.

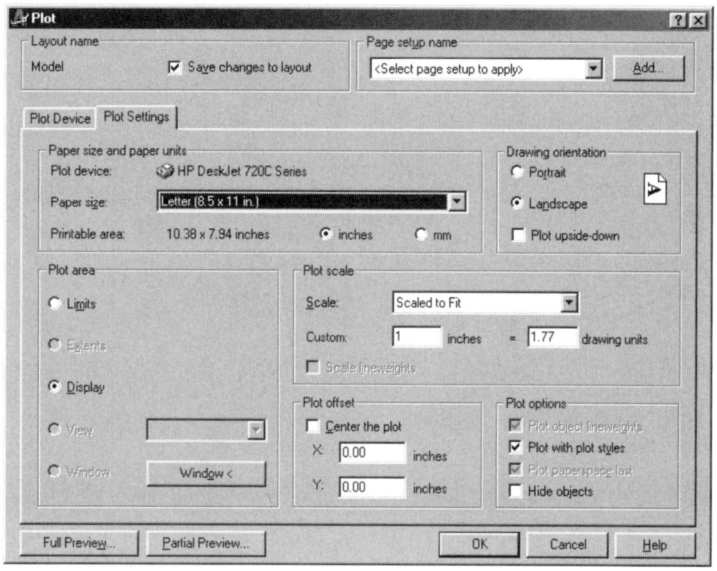

Figure 9–2
Plot dialog box.

If you need to edit lineweight or other variables associated with the drawing objects, click on edit in the Plot style table option. A dialog box (see Figure 9–4) will appear that allows you to further customize your settings.

If you want to save your plot configuration, click on the add button in the Page setup name option. A dialog box will appear that gives you the option to save the page setup variables.

The Plot to a file option lets you output the drawing to a file rather than to a plotter or printer. A plotter file will save the drawing name with a .plt file extension.

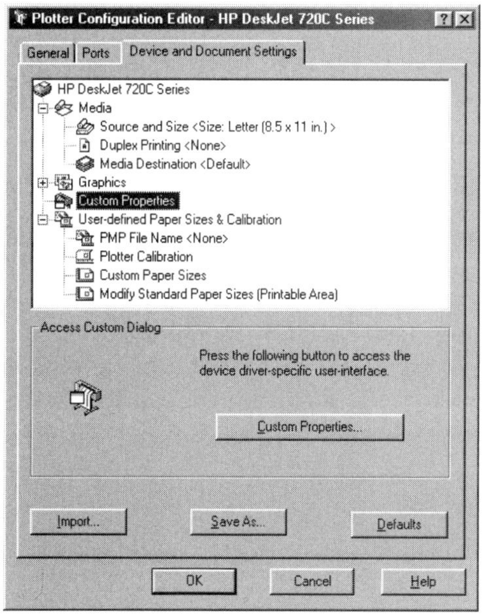

Figure 9–3
Properties configuration dialog box.

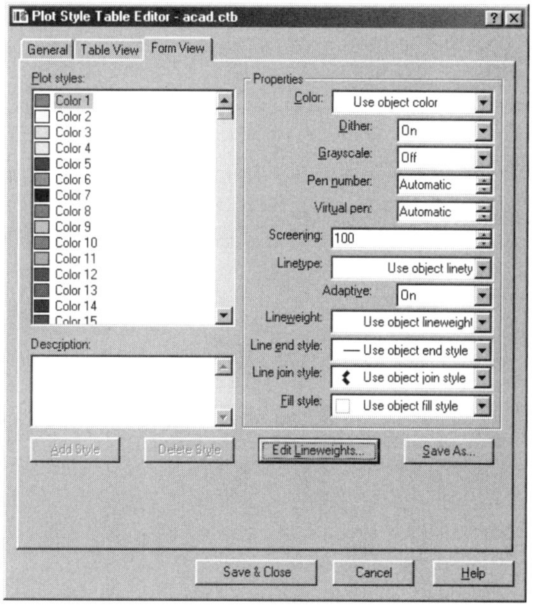

Figure 9–4
Plot Style Table dialog box.

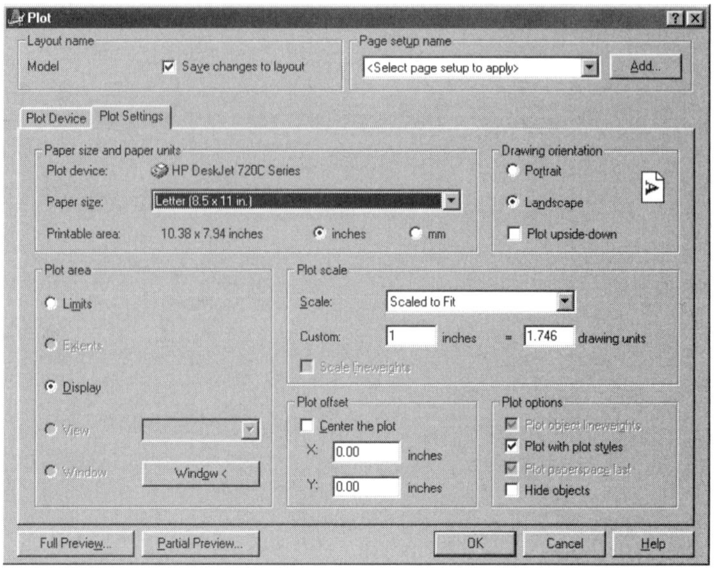

Figure 9–5
Plot Settings options.

PLOT SETTING TAB

The Plot Settings options include paper size and units, drawing orientation, plot area, plot scale, plot options, and plot offset (see Figure 9–5). Paper size is limited by the physical limits of the printer/plotter. In Figure 9–5, the default setting for the paper size was 8.5 × 11 inches; however, the actual printable area was 10.38 × 7.94 inches. There are three options for drawing orientation: Portrait, Landscape, or Plot upside-down. Typically you will choose either landscape or portrait.

In the Plot area section of the dialog box, there are two options: you can plot either the limits of the drawing or the screen display. The Display option was selected in Figure 9–5. To the right of the Plot area section is the Plot scale section of the dialog box. Scaled to Fit was selected in Figure 9–5, which means that AutoCAD will automatically scale the drawing area to the printable area. In this case 1″ is equal to 1.746 drawing units.

The Plot offset option determines how the plot will be placed on the sheet of paper. You can enter offset values, or you can select the Center the plot option. In order to view how the drawing will fit on the sheet of paper, click on either the Full Preview or the Partial Preview button located near the lower left corner of the dialog box (see Figure 9–5). The full preview mode shows the drawing in detail and how it fits on the sheet of paper (see Figure 9–6), whereas the partial preview mode shows only an outline of the boundaries of the drawing (see Figure 9–7).

TRY THIS

Check the **Default Printer** in the Plot dialog box.

1. Open the AutoCAD software program.
2. Select **Start from Scratch**.

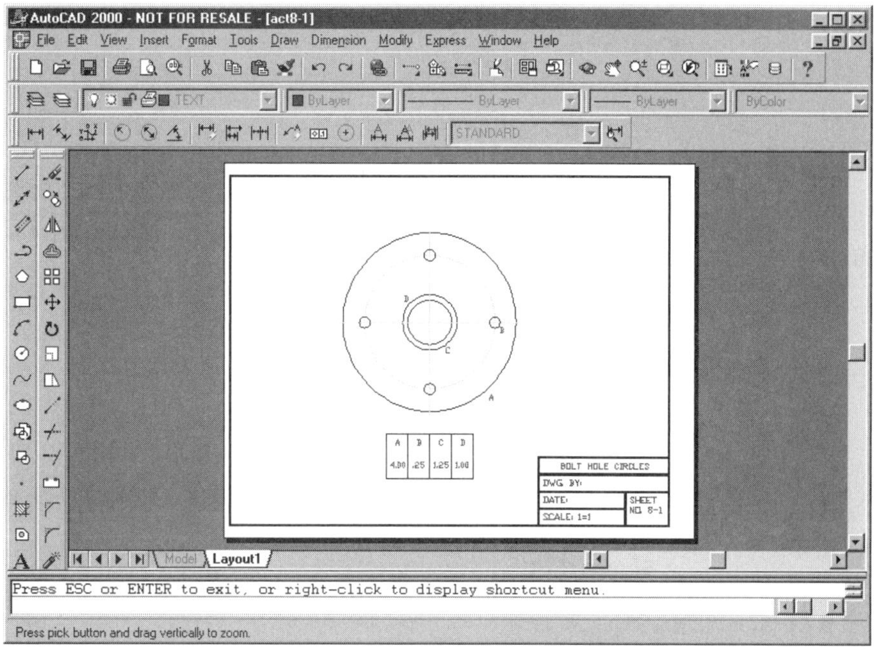

Figure 9–6
Full preview mode.

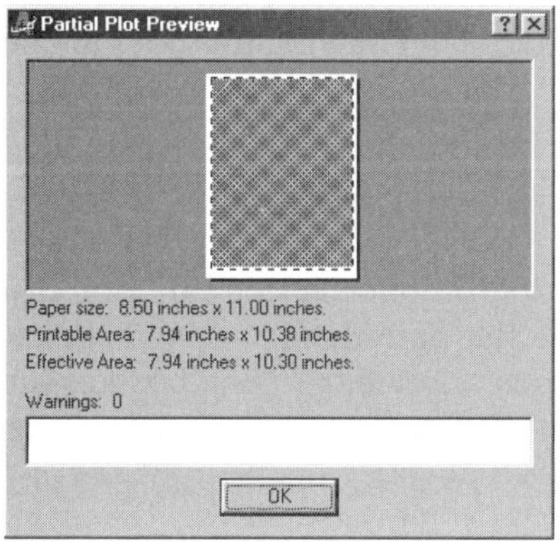

Figure 9–7
Partial preview mode.

3. From the File pull-down menu, select **Plot**.
4. Select the **Plot Device** tab.
5. Identify the printer/plotter options available.

Plot styles can be used to change the way objects in your drawing look when you plot. You can plot the same drawing in different ways, emphasizing different elements of construction in each plot. A plot style consists of overrides for color, dithering, gray scale, pen assignments, screening, linetype, lineweight, end styles, join styles, and fill styles. A plot style can be assigned to any object or layer.

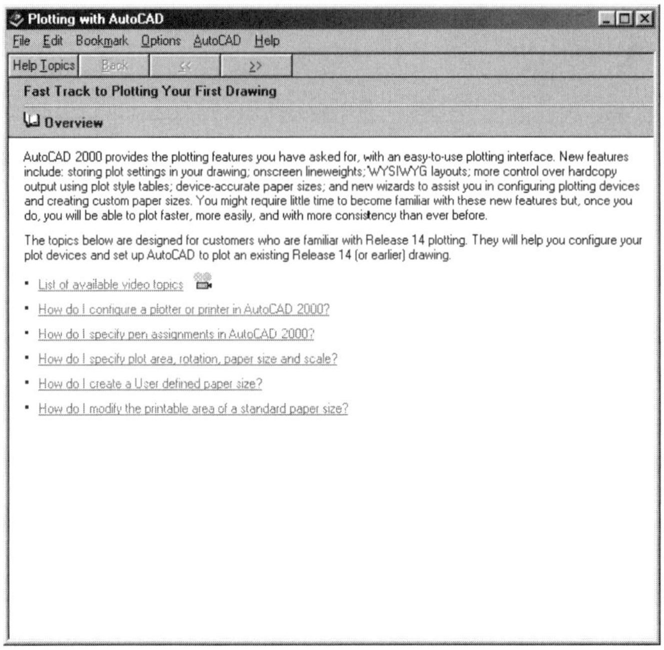

Figure 9–8
Fast Track to Plotting Your First Drawing dialog box.

In the AutoCAD 2000 Help pull-down menu, the option Fast Track to Plotting Your First Drawing provides an in-depth look at the variables associated with plotting (see Figure 9–8).

OTHER PLOT OPTIONS

The Page Setup option in the File pull-down menu was designed to help you define the parameters associated with plotting the drawing. When Page Setup is selected, a dialog box appears that has two tabs, Plot Device and Layout Settings (see Figure 9–9). Page setup allows you to define the plot options that you want to apply to a drawing.

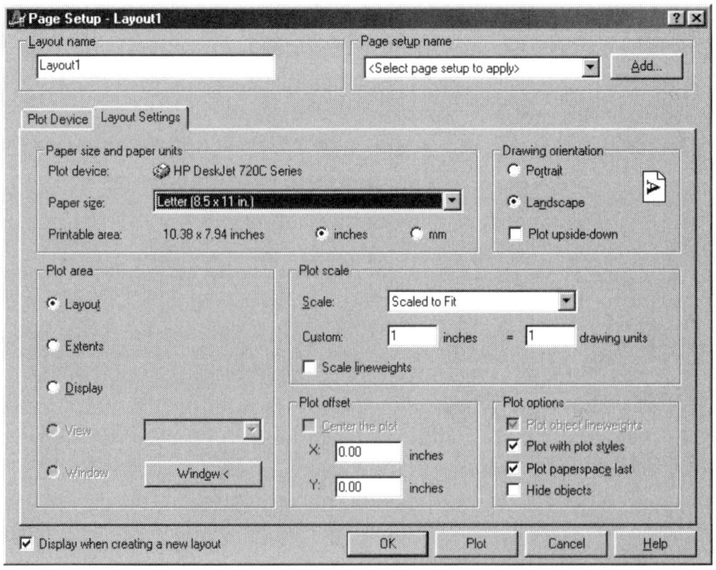

Figure 9–9
Page Setup dialog box.

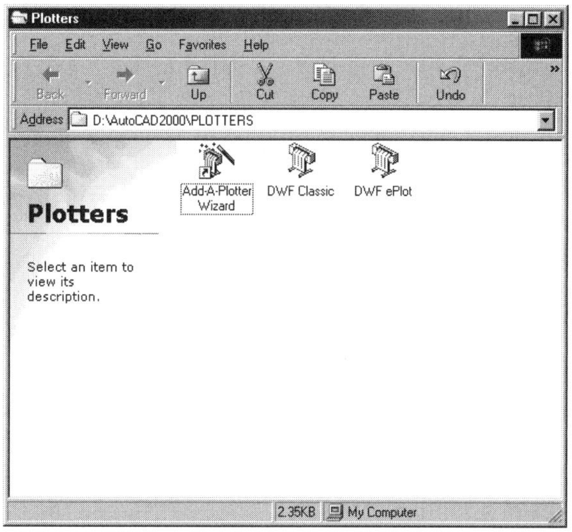

Figure 9–10
Plotter Manager window.

The Plotter Manager was designed to let you add various plotters that are available for use. The Plotter Manager includes the Add a Plotter Wizard (see Figure 9–10), which allows you to define a plotter output device. Multiple printers/plotters can be defined for use in the Plotter Manager. The Plotter Manager command can be found in the File pull-down menu.

Chapter 9 ■ Activities

Activity 9–1

ACTIVITY STEPS

1. Enter AutoCAD 2000 and click on the Help pull-down menu.
2. Select Learning Assistance.
3. Select Tutorials.
4. Select Fast Track to AutoCAD2000.
5. Select Fast Track to Plotting.
6. Review the various topics associated with Fast Track to Plotting.

Activity 9–2

From the Chapter 2 activities, open the Entities drawing. Select Plot from the File pull-down menu. Set the necessary plot parameters based on the available output device attached to your computer or network.

ACTIVITY STEPS

1. Check Device to determine if the appropriate printer/plotter has been selected.
2. Check Page setup options for Layout1.
3. Plot drawing Limits.
4. Make sure Inches is selected and check for correct paper size.
5. Set Orientation to 0 and set the X and Y origin offsets to 0.
6. Plot the drawing full scale, 1=1.
7. Do a Full Preview of the drawing to check its location on paper.
8. Make any adjustments necessary.

The drawing should fit on an A-size sheet of paper.

Activity 9–3

Repeat Activity 9–2 for the shim drawing that was created at the end of Chapter 2.

CHAPTER

10

System Dimension Variables

AFTER READING THIS CHAPTER, YOU WILL BE ABLE TO:

- Understand better the system dimension variables and how drawing entities are affected by drawing scales.

KEY CONCEPTS

Dimension system variables
Limits
Ltscale

ESTABLISHING DRAWING LIMITS

The **drawing limits** are two-dimensional (X,Y) points in the world coordinate system that represent a lower-left corner of the drawing area and an upper-right corner of the drawing area. Drawing limits also determine the area of the drawing that can display grid dots.

Before you begin any drawing, it is important to establish certain drawing parameters. Determining the **drawing limits** is one of the most important parameters to establish before starting any drawing activity. The relationship between the drawing limits set in model space and the paper size established in layout is critical for printing or plotting a drawing to scale. Because drawing entities are typically drawn full scale in AutoCAD it is necessary to correctly scale a drawing created in model space to the paper size set in layout. When drawings are scaled, certain drawing entities are affected. Architectural drawing activities will be used to illustrate the various topics discussed in this chapter. If you were going to plot or print a drawing on B-size paper (17″ × 11″) you would first have to account for the mechanical limits of the printer/plotter to establish the actual plot area of the sheet of paper.

For example, let's say that you have determined that you will create a drawing using $\frac{1}{4}''$ = 1′ as the scale. If you are going to output this drawing on B-size paper, the drawing limits will be 62′ × 40′ (15.5 × 10). These limits were determined by multiplying the size of the sheet of paper (15.5 × 10) by 4, taking into account the printer/plotter requirements.

If you had selected $\frac{1}{8}''$ = 1′ as the drawing scale, then the model space drawing limits would have been 124′ × 80′ for B-size paper. In order to select the correct drawing scale, it is necessary to have some understanding of the size of the drawing area needed to create the drawing entities.

TRY THIS

Calculate the appropriate limits for the following drawing scales.

1. $\frac{1}{16}''$ = 1′ for a drawing to be plotted on B-size paper (15.5 × 10).
2. $\frac{1}{8}''$= 1″ for a drawing to be plotted on A-size paper (10 × 7.7).
3. $\frac{1}{8}''$ = 1′ for a drawing to be plotted on B-size paper (15.5 × 10).

SETTING DIMENSION SYSTEM VARIABLES

Drawing scales also affect the settings of the dimension system variables, which control the appearance of dimensions. You can set dimension system variables on the command line or through the Dimension Style Manager (DDIM) dialog box (see Figure 10–1). You can also enter DDIM at the com-

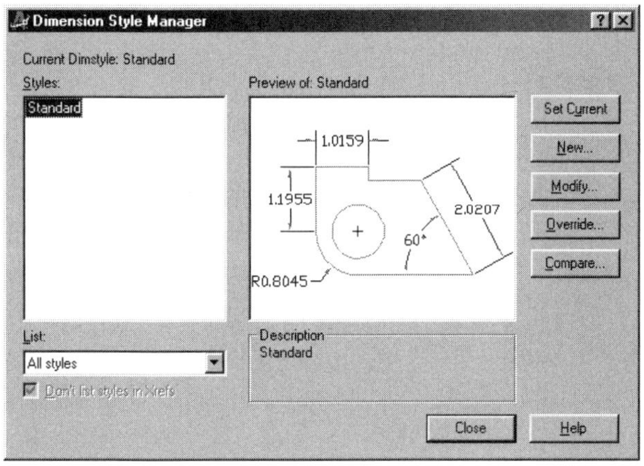

Figure 10–1
Dimension Style Manager dialog box.

mand prompt line, or select Style from the Dimension pull-down menu. The DDIM dialog box will appear on screen.

Dimension system variables must be set to account for any scale factor used to create a drawing, and certain standards for dimension variables need to be followed when creating a drawing. For instance, a typical text height on a drawing is $\frac{1}{8}''$ (0.125) tall. Table 10–1 lists the relationships between text size and drawing scale. You would set the same scale factor values to generate dimension arrowheads or tick marks that would print or plot at $\frac{1}{8}''$ (0.125).

In order to set the size of the most commonly used variables, select the Modify button in the Dimension Style Manager dialog box. A dialog box (see

Table 10–1

Correlating Scale Factors with Text Size

SCALE	SCALE FACTOR	TO PLOT TEXT SIZE AT...	SET DRAWING TEXT SIZE TO...
$\frac{1}{8}''$ = 1′-0″	96	$\frac{1}{8}''$	12″
$\frac{3}{16}''$ = 1′-0″	64	$\frac{1}{8}''$	8″
$\frac{1}{4}''$ = 1′-0″	48	$\frac{1}{8}''$	6″
$\frac{3}{8}''$ = 1′-0″	32	$\frac{1}{8}''$	4″
$\frac{1}{2}''$ = 1′-0″	24	$\frac{1}{8}''$	3″
$\frac{3}{4}''$ = 1′-0″	16	$\frac{1}{8}''$	2″
1″ = 1′-0″	12	$\frac{1}{8}''$	1.5″
$1\frac{1}{2}''$ = 1′-0″	8	$\frac{1}{8}''$	1.0″

Figure 10–2) appears with tabs that allow you to set the following dimension system variables: Lines and Arrows, Text, Fit, Primary Units, Alternate Units, and Tolerances.

There are four lines and arrows categories in which variables can be set, namely, Dimension Lines, Extension Lines, Arrowheads, and Center Marks for Circles. In Figure 10–2, the color and lineweight for dimension lines and extension lines will be determined by the layer properties where they are found. If the Suppress option is selected for either dimension lines or extension lines, those elements will not be displayed on the drawing. For instance, in Figure 10–3, the first extension line was suppressed because the object line served as the termination point of the dimension line.

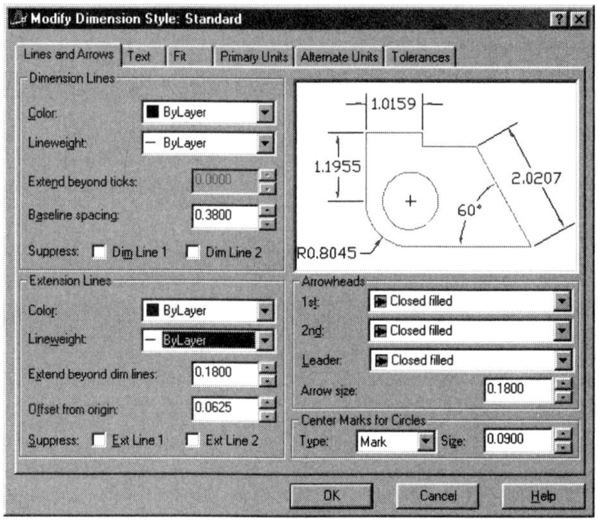

Figure 10–2
Modify Dimension Style dialog box options.

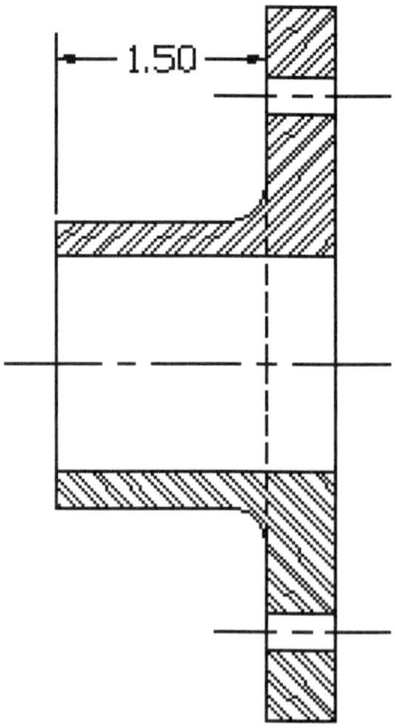

Figure 10–3
Extension line suppression.

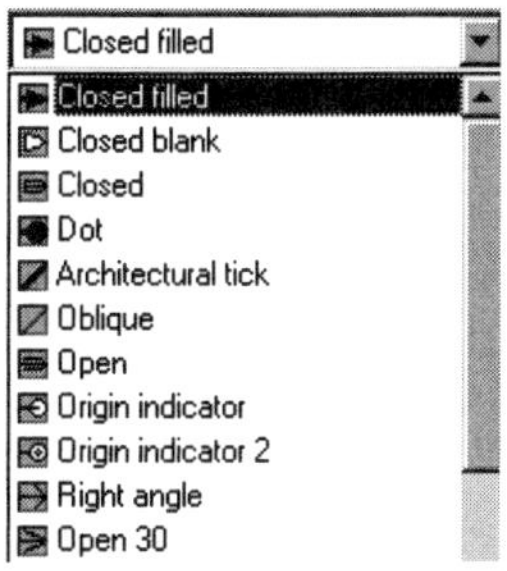

Figure 10–4
Arrowhead styles.

Arrowheads

The options for arrowheads include determining the style of arrowhead as well as the size of the arrowhead. Figure 10–4 displays a listing of a few arrowhead styles.

Center Marks

The center mark displays the center of an arc or circle. This option lets you set a value that affects the display of a center mark. In Figure 10–5 a negative value of −0.0625 was entered. The resulting center mark included a $\frac{1}{8}''$ center mark as well as center lines that extended past the edge of the object. In Figure 10–6 a positive center mark value of 0.0625 was entered. When a positive value is entered, only the center mark appears without the center lines.

TRY THIS

Set the following dimension system variables in the Dimension Style Manager dialog box.

1. From the Dimension pull-down menu select **Style.**
2. In the Dimension Style Manager box select **Modify,** then select the **Lines and Arrows** tab.
3. Set the Arrow size: to **.125.**
4. Set the Extend beyond dim lines: **.125.**
5. Select **Line** in the Center Marks for Circles option and change the size to **.0625.**
6. Choose **OK** to exit the Lines and Arrow dialog box.
7. Choose **Close** to exit the Dimension Style Manager dialog box.

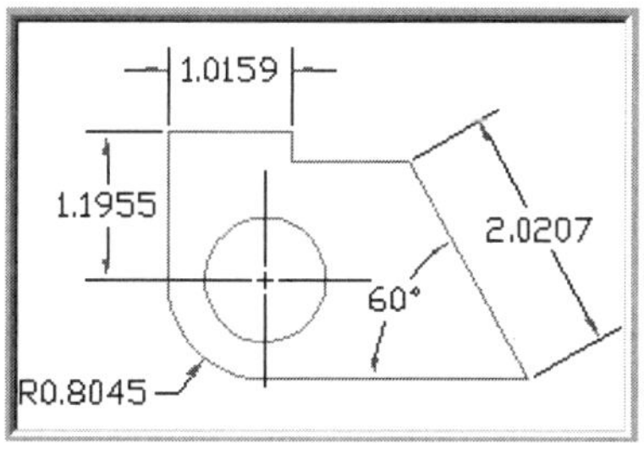

Figure 10–5
Negative center mark value.

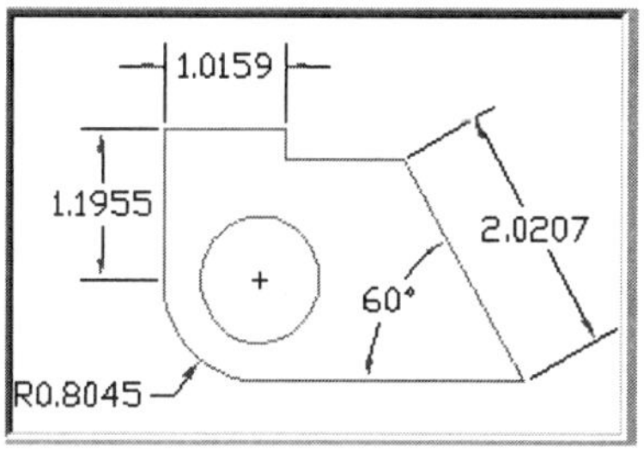

Figure 10–6
Positive center mark value.

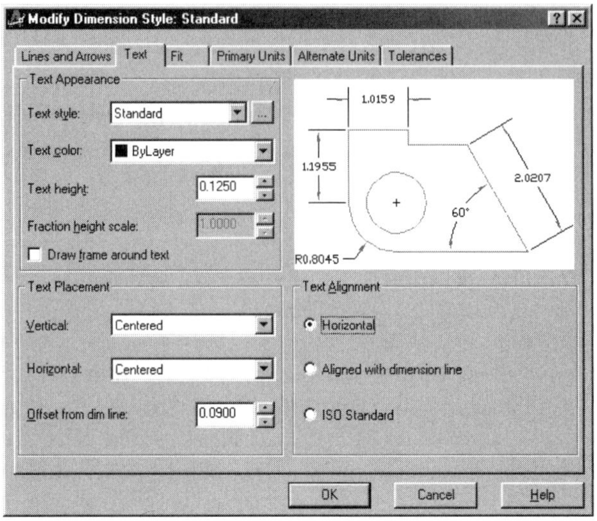

Figure 10–7
Dimension text variable.

Text

The dimension text variables that can be set include text style, text color, text height, text alignment, and text placement (see Figure 10–7). Text style and color are typically set according to the layer where they are located. With the Text Placement option you can set where the text will be displayed in relation to either the dimension line or the extension line. There are three alignment styles that can be selected for format, namely, horizontal, aligned with dimension line, or ISO Standard.

Fit

The Fit option for placing dimensions is used when there is not enough room to fit either text or arrowheads on the dimension line. Numerous options are available for fitting either text or arrowheads (see Figure 10–8). One very

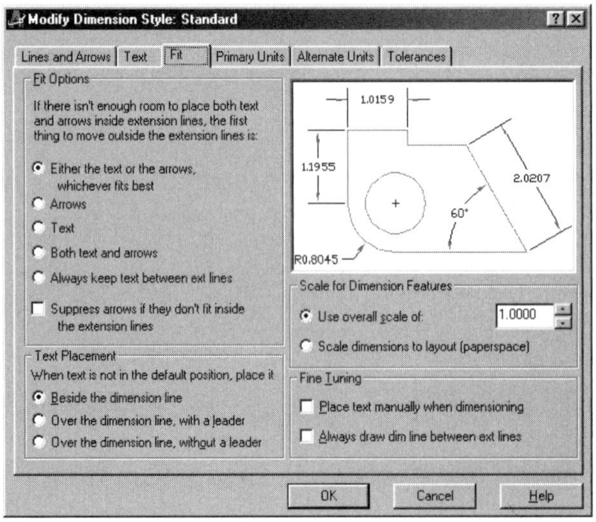

Figure 10–8
Fit dimension options.

important option of Fit is the Scale for Dimension Features option. If a drawing is going to be scaled, those elements associated with dimensions will also have to be scaled. The scale option lets you set a scale factor that applies to all dimension variables. For example, if you had previously determined that your drawing scale was $\frac{1}{4}$″ = 1′, then the dimension scale value would be 48. All the dimension variables would be scaled by a factor of 48.

Primary Units

The options in Primary Units allow you to can set the format and precision of linear and angular dimension units. Unit format options for linear dimensions include Scientific, Decimal, Architectural, Fractional, and Engineering. Other options that can be set for linear dimensions include precision level (number of decimal places), decimal separator, round off value, and any prefix or suffix you might want to add. The measurement scale factor option allows you to scale your dimension scale variables to match the overall scale value of the drawing. For instance, if the overall scale value of the drawing was $\frac{1}{8}$″ = 1′, the measurement scale value would be set to 96. All the dimension variables would be multiplied by a value of 96 in order to be plotted correctly.

Options in the Angular Dimensions portion of the Primary Units dialog box (see Figure 10–9) include setting variables that affect how angular dimensions are displayed. The Units format for angular dimensions includes Decimal Degrees, Degrees Minutes Seconds, Gradians and Radians. The precision level of angular dimensions can also be set.

Alternate Units

The alternate dimension units option lets you determine the dimension in an additional measurement system. Options include the displaying of the metric equivalent for imperial dimensions, or the imperial version for metric dimensions. Alternate dimension units are displayed in square brackets

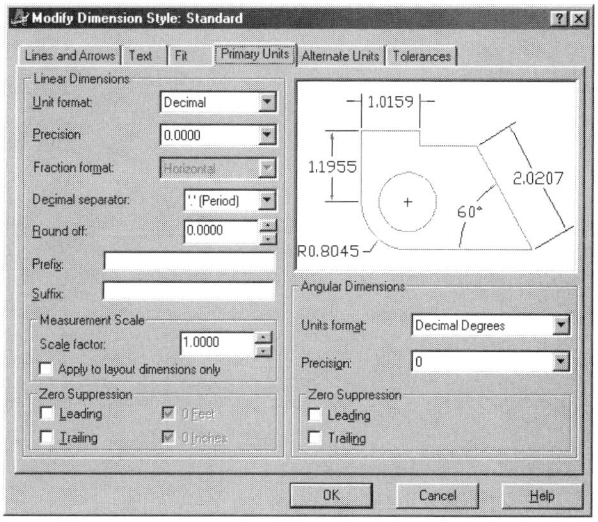

Figure 10–9
Primary Units dialog box.

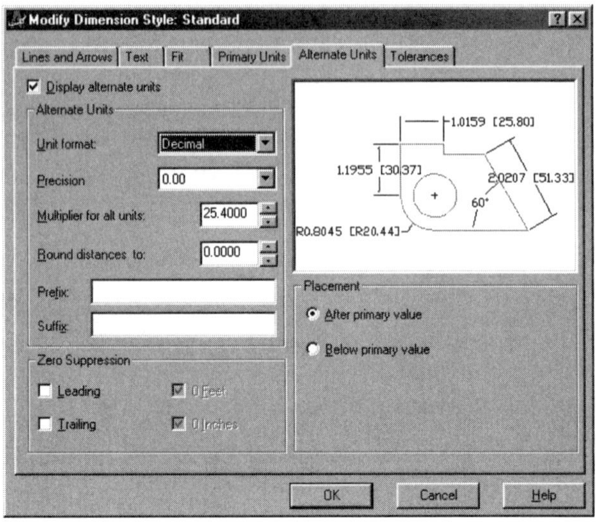

Figure 10–10
Alternate Units dialog box.

[ ] next to the primary units in the dimension text. You use the Alternate Units tab in the Modify Dimension Style dialog box (see Figure 10–10) to format alternate dimension units.

Tolerances

Under the Tolerance Format you can set the following various tolerance display options: Method sets the tolerance method. None turns off display of tolerances. You can use Symmetrical when the tolerance plus or minus values are the same, and Deviation when plus or minus values differ. Limits incorporates plus or minus values into the dimension value and displays the maximum dimension over the minimum. Basic draws a box around the dimension text, a format often used to indicate theoretically exact dimensions. Basic is also controlled by the Draw Frame Around Text option on the Text tab. Changing one of these options changes the other. The options associated with Tolerances are displayed in Figure 10–11.

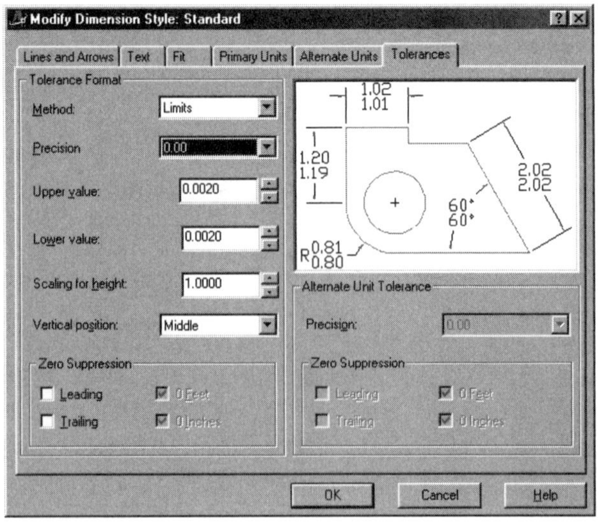

Figure 10–11
Tolerance dialog box.

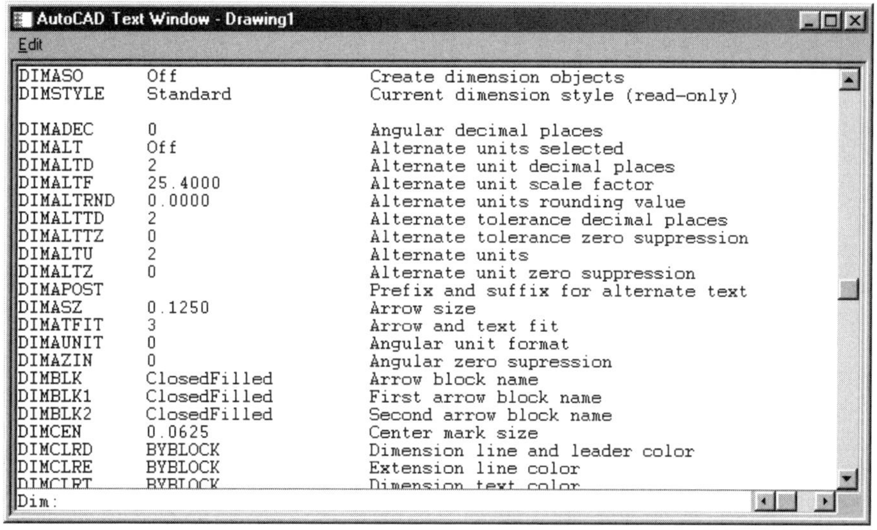

AutoCAD Text Window - Drawing1

Edit

```
DIMASO      Off            Create dimension objects
DIMSTYLE    Standard       Current dimension style (read-only)

DIMADEC     0              Angular decimal places
DIMALT      Off            Alternate units selected
DIMALTD     2              Alternate unit decimal places
DIMALTF     25.4000        Alternate unit scale factor
DIMALTRND   0.0000         Alternate units rounding value
DIMALTTD    2              Alternate tolerance decimal places
DIMALTTZ    0              Alternate tolerance zero suppression
DIMALTU     2              Alternate units
DIMALTZ     0              Alternate unit zero suppression
DIMAPOST                   Prefix and suffix for alternate text
DIMASZ      0.1250         Arrow size
DIMATFIT    3              Arrow and text fit
DIMAUNIT    0              Angular unit format
DIMAZIN     0              Angular zero supression
DIMBLK      ClosedFilled   Arrow block name
DIMBLK1     ClosedFilled   First arrow block name
DIMBLK2     ClosedFilled   Second arrow block name
DIMCEN      0.0625         Center mark size
DIMCLRD     BYBLOCK        Dimension line and leader color
DIMCLRE     BYBLOCK        Extension line color
DIMCLRT     BYBLOCK        Dimension text color
Dim:
```

Figure 10–12
Text window listing all the dimension system variables and their settings.

Text Display of Dimension Variables

One method of checking all the dimension system variables in a text dialog box is to type dim at the command prompt and then type Status. A listing of the dimension system variables and setting of each variable will be listed in a text dialog box (see Figure 10–12). The acronym of each dimension system variable can also be entered at the command prompt to determine the existing setting.

SETTING LTSCALE VALUES

Scaling can also affect the appearance of lines. In order to compensate for scaling, AutoCAD uses the **Ltscale** command for changing the appearance of lines. Ltscale stands for linetype scale. The Ltscale command is used to determine the spacing between dashes, dots, and other elements in a linetype. Just as text is affected by the scale of a drawing, so are linetypes. The length of dashes, dots, and the gaps between the dashes should not be too short or exaggerated on a drawing. The smaller the scale, the more repetitions that occur for each drawing unit. The default ltscale is 1.0. The following list of commands will help you set the ltscale.

1. From the Format pull-down menu select Linetype.
2. In the Linetype Manager dialog box select Details.
3. In the Details section of the dialog box (see Figure 10–13), enter the values for the Global scale factor and the Current object scale. The global scale factor affects the scale factor for all new and existing linetypes. The current object scale changes the linetype scale of any subsequently drawn objects relative to the global scale.
4. Check the Use paper space units for scaling box to make the scaling current for paper space linetype scaling.

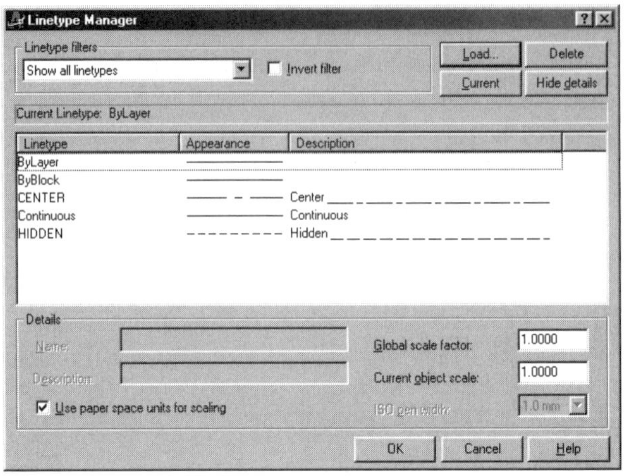

Figure 10–13
Linetype Manager dialog box.

You may need to adjust the ltscale several times in order for the lines to appear correctly. Be sure to view the drawing entities in paper space after you have changed the ltscale to see how the lines are represented.

TRY THIS

Start a new drawing and create a centerline and hidden line. Use the Ltscale command to change the appearance of the lines.

1. Open a new drawing.
2. Change the units to **Architectural.**
3. In Model space set the limits to **80', 62'.**
4. **Zoom all** to view all the area defined by your limits setting.
5. Set your Grid to a value of **4'.**
6. Open the Linetype Manager dialog box.
7. Load the **Centerline** linetype, and exit the Linetype Manager dialog box.
8. Open the Layer Control dialog box.
9. Click on the **New** button and create a new layer called **Centerline.**
10. Double click on the linetype and assign the **Centerline** linetype to the **Centerline** layer.
11. Set the **Centerline** layer as the current layer.
12. Choose **OK.**
13. Draw a horizontal line of any length.
14. Depending on the length of the line, it may appear as a solid line.
15. At the command prompt, type **Ltscale.**
16. Enter the value **96** and press **<Enter>.**

The line should change in appearance: short and long dashes should be displayed.

Activity 10–1

Draw a Bike Rack

Plotter paper size: B

Suggested settings:	Grid	2′
	Snap	3″
	Layers (7)	**0** (default border) **Hatch**, Linetype continuous, Color: cyan **Object (obj)**, Linetype continuous, Color: black **Hidden (hid)**, Linetype hidden, Color: magenta **Tbk (title block)**, Linetype continuous, Color: red **Txt (text)**, Linetype continuous, Color: green **Dim (dimensions)**, Linetype continuous, Color: green
	Units	Architectural
	Model space limits	31′, 20′

Hints:

1. Open the B-size drawing template that you created in Chapter 2. After it has completed loading, use the SAVEAS command to rename the drawing file ACT10-1.
2. Change the units to Architectural.
3. Set the model space limits to 31′, 20′.
4. Set the grid to 2′.
5. In model space execute a Zoom All (a).
6. Create the bike rack drawing in Figure 10–14 on p. 166.
7. Include all hatches and dimensions shown in the figure.
8. Switch to layout to print or plot the drawing.

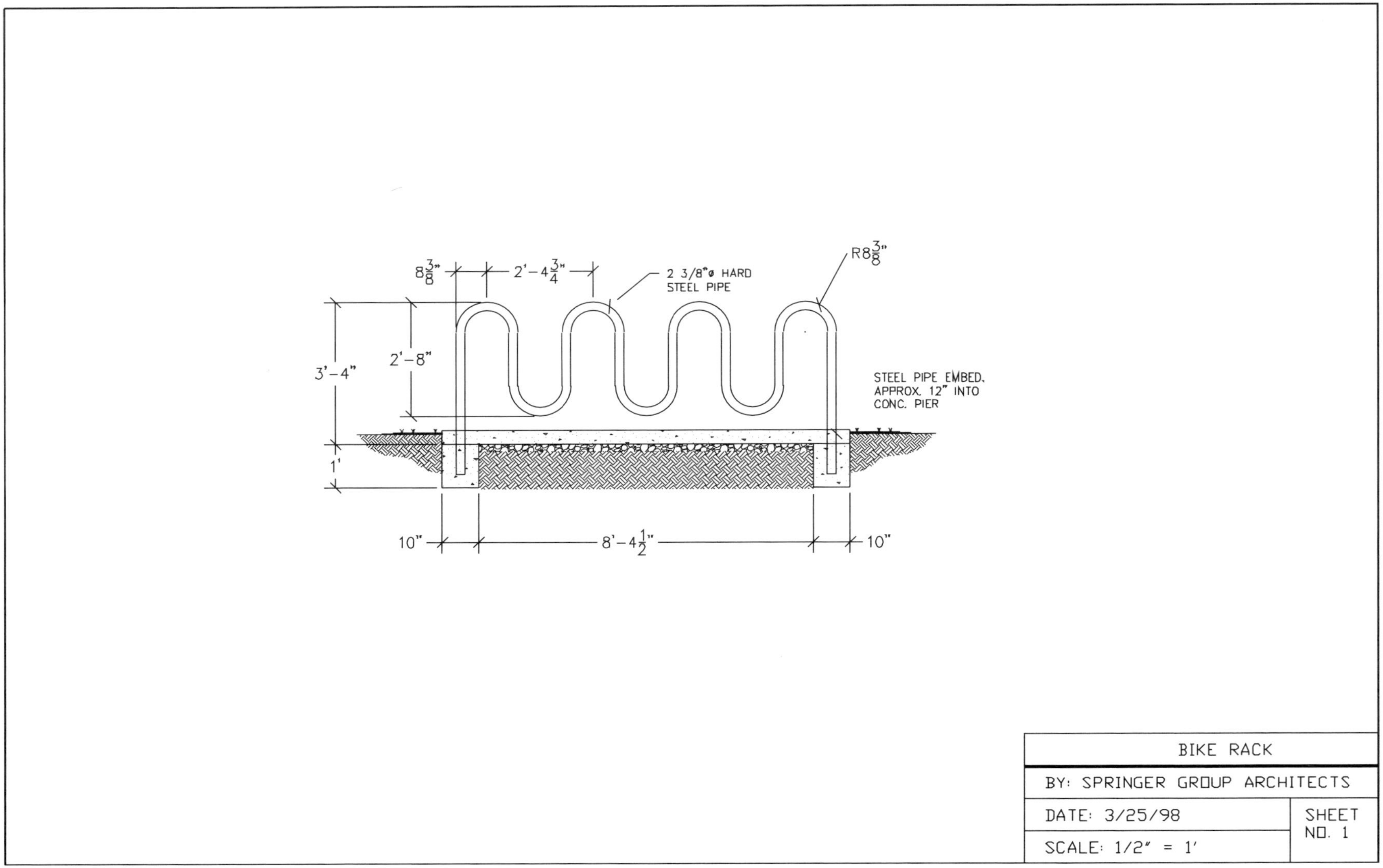

Figure 10–14
Activity 10–1

ACTIVITY 10–2

Draw a Curb Detail

Plotter paper size: B

Suggested settings:	Grid	6″
	Snap	3″
	Layers (7)	**0** (default border)
		Hatch, Linetype continuous, Color: cyan
		Object (obj), Linetype continuous, Color: black
		Hidden (hid), Linetype hidden, Color: magenta
		Tbk (title block), Linetype continuous, Color: red
		Txt (text), Linetype continuous, Color: green
		Dim (dimensions), Linetype continuous, Color: green
	Units	Architectural
	Model space limits	124″, 80″

Hints:

1. Open the B-size drawing template that you created in Chapter 2. After it has completed loading, use the SAVEAS command to rename the drawing file ACT10-2.
2. Change the units to Architectural.
3. Set the model space limits to 124″, 80″.
4. Set the grid to 6″.
5. In model space execute a Zoom, then All (a).
6. Create the curb detail drawing in Figure 10–15 on p. 168.
7. Include all hatches and dimensions shown in the figure.
8. Switch to layout to print or plot the drawing.

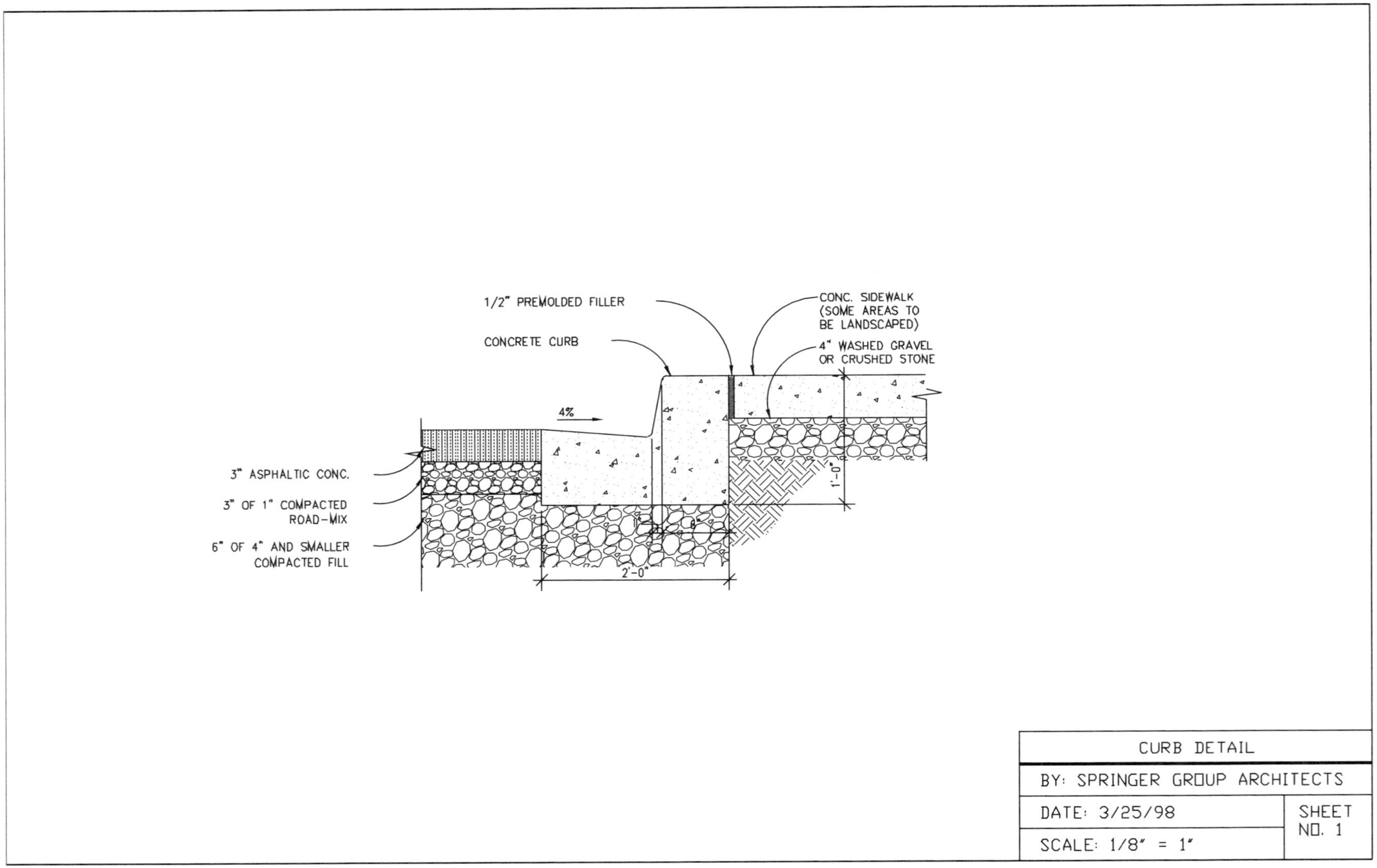

Figure 10–15
Activity 10–2

ACTIVITY 10-3

Draw a Wall Detail

Plotter paper size: A

Suggested settings:	Grid	6″
	Snap	3″
	Layers (7)	**0** (default border) **Hatch**, Linetype continuous, Color: cyan **Object (obj)**, Linetype continuous, Color: black **Hidden (hid)**, Linetype hidden, Color: magenta **Tbk (title block)**, Linetype continuous, Color: red **Txt (text)**, Linetype continuous, Color: green **Dim (dimensions)**, Linetype continuous, Color: green
	Units	Architectural
	Model space limits	10′, 7.7′

Hints:

1. Open the A-size drawing template that you created in Chapter 2. After it has completed loading, use the SAVEAS command to rename the drawing file ACT10-3.
2. Change the units to Architectural.
3. Set the model space limits to 10′, 7.7′.
4. Set the grid to 6″.
5. In model space execute a Zoom, then select All (a).
6. Create the wall detail drawing in Figure 10–16 on p. 170.
7. Include all hatches and dimensions shown in the figure.
8. Switch to layout to print or plot the drawing.

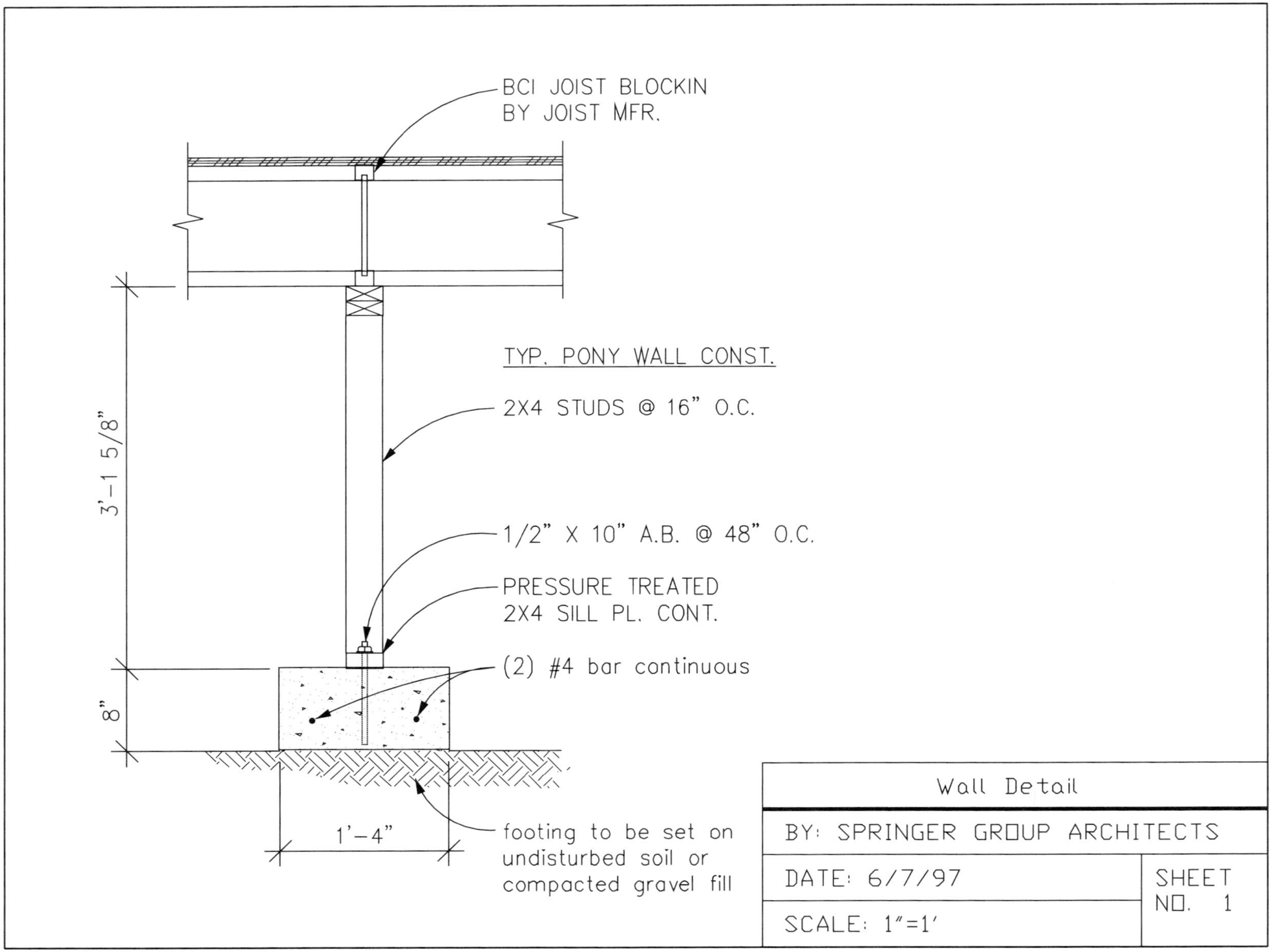

Figure 10–16
Activity 10-3

CHAPTER

11

More Drawing Aids

AFTER READING THIS CHAPTER, YOU WILL BE ABLE TO:

- Work more efficiently with drawings.

KEY CONCEPTS

- Area
- Block
- Change and DDchprop
- Dist
- List

BLOCK

A **block** is a collection of objects you can group together to form a single object, or a block definition.

If you are going to use drawing objects repetitively, it is useful to create a library of symbols that can be inserted into any drawing. Typically these libraries are composed of drawing objects known as **blocks**. A block is a collection of objects that are grouped together to form a single object. A block can be saved with a current drawing, or a block can be inserted into a different drawing.

There are two commands associated with blocks: **Block** and **Wblock**. The Block command is selected from the draw pull-down menu or entered at the command prompt line. Those objects that you want included in a Block will have to be drawn prior to executing the Block command. When the Block command is executed, a dialog box (see Figure 11–1) will appear and you will be asked for a block name and a block base point for insertion. The insertion point is a reference point for placing the newly created block in a drawing. After entering the insertion point, you select those objects that will be included in the block (see Figure 11–1).

Once the desired objects have been selected, a block has been created. Multiple blocks can exist in the same drawing.

TRY THIS

Create a block.

1. Open the AutoCAD software program and select **Start from Scratch.**
2. Draw a six-sided polygon that is inscribed within a 1″-radius circle.
3. From the Draw pull-down menu select **Block,** then **Make.**
4. Enter **Polygon** as the name for the block.
5. Pick near the center of the polygon as the base point for insertion.
6. Use **Select objects** to select any portion of the object.
7. In the description section of the dialog box, type **six-sided polygon.**
8. Exit the dialog box.

The six-sided polygon should still be displayed on the screen.

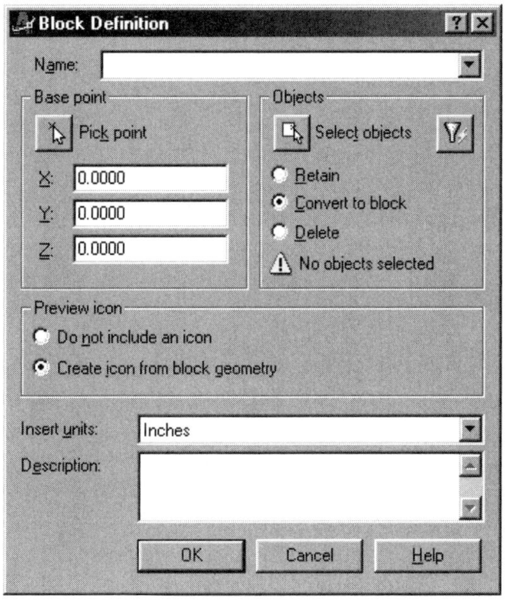

Figure 11–1
Block Definition dialog box.

TRY THIS

Create a block.

1. Open the AutoCAD software program and select **Start from Scratch.**
2. Draw an eight-sided polygon that is inscribed within a 1.5″-radius circle.
3. From the Draw pull-down menu select **Block,** and then **Make** (or type **block** at the command prompt).
4. Enter **Poly8** as the name for the block.
5. Pick near the center of the polygon as the reference point for insertion of the block.
6. Select any line of the block and press **<Enter>.**
7. Save the drawing as **Block2** and exit.

The eight-sided polygon should still be displayed on the screen.

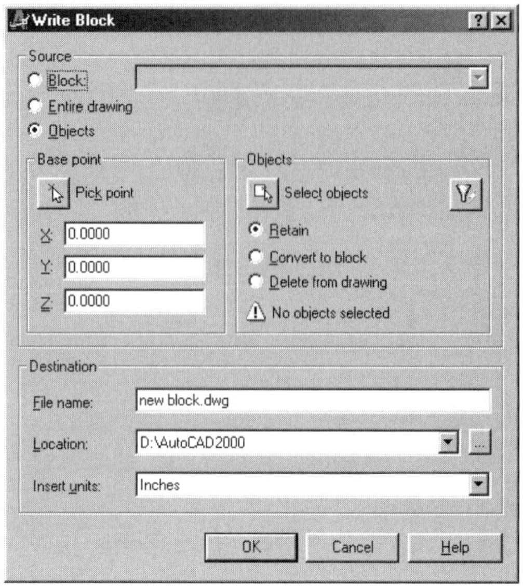

Figure 11–2
Write Block dialog box.

The blocks created from the Block command can be inserted only into the drawing from which they originated.

If you wish to insert a block into another drawing, use the **Wblock** command. The Write Block dialog box appears when the Wblock command is executed (see Figure 11–2), and a new drawing file is created. You must provide a name for the drawing file as well as the name of the block that you wish to use.

Options in the Write Block dialog box include defining the source of the Wblock, which includes using an existing block, objects, or the entire drawing as a block. As with the block command, you must designate a base point. Select objects options include retaining the object in the current drawing, converting an object to a block, or deleting the selected objects from the existing drawing. In the Destination section of the dialog box you can rename the drawing as well as the directory path where you want the drawing file saved as shown in Figure 11–3.

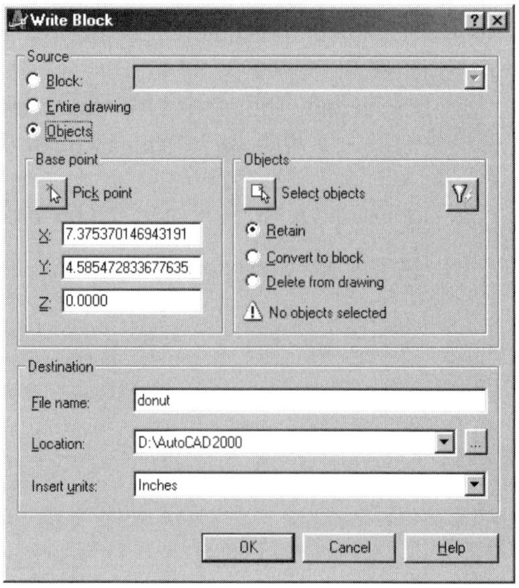

Figure 11–3
Creating a new drawing file with the Wblock command.

TRY THIS

Create a new drawing file with the Wblock command.

1. Open AutoCAD and select **Open a Drawing.**
2. Open the drawing from Activity 2-1 (Entities).
3. Type **WBlock** at the command prompt).
4. Enter **Donut** as the name for the block.
5. Select the donut as the object that will define the block.
6. Select any edge of the donut and press **<Enter>.**
7. Close the drawing without saving the changes.
8. Exit the program.

A new drawing file called Donut should have been created.

The **Explode** command when used for exploding blocks separates those elements making up the block.

Blocks can be scaled and rotated on the X axis, on the Y axis, or proportionately. If you want to edit a block, you must **Explode** it. To explode a block, from the Modify pull-down menu select Explode or select the explode icon from the Modify toolbar. At the Select Object: prompt Pick the object to explode.

If a block is exploded, all objects that were grouped together to form a block are separated and take on their individual characteristics. If a block is redefined in a drawing, all references to that block are updated in the drawing.

The command used to place a block in a drawing is Insert. This command is a submenu option in the Insert pull-down menu, or you can type insert at the command prompt. If you use the Insert command from the pull-down menu, a dialog box will appear (see Figure 11–4). Options in the Insert dialog box include block name, an insertion point, scale factor, rotation, and an option to explode the block.

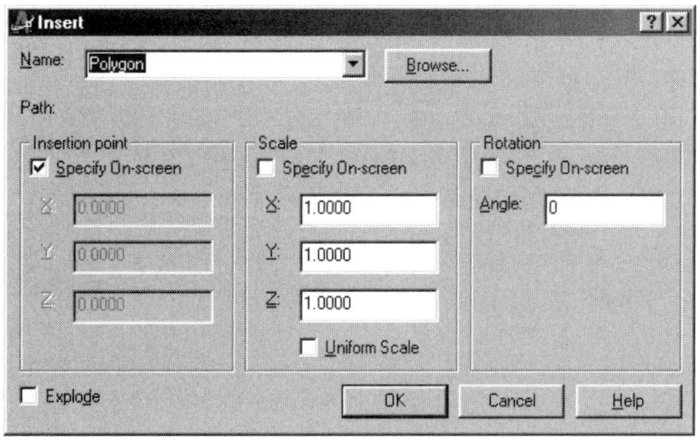

Figure 11–4
Insert dialog box.

TRY THIS

Inserting a block.

1. Open AutoCAD and select **Open a Drawing.**
2. Open drawing **Polygon.**
3. From the Insert pull-down menu, select **Block.**
4. Enter **Polygon** as the name for the block.
5. Select a point in the drawing to place the new polygon.
6. Press **<Enter>** three times to accept the default X,Y scale factor and rotation.
7. Exit the program.

TRY THIS

Inserting a file saved as a Wblock.

1. Open the AutoCAD software program and select **Start from Scratch.**
2. From the Insert pull-down menu, select **Block.**
3. Enter **Donut** as the name for the block.
4. Randomly pick a point to place the donut.
5. Press **<Enter>** three times to accept the default X,Y scale factor and the default rotation.
6. Exit the program.

CHANGING OBJECT PROPERTIES

While drawing you may inadvertently create objects on the wrong layer, or after you have drawn them you may want to change the color, linetype, ltscale, elevation, thickness, or layer. Rather than redrawing the objects, you can use either the Change or DDchprop command to change certain object characteristics. The DDchprop command uses a dialog box for executing any editing commands (see Figure 11–5). The Change command does not use a dialog box; instead, options are typed at the command prompt (see Figure 11–6).

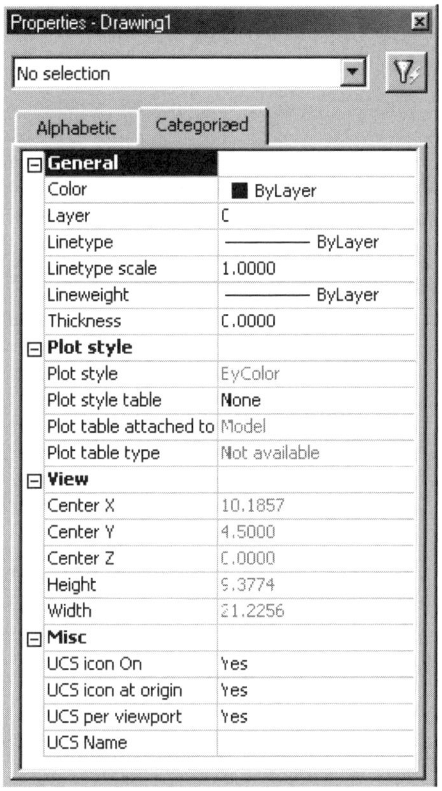

Figure 11–5
Properties dialog box.

TRY THIS

Change object properties.

1. Start the AutoCAD software program and select **Open a Drawing.**
2. Open drawing file **ACT6-2** (slider bracket).
3. From the Modify pull-down menu, select **Properties.**
4. Select any solid line of the object, and press **<Enter>.**
5. The Properties dialog box should appear.
6. Change the Layer to **Dim.**
7. The object should have changed color to green, since that was the color assigned to the Dim layer.
8. Repeat the command again, and practice changing linetypes and colors.
9. Exit the program without saving the changes.

```
Command: chprop
Select objects: 1 found
Select objects:
Enter property to change [Color/LAyer/LType/ltScale/LWeight/Thickness]:
```

Figure 11–6
Chprop options.

DIST

Figure 11–7
Distance command icon.

In addition to changing object properties, often it is necessary to check certain object properties while drawing. AutoCAD 2000 includes commands that give you the ability to do this. If you need to measure the length of a line, for example, you can use the **Dist** (distance) command. You can start the Dist command from the Inquiry flyout on the toolbar (see Figure 11–7), or you can type dist at the command prompt. The command sequence is as follows:

> Command: dist
> First point: Specify a point (1).
> Second point: Specify a point (2).
> Distance = calculated distance
> Angle in XY plane = angle Angle from XY plane = angle
> Delta X = change in X, Delta Y = change in Y, Delta Z = change in Z

Figure 11–8 shows how the Dist command might be used to measure a horizontal line. In this example the Osnap end command was used to select the endpoints of the lines.

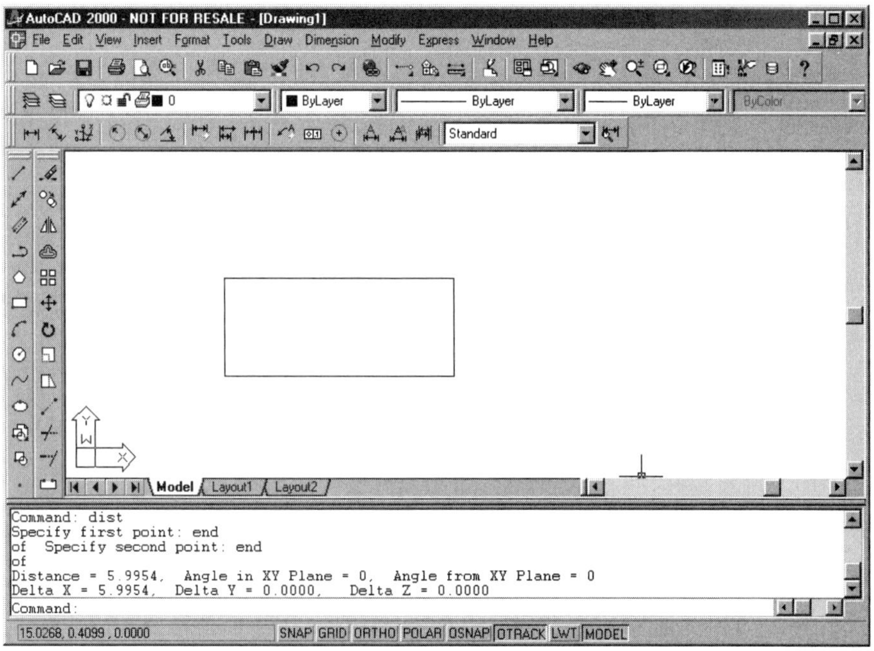

Figure 11–8
Dist command.

TRY THIS

Measure lines using the Dist command.

1. Open the AutoCAD software program and select **Start from Scratch.**
2. Draw horizontal lines of varying lengths.
3. Use the **dist** command to measure the lines.
4. Exit the drawing without saving it.

AREA

Another object property that can be measured is area. The **Area** command will calculate the area and outside circumference of an enclosed polygon. You can select the Area command from the Tools menu Inquiry option or you may type Area at the command prompt. Area command options include the following selections.

<First point> / Object / Add / Subtract:

In Figure 11–9 the area of the polygon was calculated. The perimeter of the polygon was also calculated.

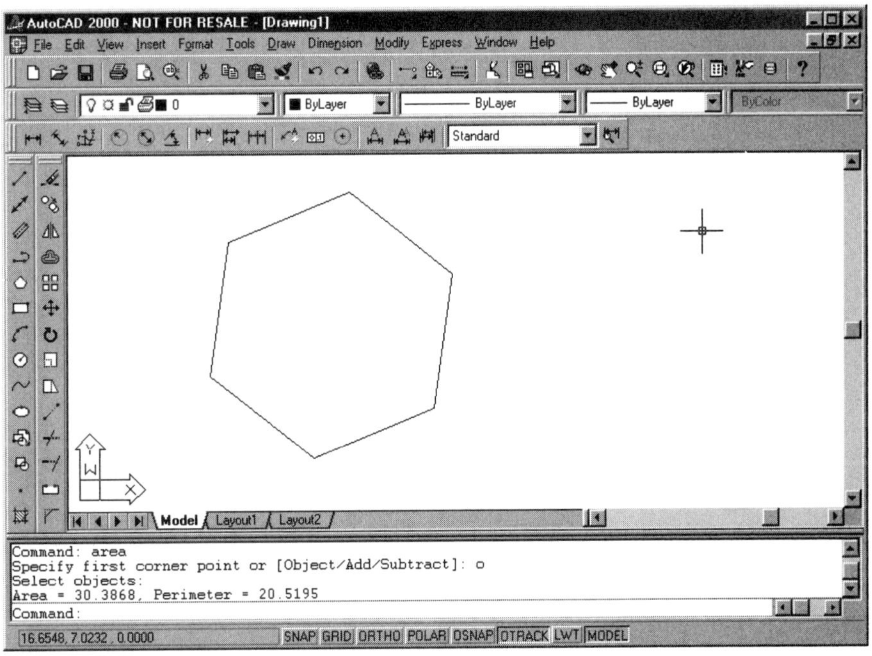

Figure 11–9
Area command.

TRY THIS

Calculate the area of a polygon.

1. Open the AutoCAD software program and select **Start from Scratch.**
2. Draw polygons of varying sizes.
3. Use the **Area** command to calculate the area of the polygons.
4. Exit the drawing without saving it.

LIST

Another command used to check object properties is **List**. The List command describes the object type, object layer, and X,Y,Z position relative to the current UCS and whether the object is in model space or paper space. The List command may be selected from the Tools pull-down menu under Inquiry, or list may be typed at the command line. After starting the command, you will select an object. Once the object has been selected, a dialog box will appear that lists the object properties. The List command is often used to determine the properties of a certain object. In Figure 11–10, the list dialog box displays information about the hatch pattern of the object.

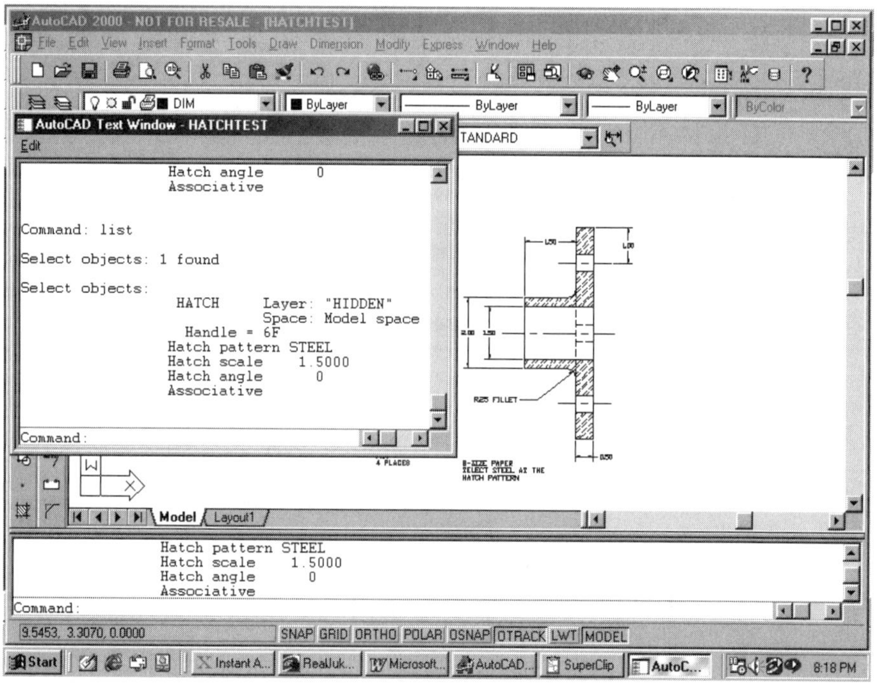

Figure 11–10
List command.

TRY THIS

Use the List command to identify characteristics of an object.

1. Open the AutoCAD software program and select **Open a Drawing.**
2. Open the **Oceanarium.dwg** from the Samples subdirectory of AutoCAD.
3. Type **List** at the command prompt and select an object.
4. Repeat the command for different objects in the drawing.
5. Exit the drawing without saving it.

Chapter 11 ■ Activities

Activity 11–1

Practice Using Block Commands

Open drawing ACT8-2 (Flange Bushing). Make the 0 layer the current layer and turn off the text layer. Use the Block command to make a block of the right side of the drawing, which will include only the object lines, centerlines, and hidden lines of the object in the block. Name the block Flange. In the Bmake dialog box use the Select Point option to determine the point to which the block will be referenced for insertion into the drawing. Use Osnap int (intersection), and pick the lower left corner of the object as the reference point.

Use the Insert command and insert the block (Flange) into the same drawing. Randomly place the block in the drawing.

Do not save changes when exiting the drawing.

Activity 11–2

Practice Using the Dist Command

Open the AutoCAD software program and select Start from Scratch. Draw horizontal and vertical lines of various lengths. Use the Dist command to measure each of the lines you created. Use Osnap endp (endpoint) to select the ends of the lines.

Do not save changes when exiting the drawing.

Activity 11–3

Practice Using the Area Command

Open AutoCAD and select Start from Scratch. Draw a number of polygons of various sizes. Use the Area command to calculate the area of each polygon.

Do not save changes when exiting the drawing.

ACTIVITY 11–4

Practice Changing Object Properties

Start AutoCAD and open drawing ACT6-4 (Grate). Use the DDchprop or the Chprop command to change the color of the interior squares to red and the linetype to hidden.

Do not save changes when exiting the drawing.

Index

TOOLBARS

Standard Toolbar

New, Open, Save, Print, Print Preview, Spelling, Cut, Copy, Paste, Match Properties, Undo, Redo, Launch Browser, Object Snap Flyout, UCS Flyout, Inquiry Flyout, Redraw All, Aerial View, Viewpoint Flyout, Pan Realtime, Zoom Realtime, Zoom Flyout, Zoom Preview, Help

Draw Toolbar

- Line
- Construction Line
- Multiline
- Polyline
- Polygon
- Rectangle
- Arc
- Circle
- Spline
- Ellipse
- Insert Block
- Make Block
- Point
- Hatch
- Region
- Multiline Text

Modify Toolbar

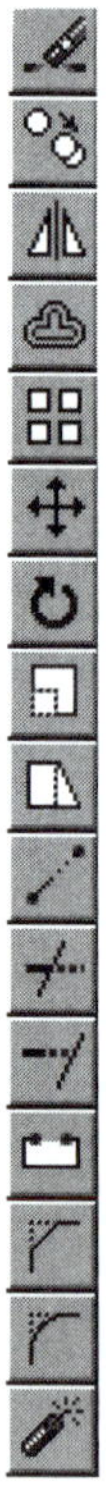

- Erase
- Copy Object
- Mirror
- Offset
- Array
- Move
- Rotate
- Scale
- Stretch
- Lengthen
- Trim
- Extend
- Break
- Chamfer
- Fillet
- Explode